THE FATHERS OF THE CHURCH

A NEW TRANSLATION

VOLUME 59

THE FATHERS
OF THE CHURCH

A NEW TRANSLATION

ROY JOSEPH DEFERRARI
Editorial Director Emeritus

EDITORIAL BOARD

BERNARD M. PEEBLES
The Catholic University of America
Editorial Director

PAUL J. MORIN
The Catholic University of America
Managing Editor

ROBERT P. RUSSELL, O.S.A.
Villanova University

THOMAS P. HALTON
The Catholic University of America

MARTIN R. P. MCGUIRE
The Catholic University of America

WILLIAM R. TONGUE
The Catholic University of America

HERMIGILD DRESSLER, O.F.M.
The Catholic University of America

SR. M. JOSEPHINE BRENNAN, I.H.M.
Marywood College

MSGR. JAMES A. MAGNER
The Catholic University of America

REDMOND A. BURKE, C.S.V.
The Catholic University of America

SAINT AUGUSTINE

THE TEACHER

THE FREE CHOICE OF THE WILL

GRACE AND FREE WILL

Translated by
ROBERT P. RUSSELL, O.S.A.

Villanova University

THE CATHOLIC UNIVERSITY OF AMERICA PRESS
Washington, D.C. 20017

IMPRIMI POTEST:

    JAMES G. SHERMAN, O.S.A.
    Prior Provincial

NIHIL OBSTAT:

    JOHN C. SELNER, S.S., S.T.D.
    Censor Librorum

IMPRIMATUR:

    ✠PATRICK CARDINAL A. O'BOYLE, D.D.
    Archbishop of Washington

September 5, 1967

The *nihil obstat* and *imprimatur* are official declarations that a book or pamphlet is free of doctrinal or moral error. No implication is contained therein that those who have granted the *nihil obstat* and the *imprimatur* agree with the content, opinions, or statements expressed.

Library of Congress Catalog Card No.: 67-30350

Copyright © 1968 by
THE CATHOLIC UNIVERSITY OF AMERICA PRESS, INC.
All rights reserved
Reprinted 1990
First Paperback Reprint 2004
ISBN 0-8132-1414-9
ISBN-13: 978-0-8132-1414-6 (pbk.)

TO MY SISTER

CONTENTS

	Page
THE TEACHER	1
THE FREE CHOICE OF THE WILL	63
GRACE AND FREE WILL	243
INDICES	309

THE TEACHER

(De magistro)

INTRODUCTION

THE SHORT BUT HIGHLY SIGNIFICANT WORK, entitled *The Teacher*, is next to the last in a series of Dialogues begun at Cassiciacum, near Milan, where Augustine had gone in the autumn of 386 to prepare for baptism. The present Dialogue reproduces, at least in substance, discussions held with his son shortly after their return to Tagaste in 388 and is the only one in which Adeodatus is the sole interlocutor.[1] In *The Confessions* Augustine describes the origin of the work as follows: "There is a book of mine called *The Teacher* in which Adeodatus himself converses with me. You know, O God, that all the thoughts expressed there as coming from the second party to the Dialogue are his own, though he was only sixteen years old."[2] The actual composition of the work, which may have been intended as a literary memorial to this precocious young man, is commonly assigned to the year 389, not long after the premature death of Adeodatus.

The central theme of the Dialogue is succinctly stated in the *Retractations,* a chronological review of the Saint's works, exclusive of *Sermons* and *Letters,* composed between 426 and 427. "During this same period," he writes, "I composed a book called *The Teacher* where, after some discussion and inquiry, we find that it is God alone who teaches men knowledge, all of which is also in accord with what is written in the Gospel: 'One is your teacher, Christ.' "[3] Although the focal

---
1 Adeodatus was present at the discussions recorded in *The Happy Life,* composed at Cassiciacum to mark Augustine's birthday on November 13. In it Augustine refers to him as follows: "My son, Adeodatus, the youngest of us all, was also with us. Unless my affection deceives me, his talent gives promise of great success" (1.6).
2 *Conf.* 9.6.14.
3 *Retract.* 1.12.

problem concerns the role of the teacher and the function of signs and language, the discussion quite logically leads to a consideration of the origin of man's intellectual knowledge.

In general, however, the Dialogue is given over to the refutation of the view that signs and words can of themselves engender truth in the mind of the pupil or ordinary listener. At first it might appear that Augustine's entire line of reasoning is directed against the very institution of teaching as this is commonly understood and accepted. Nothing could be further from his true purpose, and, indeed, the lesson of the Dialogue would be lost if one were to infer that the role of the teacher has been rendered superfluous or negligible. For it is precisely by the kind of skillful and timely questioning on the part of the teacher, so well exemplified in *The Teacher* itself, that enables the pupil to discover the truth for himself. And if Augustine stresses the instrumental role of the human agency in learning, it is only to bring into greater relief the central thesis summarized by Adeodatus at the conclusion of the Dialogue, namely, that it is Christ, the "indwelling Truth" who alone teaches men truth.

The epistemological import of this conclusion is significant, representing, as it does, an important and decisive moment in the history and development of Augustine's celebrated doctrine of "divine illumination."[4] In two earlier dialogues, *Soliloquies* and *The Greatness of the Soul*, there is an apparent tension between vestiges of a Platonic reminiscence and vague adumbrations of his later and definitive teaching of illumination. In the present Dialogue the latter is clearly delineated for the first time in those essential aspects which find their fuller development and classical expression within the rich

---

4 This is particularly noticeable in the *Soliloquies* where the notion of "illumination" is clearly suggested (1.8.5), while Platonic reminiscence is implied in a later passage (2.20.35). In a letter to his friend Nebridius, composed during the same year as *The Teacher*, Augustine seems to accept the doctrine of reminiscence (cf. *Ep.* 7.1.2).

psychological context of that great masterpiece, *The Trinity*.⁵ All further traces of the Platonic doctrine disappear, except for the term "memory," which Augustine appropriates in a sense altogether different and original.

When one considers the importance of this work in the Middle Ages⁶ as well as its valuable pedagogical insights and its relevance to modern semantic inquiry,⁷ it is not difficult to appreciate the lasting influence of this rich and stimulating Dialogue. The fact, too, that contemporaries of Augustine preferred to call him *Magister*⁸ may well have been inspired in part by this delightful encounter between so loving and gifted a father and a son of great but unfulfilled promise.

The present translation has been made from the critical text of G. Weigel, published in the *Corpus scriptorum ecclesiasticorum latinorum* (Vienna 1961). In the present work, as well as in the remaining works of this volume, Scriptural quotations follow the Challoner revision of the Douay Bible for the Old Testament and the Confraternity of Christian Doctrine Edition for the New Testament. Occasional minor adaptations have been made wherever warranted by Augustine's own reading of the biblical text.

---

5 In chapter 15 of Book Twelve—a *locus classicus* for his teaching on "illumination"—Augustine expressly rejects the theory of reminiscence proposed in Plato's *Meno*. "But we ought rather to believe," he says, "that the nature of the intellectual mind is so formed as to see those things which, according to the design of the Creator, are subjoined to intelligible realities in the natural order, in a kind of incorporeal light of its own kind *(sui generis)*. . . ."
6 In the *Disputed Questions* St. Thomas raises the same problem dealt with in Augustine's *De magistro* under the heading: *Utrum homo docere alium possit et dici magister, vel Deus solus* (11.1). Both treatises, which reach the same conclusion from different epistemological premises, have occasioned a number of comparative studies. For example, J. Colleran, *The Treatises "De magistro" of Saint Augustine and Saint Thomas* (Diss., Rome 1945).
7 Cf. G. Leckie, *Concerning the Teacher and On the Immortality of the Soul by Aurelius Augustine* (New York 1938) ix-xxviii.
8 Cf. P. Courcelle, "A propos du titre 'Augustinus Magister': Le 'maître' Augustin," *Augustinus Magister* (Paris 1954) 3.9-11.

SELECT BIBLIOGRAPHY

Text:

Maurist Edition: *Sancti Augustini Hipponensis episcopi Opera* 1 (Paris 1689) 541-564. Reproduced, with few variants, by:
Migne, J. P. *Patrologia Latina* 32 (Paris 1845) 1193-1220.
Weigel, G. *Corpus scriptorum ecclesiasticorum latinorum* 77 (Vienna 1961).
Cassoti, M. *Sanctus Augustinus: De magistro,* Italian trans. A. Faggi (3 ed. Brescia 1958).
Mura, A. *Sant' Agostino: Il maestro* (Rome 1965).

Translations:

Colleran, J. *Saint Augustine: The Greatness of the Soul, The Teacher* (Ancient Christian Writers 9; Westminster, Md. 1950) 113-186; 221-240.
Hornstein, H. *Aurelius Augustinus: Vom Lehrmeister* (Düsseldorf 1957).
Leckie, G. *Concerning the Teacher and On the Immortality of the Soul by Aurelius Augustine* (New York 1938).
Martinez, M. *Del maestro* (Biblioteca de Autores Cristianos 21: Obras de San Agustín 3 [Madrid 1951] 667-759).
Perl, C. *Aurelius Augustinus: Der Lehrer* (Paderborn 1959).
Thonnard, F. *Le maître* (Bibliothèque Augustinienne: Oeuvres de saint Augustin 6.3 [2 ed. Paris 1952] 14-121; 481-495).
Tourscher, F. *The Philosophy of Teaching: A Translation of Saint Augustine's "De magistro"* (Villanova, Pa. 1924).

Secondary Works:

Colleran, J. *The Treatises "De magistro" of Saint Augustine and Saint Thomas* (Diss. Pontif. Inst. 'Angelico,' Rome 1945).
Gilson, E. *Introduction à l'étude de saint Augustin* (3 ed. Paris 1949). English trans., *The Christian Philosophy of Saint Augustine* (New York 1960).
Kevane, E. *Augustine The Educator* (Westminster, Md. 1964).
_____. "Augustine's 'De doctrina christiana': A Treatise on Christian Education," *Recherches Augustiniennes* 4 (1966) 97-133.
Pépin, J. "Le problème de la communication des consciences chez Plotin et saint Augustin," *Revue de métaphysique et de morale* 55 (1950) 128-148.
Rosenstock-Huessy, E. *Der Atem des Geistes* (Frankfurt 1951).

THE TEACHER

Chapter 1

1. *Augustine.* What would you say we are trying to do whenever we speak?

Adeodatus. As it strikes me right now, we want either to teach[1] or to learn.

Aug. I see, and I agree with one of these, but how does this hold for learning?

Ad. How in the world do you suppose we learn, if not by asking questions?

Aug. I think that even then we simply want to teach. Now I am inquiring of you whether you ask a question for any other reason than to teach the person asked what it is you want to know.

Ad. What you say is true.

Aug. So you see that our aim in speaking is simply to teach.

Ad. I do not see this clearly. If speaking is no more than uttering words, I see we do that whenever we sing. And as we often sing when we are alone where no one else is present, I do not think we wish to teach anything.

Aug. For my part, I think there is a form of teaching by way of recalling, and a really important one, which the very subject under discussion will bring to light. But if you do not think that we learn by recalling or that we teach when we bring something to one's mind, I will not oppose you. And I will now take the position that the two reasons for speaking are either to teach or to recall something, whether to others

---

[1] Throughout the Dialogue, the term "teach" is used to include any form of personal communication for the purpose of instruction.

or to ourselves. And this we do even when we are singing. Would you not say so?

Ad. Not entirely, for I very seldom sing to call something to my mind. I do it only for pleasure.

Aug. I see what you mean. But you notice, do you not, that what pleases you in singing is a certain melodious ordering of sound? Since this can be joined to words, or removed from them, is singing not one thing and speaking something else? Melody can be produced by the flute and harp; birds sing too, and there are times when we hum a musical piece without words. This can be called singing, but not speech. Do you have any objection to raise?

Ad. None whatever, really.

2. *Aug.* Do you think then that language has been introduced solely in order to teach or to recall?

Ad. I would were it not for the difficulty that, in praying, we are actually speaking, and yet it is not right to believe that God is taught anything by us, or that we recall something to His mind.

Aug. You do not realize, I think, that the command to pray in the secrecy of our chamber[2]—a term signifying the innermost recesses of the soul—was given only for this reason, that God does not need to be reminded or taught by us in order to give us what we desire. When a person speaks, he gives an outward sign of what he wants by means of an articulated sound. But we must seek and pray to God in the innermost court of the rational soul which is called the "interior man," for it is here that He has wished to make His temple. And have you not read in the Apostle: "Know you not that you are the temple of God and that the Spirit of God dwells in you,"[3] and that "Christ dwells in the inner man"?[4] And have you not noted the words of the Prophet: "Speak in your

---

2 Cf. Matt. 6.6.
3 1 Cor. 3.16.
4 Cf. Eph. 3.16,17.

hearts and repent in your chambers; offer the sacrifice of justice and hope in the Lord"?[5] Where do you think the "sacrifice of justice" is to be offered, if not in the "temple" of the soul and in the "chambers" of the heart? Now we have to offer sacrifice there where we are to pray. Hence there is no need, when we pray, for language, that is, for the spoken word, except, perhaps, to express one's thoughts, the way priests do, not so God may hear, but in order that men may hear and, by this verbal reminder, fix their thoughts upon God by a unity of heart and mind. Or do you have another view?

Ad. I am in complete agreement.

Aug. Are you then not concerned by the fact that the greatest Teacher of all taught us certain words to say when He was teaching the disciples how to pray?[6] In so doing, He apparently did nothing else than teach them what they should say when praying.

Ad. That does not trouble me at all, for He did not teach the disciples words, but realities by means of words. In this way they were to call to mind to whom to pray and what to pray for when, as you said, they pray in the inner sanctum of the soul.

Aug. You have the right idea. I believe you notice at the same time that even when a person is trying hard to think, although we utter not a sound, yet because we are thinking of the words themselves, we are speaking inwardly in our minds. So, too, by speaking, we merely call something to mind since, in turning over the words stored therein, memory brings to mind the realities themselves which have words for their signs.

Ad. I understand, and I follow you.

---

5 Ps. 4.5-6.
6 A reference to the Lord's Prayer (cf. Matt. 6.9-13). In his commentary *On the Lord's Sermon on the Mount* (2.4.15-37), as well as in *Sermon 56*, Augustine provides a lengthy and beautiful exposition of this prayer. Cf. *Fathers of the Church* 11.122-148; 239-257.

Chapter 2

3. *Aug.* Do we agree then that words are signs?
Ad. We do.
Aug. Well, can there be a sign unless it signifies something?
Ad. No.
Aug. How many words are there in this verse? *Si nihil ex tanta superis placet urbe relinqui*[1] (If it please the gods that nothing remain of so great a city).
Ad. Eight.
Aug. Are there eight signs, then?
Ad. Yes.
Aug. I believe you grasp the meaning of this verse.
Ad. Well enough, I think.
Aug. Tell me what the words mean, one by one.
Ad. I certainly understand what *si* signifies, but I find no other word to explain it.
Aug. Whatever it signifies, do you at least know where it occurs?
Ad. It seems to me that *si* signifies doubt, and where, except in the mind, can doubt exist?
Aug. I will accept that for the time being. Go on to the other words.
Ad. Nihil—what else does it signify except what does not exist?
Aug. Perhaps what you say is true, but I am held back from agreeing by something you granted before, namely, that nothing is a sign unless it signifies something. But what does not exist cannot possibly be something. Therefore, the second word in this verse is not a sign because it does not signify something, and we were wrong in agreeing that all words are signs, or that every sign signifies something.
Ad. I am really hard pressed by what you say. But it is certainly sheer folly for us to utter a word when we have nothing

---
1 Vergil, *Aeneid* 2.659

to say. Yet, even as you speak with me now, I do not believe you are making empty sounds, but by every sound coming from your lips you are giving me a sign enabling me to understand something. Consequently, you should not utter those two syllables, when speaking, if you do not signify something by them. But if you see they are necessary to make a meaningful statement and that they teach or call something to our mind when they strike the ear, then you will really see what I want to say, but am unable to explain.

Aug. What, then, are we to do? Instead of saying that *nihil* signifies something which is nothing, shall we say that this word signifies a certain state of mind when, failing to perceive a reality, the mind nevertheless finds, or thinks it finds, that such a reality does not exist?

Ad. Maybe that is the very thing I was trying so hard to explain.

Aug. Be that as it may, let us go on from here so we will not find ourselves in a most absurd situation.

Ad. What in the world is that?

Aug. That "nothing" is holding us back and causing us delay.[2]

Ad. That is certainly ridiculous, and yet I realize that it can happen, I know not how. Yes, I see plainly that it has happened.

4. *Aug.* We shall, God permitting, have a clearer understanding of this sort of contradiction in its proper place. For now, return to that verse and try to explain as well as you can what the rest of the words signify.

Ad. The third word is the preposition *ex,* for which I think we can substitute the preposition *de.*

Aug. I am not asking you to substitute one familiar word for another equally familiar, of the same meaning, if, in fact, it does have the same meaning. But let us grant that for now. To be sure, if the poet had not said *ex tanta urbe,* but *de*

---

2 Cf. chapter 8.21.

tanta, and I were to ask you what *de* means, you would say *ex,* since these are two words, that is, signs, which you suppose mean the same thing. But I am looking for the one thing itself, whatever it is, which is signified by these two signs.

Ad. I think that *ex* signifies a separation of one thing from something in which it had been present and which is now said to be "from" the first; whether this no longer remains, as in that verse where, though the city did not survive, some Trojans were able to depart "from" it, or where it still remains, as when we say there are traders in Africa "from" the city of Rome.

Aug. Granted that this is true, without enumerating many examples that might possibly be cited as exceptions to your rule, nevertheless you will readily notice this one point, at least, namely, that you have been explaining words by words, that is, signs by signs, and what is familiar by what is equally familiar. But I would like you to point out to me, if you can, the realities themselves of which these are signs.

Chapter 3

5. *Ad.* I am astonished that you do not know, or rather, that you pretend not to know, that your request cannot possibly be met by any answer of mine. Actually, we are holding a conversation where we can only reply by means of words. But you are looking for those realities which, whatever else they are, are certainly not words, and yet you are also using words to ask me about them. So you will first have to ask a question without words so I can then reply in the same manner.

Aug. You have a right to do this, I admit. But suppose I should ask you what was signified when these three syllables *paries* [wall] are spoken, could you not point with your finger so I could see clearly the reality itself, of which this three-syllable word is a sign. You would be showing it to me, but without the use of words.

Ad. I grant that this is possible only for names signifying bodily objects, provided these are present.

Aug. Are we going to call color a body? Do we not rather speak of it as a quality of bodies?

Ad. That is right.

Aug. Here again, why can it not be indicated with the finger? Or do you also include with bodies the qualities of bodies, so that these, as well as bodies, can be shown without words, whenever they are present?

Ad. When I said "bodies," I intended that all things corporeal should be understood, namely, everything which the senses perceive in bodies.

Aug. But consider whether even here you should allow for exceptions.

Ad. That is sound advice. For I should not have said all things corporeal, but all things visible. I indeed acknowledge that though sound, odor, taste, weight, heat, and other qualities pertaining to the senses other than sight, cannot be perceived apart from bodies, and are therefore corporeal, yet they cannot be indicated with a finger.

Aug. Have you never noticed how men converse, as it were, with deaf people by gestures and how the deaf themselves in turn use gestures to ask and answer questions, to teach and to make known either all their wishes or, at least, a good many of them? When this is done, visual qualities are not the only ones indicated without the use of words, but also sound, taste, and other such qualities. And there are actors in the theaters who often unfold and act out whole stories by dancing, without the use of words.

Ad. I have no objection, except to note that not only I, but also your dancing actor himself, could not show you what the preposition *ex* signifies without using words.

6. *Aug.* Perhaps what you say is true. But let us suppose that he can. You will have no doubt, I think, that no matter what the bodily movement may be by which he tries to point out for me the reality signified by this word, it will not be the reality itself, but a sign. Therefore, he will be indicating, not indeed one word by another, but still one sign by another so that the monosyllable *ex* and the bodily gesture will signify some one thing which I would like to have pointed out to me without the use of a sign.

Ad. I ask you, how is such a thing possible?

Aug. The same way that it was possible in the case of the wall.

Ad. Even that cannot be indicated without a sign, as the course of our reasoning has shown. For the pointing of the finger is certainly not the wall, but a sign made to indicate the wall. Nothing, therefore, can be made known, as I see it, without the use of signs.

Aug. Suppose I should ask you what walking is, and you were to get up and walk? Would you not be using the reality itself rather than words, or any signs, to teach me?

Ad. I acknowledge that this is so, and I am ashamed that I failed to see something so obvious. From this example, thousands of other things come to mind which can be made known of themselves, and not through signs, such as eating, drinking, sitting, standing, shouting, as well as numberless other cases.

Aug. Well, now, answer me this. Suppose I were completely ignorant of the meaning of this word and were to ask you what walking is while you were walking, how would you teach me?

Ad. I would walk a little faster, so that this new factor, introduced after your question, would bring it to your attention; and all the while, nothing else would be going on except the very thing that had to be made known.

Aug. Do you not realize that walking and hurrying are two different things? A man who walks is not thereby hurrying, and one who hurries is not necessarily walking. For we also speak of hurrying in connection with writing and reading, and for countless other things. Therefore, if you did what you were doing a little more quickly, in response to my question, I might suppose that there is no difference between walking and hurrying. For this acceleration of your pace was the new factor you introduced, and I would be misled on this account.

Ad. I admit that we cannot indicate something without a sign if we are asked about it at the time we happen to be doing it. For if we do not add something to what we are doing, our questioner will take it that we are unwilling to show him and that, having ignored him, we continue what we are doing. But if he asks about things we are able to do, but not at the time we are doing them, then, by performing the act after his question, we can show him what he wants to know by the thing itself, rather than by a sign—unless he chances to ask me what speaking is while I am speaking. For, in that case, no matter what I should say to teach him, I will have to speak. From this point, I shall go on teaching him until I make plain to him what he wants to know, without deviating from the thing itself which he wanted to have shown him, and without looking for signs to indicate it, except for the sign of language itself.

Chapter 4

7. *Aug.* A very keen observation, indeed! See, then, whether we are agreed that those things can be indicated without signs which we are either not doing when asked about them, but can do right away, or those which are perhaps signs themselves while we are making them. When talking, for example, we are making signs, from which the term "signify" is derived.

Ad. We agree.

Aug. When, therefore, a question is asked about certain

signs, these can be indicated by means of signs. If, however, the question concerns things that are not signs, these can be indicated either by doing them after being questioned, if this is possible, or by making signs to direct attention to them.

Ad. That is correct.

Aug. Within this three-fold division of signs, let us first consider, if you will, that class in which signs are indicated by signs. Words are not the only signs, are they?

Ad. No.

Aug. I think that in speaking we use words to signify words themselves or other signs, as when we say "gesture," or "letter," for these two words are also signs. Or we use words to signify something else which is not a sign, as when we say "stone." Since it signifies something, this word is a sign, but what it signifies is not in turn a sign. But this kind of sign, namely, that where words signify things that are not signs, does not belong to the class of sign now under discussion. For we proposed to consider the class of signs where signs are indicated by means of signs. We found that this included two sub-divisions, since by means of signs we teach or call to mind either the same signs or different signs. Do you not think so?

Ad. It is perfectly clear.

8. *Aug.* Tell me, then, to which sense those signs pertain which are words?

Ad. To hearing.

Aug. And gestures?

Ad. To sight.

Aug. What about words we find written? Are they words, or are they more properly thought of as signs of words? To be a word, something must be uttered with articulated sound and have some meaning, and sound can be perceived by no other sense than hearing. Consequently, when a word is written, the eyes are given a sign by which something pertaining to hearing is brought to mind.

Ad. I fully agree.

Aug. You will also agree, I think, that when we say "noun," we are signifying something.

Ad. That is true.

Aug. Well, what is that?

Ad. That, precisely, which anything is called, as Romulus, Rome, virtue, river, and numberless other things.

Aug. Do these four nouns not signify something?

Ad. They do, indeed.

Aug. And is there any difference between these nouns and the things they signify?

Ad. Yes, there is a big difference.

Aug. I would like to hear from you what that difference is.

Ad. First of all, nouns are signs, things are not signs.

Aug. Would you agree if we call things that can be signified by signs, but are not signs, "signifiables," just as we call things that can be seen "visible"? This will enable us to deal with these matters more easily from here on.

Ad. I would certainly agree.

Aug. Well, what about those four signs you mentioned a short while ago? Can they be signified by any other signs?

Ad. I am surprised that you think I have already forgotten that we found that written words are signs of other spoken signs.

Aug. Tell me the difference between them.

Ad. The former are visible, the latter, audible. Why not allow the term "audible," if we have allowed the term "signifiables"?

Aug. I am quite pleased to allow it. But I ask you again whether those four signs can be signified by any other audible sign, as you recalled was the case for visible signs?

Ad. I recall that this was also mentioned a short while ago. I replied that a noun signifies some thing, and included those four things under its heading. I also realize that both "noun" and those four nouns become audible signs when they are expressed vocally.

Aug. What is the difference then between an audible sign and the audible reality signified, which, again, is a sign?

Ad. I see there is this difference between what is called a noun and those four things included under its meaning. The former is an audible sign of other audible signs, while the latter, though real signs, are nevertheless not signs of signs, but signs of things. Some are visible, such as Romulus and Rome, others are intelligible, such as virtue.

9. *Aug.* I am satisfied to accept this. But are you aware that everything expressed by articulate sound, with meaning, is a word?

Ad. I am.

Aug. Therefore, a noun is also a word, since, as we see, it is expressed by articulate sound, with meaning. And when we say that an eloquent man uses choice words, he is, to be sure, also using nouns. When the slave in Terence's play replied to his old master, "Fair words, I pray you,"[1] the master had used many nouns also.

Ad. I agree.

Aug. Then you will grant that when we utter the two syllables *verbum* (word), we are also signifying "noun," and that the former is therefore a sign of the latter.

Ad. That I grant.

Aug. I would like you to answer this question too. You said that "word" is a sign of "noun" and "noun" is a sign of "river" and "river" is the sign of a reality that we can see; also, that there is a difference between the reality and "river," which is its sign, and between this sign and "noun," which is the sign of this sign. Tell me, then, what difference you think there is between the sign of "noun," which was found to be a "word," and "noun" itself, which is its sign.

Ad. I see there is this difference. Things signified by "noun" are also signified by "word," for just as "noun" is a word, so also is "river" a word. On the other hand, not everything sig-

---

[1] *Andria* 204.

nified by "word' can also be signified by "noun." For both the term "if," at the opening of the verse you quoted, and the term "from," are words but not nouns, though they have been occupying our attention for such a long time and have now, with reason as our guide, led us to the present subject. And there are many such cases to be found. Consequently, since all nouns are words but not all words are nouns, I think the difference between "word" and "noun" is plain, namely, the difference between the sign of a sign not signifying other signs, and a sign of a sign which itself signifies other signs.

Aug. Would you grant that while every horse is an animal, not every animal is a horse?

Ad. Who would doubt it?

Aug. Then the difference between "noun" and "word" is the same as that between "horse" and "animal." Perhaps what keeps you from agreeing is the fact that we also use the term *verbum* [word] in another sense to signify verbs that are conjugated throughout the various tenses, such as: I write, I wrote, I read, I have read. Obviously, these are not nouns.

Ad. You have indicated precisely the very thing that made me hesitate.

Aug. Do not let that disturb you. We do, in fact, speak of signs in a general way, to embrace whatever can signify anything, and here, as we see, words are also included. We likewise speak of "military insignia" [*signa militaria*], which are properly called signs, but do not include words. Yet, were I to tell you that just as every horse is an animal but not every animal is a horse, so too, while every word is a sign, not every sign is a word, I think you would not hesitate to agree.

Ad. I now see and fully agree that there is the same difference between "words," taken in a general sense, and "noun," as between "animal" and "horse."

10. *Aug.* Do you likewise see that when we articulate this three-syllable word "animal," the noun is one thing, what it signifies is something else?

Ad. I already granted that before for all signs and things capable of being signified.

Aug. Do you think that all signs signify something other than what they are themselves, in the way that the three-syllable word "animal," when spoken, does not signify the word itself?

Ad. Of course not. For whenever we say "sign," it signifies not only other signs, whatever they are, but also itself, because "sign" is a word, and all words are certainly signs.

Aug. But does not something similar occur when we pronounce the two-syllable word *verbum* [word]? For if it signifies whatever has meaning and is articulated, then it also comes under the heading of "word."

Ad. That is correct.

Aug. But does not the same thing hold true for "noun"? It also signifies nouns of all genders and is itself a noun of neuter gender. If I should ask you what part of speech "noun" is, could you give any other correct answer except a "noun"?

Ad. What you say is true.

Aug. Then there are signs which, among the other thing they signify, also signify themselves.

Ad. There are such signs.

Aug. Do you think the case is similar when we pronounce the four-syllable term *conjunctio* [conjunction]?

Ad. Not at all. For it does not signify nouns, but it is itself a noun.

Chapter 5

11. *Aug.* You have been paying close attention. Consider now whether signs can be found which mutually signify each other in such a way that the first signifies the second, and the second, the first. This mutual relation does not obtain between the four-syllable word *conjunctio* [conjunction] and what it signifies, as when we say, "if," "or," "for," "yet," "unless," "therefore," "since," and the like. For the one word "conjunction" signifies them all, but no one of them signifies that four-syllable word itself.

Ad. I understand, and I am eager to know what those signs are which mutually signify each other.

Aug. Then you fail to see that by saying "noun" and "word," we are expressing two words?

Ad. I see that.

Aug. Why, then, do you fail to see that by saying "noun" and "word," we are expressing two names?

Ad. I see that too.

Aug. Then you know that "noun" is signified by "word" just as "word" is signified by "noun."

Ad. I agree.

Aug. Can you tell me how they differ, apart from the fact that they are spelled and pronounced differently?

Ad. Possibly I can, for it is the same difference I indicated a short time ago. When we say "words," we signify everything expressed by articulate speech and conveying some meaning. Every noun, then, even "noun" itself, is a word, but not every word is a noun, though "word" is itself a noun.

12. *Aug.* What if someone should make this statement, and prove it, namely, that just as every noun is a word, so too, every word is a noun, could you find any difference between them, apart from the different sounds of the letters?

Ad. No, I think there is no difference between them.

Aug. What if all sounds expressed by articulated speech and conveying some meaning are both words and nouns, but are designated words for one reason, and nouns for another—would there be no difference between them?

Ad. I do not see how there could be.

Aug. You will at least understand this, that everything colored is visible and everything visible is colored, though these two words have separate and different meanings.

Ad. I understand.

Aug. What, then, if the same obtains where every word is a noun and every noun is a word, though these same two nouns or words, namely, "noun" and "word," have a different meaning?

Ad. I see now that this can occur, but I am waiting for you to show me how.

Aug. You are, I think, aware that everything expressed by articulate voice and conveying some meaning must both strike the ear to be heard and be committed to the memory to be known.

Ad. I am aware of that.

Aug. So two things happen whenever we give expression to something by means of articulate sound.

Ad. That is correct.

Aug. What if words derive their name from one of the two things, and nouns from the other? Suppose, that is, that words [*verba*] come from "striking" [*verberando*], and nouns [*nomina*] from "knowing" [*noscendo*], so that the former has earned its name because of the ear, the latter, because of the mind.[1]

13. *Aug.* I will grant this when you show me that we are correct in saying that all words are nouns.

Ad. That is easy.

Aug. You learned, I suppose, and still remember, that a pronoun is so called because it can stand for a noun, though it indicates the reality less perfectly than a noun. I think this was the definition you recited to your grammar teacher, namely, that a pronoun is a part of speech which, when substituted for the noun itself, signifies the same thing, though less perfectly.

Ad. I remember the definition and think it is a good one.

Aug. So you see that according to this definition pronouns serve only for nouns and can be substituted for them only.

---

[1] Although the derivation of *nomen* from *noscere* is disputed, there appears to be no solid philological basis whatever between *verbum* and *verberare*.

When we say, for example, "this man," "the king himself," "the same woman," "this gold," "that silver," the terms "this," "himself," "same," "this," and "that," are pronouns; "man," "king," "woman," "gold," "silver," are nouns, which signify their objects more perfectly than do pronouns.

Ad. I understand this and agree.

Aug. Now, mention some conjunctions—any at all.

Ad. Et [and], *que* [and], *at* [but], *atque* [and].

Aug. Do you think that all these that you have mentioned are nouns?

Ad. By no means.

Aug. Do you think that I was at least speaking correctly when I said: "All these that you have mentioned"?

Ad. Absolutely. Now I realize how cleverly you made me see that I was giving expression to nouns, since, otherwise, it would have been incorrect to say "all *these*." But I still have the fear that you seemed to have spoken correctly only because there is no denying that these four conjunctions are also words. Consequently, they could be referred to correctly as "all these," because it is correct to say "all these words." But if you ask me what part of speech is "words," I can only reply that it is a noun. Perhaps, then, it was the inclusion of the pronoun with this noun that made your expression correct.

14. *Aug.* You have made an intelligent mistake. But that you may be mistaken no longer, pay closer attention to what I have to say, if only I can express it the way I want to. Now dealing with words by means of words is just as bewildering as intertwining and scratching one's fingers, where it is almost impossible to tell, except for the person doing it, which fingers are itching and which are relieving the itch.

Ad. See, I am all attention! That analogy has stirred my curiosity.

Aug. Words, of course, are made up of sounds and letters.

Ad. True.

Aug. Let us first of all make use of that authority so dear to us. When the Apostle Paul says: "There was not in Christ 'is' and 'is not,' but 'is' was in Him,"[2] I do not think we are to imagine that the three letters used in saying *est* [is] were in Christ, but rather what those three letters signify.

Ad. What you say is true.

Aug. So you see that when the Apostle said: "Is [*est*] was in Him," he said simply that "what was in Him is called 'is' [*est*]." It was as if he had said, "Power was in Him," which could only mean that what we call "power" was in Him. We are not to suppose that the two syllables enunciated in saying "power" are what was in Christ, but rather what these two syllables signify.

Ad. I understand and follow you.

Aug. Do you not also understand that it makes no difference whether someone says, "it is *called* virtue," or "it is *named* virtue"?

Ad. That is obvious.

Aug. Then it is just as obvious that it makes no difference whether someone says, "what was in Him is *called* 'is,'" or "is *named* 'is.'"

Ad. I see that here, too, there is no difference.

Aug. Do you also see what I am trying to point out to you?

Ad. I do not, really.

Aug. Then do you likewise fail to see that a noun is that by which a thing is named?

Ad. Clearly, nothing could be more certain.

Aug. So you see that "is" is a noun, since what was in Him is named "is."

Ad. I cannot deny it.

Aug. But if I should ask you what part of speech is "is," I think you would say it is not a noun, but a verb, though our reasoning has shown us that it is also a noun.

Ad. It is just as you say.

---

[2] 2 Cor. 1.19. Translations which follow the Greek rather than the Vulgate render the passage: "for the Son of God . . . was not now 'Yes' and now 'No,' but only 'Yes' was in him."

Aug. Do you still doubt that the other parts of speech are also nouns in the same way as we have just shown?

Ad. I do not, because I now admit that they signify something. But were you to ask, one by one, what the things they signify are called, that is, what their names are, I could only answer that they are the very parts of speech which are not called "nouns," although our reasoning has, as I now perceive, shown them to be nouns.

15. *Aug.* Are you unconcerned that someone may be found to upset your reasoning by asserting that the Apostle's authority must be allowed where realities are concerned, but not for words, with the result that the basis for this position is not so strong as we think? For, while it is possible that Paul was perfectly correct in his life and teaching, he did, nevertheless, express himself somewhat incorrectly when He said, " 'is' was in Him," all the more so, since he admits himself that he is "unskilled in speech."[3] How do you suppose we should refute such a person?

Ad. I could not gainsay such a man. I do entreat you to find someone among those experts in language whose high competence is recognized, whose authority will better enable you to accomplish your purpose.

Aug. So you think that without authorities, reason itself is incapable of proving that all the parts of speech signify something and thereby give it a designation; if it has a designation, it has a name; if it has a name, it certainly gets its name from a noun. This is readily discernible in the various languages. Anyone can see, for example, that if you ask what the Greek word is for "who," the answer is *tis;* for "wish," *thelō;* for "well," *kalōs;* for "something written," *to gegrammenon;* for "and," *kai;* for "from," *apo;* for "alas," *oi.* Now the one who asks such questions concerning all these parts of speech which we enumerated is speaking correctly, which would not be possible unless they were nouns. Accordingly,

---

[3] Cf. 2 Cor. 11.16.

since we are able to establish that the Apostle Paul spoke correctly according to this line of reasoning, without recourse to all the masters of eloquence, what need is there to look for some person to support our position?

16. But lest there be someone who will not yet yield, because he is too dull or arrogant, but declares that he will not yield at all except to authorities whose function to legislate regarding words is recognized by common consent—then, is there anything more excellent than Cicero to be found in the Latin language? Now, in his finest orations, known as the Verrines, he called the preposition *coram* (before) a noun, though it may be an adverb in this passage.[4] Since I do not quite understand the passage, it is possible that a different explanation may be advanced at another time, either by myself or by someone else. But there is one point, I think, which cannot possibly be gainsaid. The most celebrated masters of argumentation, for example, teach that a complete sentence is made up of a noun and a verb, and may be either affirmative or negative. The same Tullius refers somewhere to this form of discourse as a "proposition."[5] They also teach, and rightly so, that when the verb is in the third person, the case of the noun must be the nominative. If you examine with me such expressions as "the man sits" or "the horse runs," you will, I think, recognize that these are two propositions.

Ad. I do.

Aug. Do you see there is a separate noun in each of the propositions: "man," in the first, "horse," in the other; and also a separate verb: "sits," in the first, "runs," in the other?

Ad. I see that.

Aug. So if I were only to say "sits" or "runs," you would rightly ask me "who?" or "what?", and I would reply "a man,"

---

[4] *In Verrem* 2.2.104 (". . . totum hoc *nomen, coram* ubi facit delatum. . ."). According to H. Hagendahl, this is "a curious misinterpretation" of Cicero's Latinity; see his *Augustine and the Latin Classics* (2 vols. Studia Graeca et Latina Gothoburgensia 20:1-2; Göteborg 1967) 2.483; cf. 1.50 (test. 105).

[5] Cf. *Tusculanae disputationes* 1.7.14.

or "a horse," or "an animal," or something else, so that by joining the noun again to the verb, a complete proposition would result, namely, a sentence, whether affirmative or negative.

Ad. I understand.

Aug. Pay attention to what else I have to say. Suppose we are viewing something at a distance and are not sure whether it is an animal or a stone, or something else. If I should say to you, "Because it is a man, it is an animal," would I not be speaking rashly?

Ad. Very much so. But if you should say, "If it is a man, it is an animal," you would certainly not be speaking rashly.

Aug. You are correct. Hence the term "if" in your sentence is acceptable to both of us, while the term "because" in my sentence is unacceptable to both of us.

Ad. I agree.

Aug. See now whether these two sentences are complete propositions: " 'If' is acceptable" [*Placet si*]; " 'Because' is not acceptable" [*Displicet quia*].

Ad. They are altogether complete.

Aug. Come now, tell me which words are the verbs, and which the nouns.

Ad. I see that the verbs are "is acceptable" [*placet*] and "is not acceptable" [*displicet*], whereas the nouns can only be "if" and "because."

Aug. Then it has been sufficiently established that these two conjunctions are also nouns.

Ad. Quite sufficiently.

Aug. Can you prove by yourself that the same things hold for the other parts of speech in accordance with this same rule?

Ad. I can.

Chapter 6

17. *Aug.* Let us go on from here. Tell me now whether you

think that all names are terms [*vocabula*], and all terms are nouns, just as we found that all words are nouns and all nouns are words.

Ad. Except for the different sounds of the syllables, I really see no difference between them.

Aug. I will not object to that for now, although there are those who do make a distinction between them in meaning. But there is no need to examine their opinion just now. It must surely occur to you that we have now come to those signs which signify one another mutually, where the only difference is one of sound, and which signify themselves, together with the other parts of speech.

Ad. I do not understand.

Aug. Then you fail to understand that "noun" is signified by "term" and "term" by "noun" in such a way that, except for the sound of the letters, there is no difference between them so far as the general meaning of "noun" is concerned. For we also speak of "noun" in a particular sense, where it is found among the eight parts of speech and does not include the other seven.

Ad. I understand.

Aug. But that is the very thing I said—terms and nouns signify each other mutually.

18. *Ad.* That I understand, but I am asking what you meant by saying that these signs signify themselves, together with the other parts of speech.

Aug. Did not our reasoning show us before that all the parts of speech can be called both nouns and terms, that is to say, they can be signified both by "noun" and "term"?

Ad. That is right.

Aug. What of "noun" itself, namely, the sound expressed by the two syllables *nomen* [name]? If I ask what you would call it, would you not answer correctly that it is a "noun"?

Ad. That would be correct.

Aug. But does not the four-syllable sign, which is expressed by our saying *conjunctio* [conjunction], signify itself in this way? We cannot include this noun among the things it signifies.

Ad. Now I have it right.

Aug. That is precisely what was said, namely, that "noun" signifies itself together with the other things it signifies, and you can see for yourself that the same things hold for "term."

Ad. Now it is easy. But it occurs to me now that "noun" can be understood both in a general and in a particular sense, whereas "term" is not included among the eight parts of speech. Accordingly, I think they also differ in this respect, over and above the difference in sound.

Aug. What of *nomen* and *onoma?* Do you think there is any difference between them except for the sounds which distinguish the Latin and Greek languages?

Ad. I really see no other difference here.

Aug. We have reached this conclusion, therefore, in our discussion: there are signs which signify themselves; signs that signify each other mutually; signs that have the same extension; signs that differ only in sound. This fourth kind of sign we have just discovered; the first three were understood to apply both to "nouns" and "words."

Ad. That much has been settled.

Chapter 7

19. *Aug.* I would like you to review the results of our conversation.

Ad. I shall do the best I can. I recall, first of all, that we inquired for a time about the purpose of language and discovered that we speak either to teach or to recall. Even when we ask questions, we do nothing more than teach the person interrogated what we wish to learn from him. In the case of singing, what we are apparently doing for pleasure is not the proper function of language. In praying to God, who cannot conceivably be taught or reminded of anything, our words serve either to remind ourselves or to enable us to remind and teach others. Then, after it had been made sufficiently clear that words are merely signs, and that what fails to signify something is not a sign, you recited a verse where I should try to point out the meaning of the words, one by one. The verse was this: "If it please the gods that nothing remain of so great a city." While the second word [nihil] is familiar and perfectly obvious, we failed nevertheless to discover its meaning. And when I was of the opinion that we do not insert it in speaking without some reason, but use it to teach something to one hearing it, you did indeed reply that it possibly indicates a state of mind, whenever the mind has found, or thinks it has found, that something it was looking for does not exist. But you put off clarifying the matter for another time, and avoided probing this unexplored problem by means of a humorous remark. And do not suppose that I have forgotten what you promised.

Then, when I had all I could do to explain the third word of the verse, you kept after me not to explain one word by another of the same meaning, but to point out the reality itself signified by the words. And when I stated that this was not possible in conversation, we went on to consider things that can be indicated by pointing the finger as a reply to those who ask about them. These included, I thought, all corporeal things, but we discovered that only things visible were included. Then, somehow or other, we came to consider the case of deaf people and actors, who, without speaking, use gestures to signify not only things that can be seen, but also many other things besides, in fact, almost everything that we indicated by speech; yet, we found that gestures themselves are signs. After that, we began again to inquire how we might be able, without the use of signs, to indicate the very things signified by signs, seeing that we can indicate the wall, colors, and things visible by pointing the finger, which is also shown to be a sign. Here, after I had made the mistake of saying that no such thing was possible, we finally agreed that those things can be indicated without signs which we are not doing at the time we are asked about them, but which we are able to do once we are questioned. Speaking, however, is not included in this class, since it was perfectly clear that if we are asked what speaking is, while we are speaking, it is easy to indicate the action by the very thing itself.

20. This enabled us to see that there are signs that manifest signs, and signs that manifest things that are not signs; and again, that those things can be manifested without signs, which we are able to do after being questioned about them. We undertook a more thorough examination and discussion concerning the first of these three. It became clear from our discussion that some signs cannot in turn be signified by those signs which they signify, as is the case when we use the four-syllable word *conjunctio* [conjunction]; also, that there are other signs which can. When we say "sign," for example, we also signify "word," and when we say "word," we also signify "sign," because "sign" and "word" are two signs as well as two words. Within that class of signs, however, which signify one another mutually, we showed that some do not have the same extension, others have the same extension, while others are identical. For example, the two-syllable word expressed when we say *signum* [sign], signifies all the signs by which a thing can be signified at all. But when we say "word," this is not a sign of all signs, but only of those expressed by the articulated voice. It is clear, then, that although *verbum* [word] is signified by *signum* [sign] and vice versa, that is, the first two syllables are signified by the latter two, and the latter by the former, nevertheless, *signum* has a wider extension than *verbum*. That is to say, the first two syllables have a wider extension than the latter two.

But "word" and "noun" have the same extension when

used in a general sense. Our line of reasoning has actually shown that all the parts of speech can also be nouns, because pronouns can be used in connection with them. Also, that they name something, and that all of them can form a complete sentence by adding a verb to them. Yet, while "noun" and "word" have the same extension, since every word is also a noun, they do not have the same meaning. We did, in fact, show that it was quite probable that they are designated "words" for one reason, and "nouns" for another. We found that the first of these indicated a "striking" on the ear, and the second a recalling on the part of the mind. This can be seen, for example, from the fact that in speaking, it is perfectly correct to say: "What is the name for this thing?" whenever we want to commit it to our memory; it is not usual for us to say: "What is the word for this thing?"

On the other hand, we found that *nomen* and *onoma* are signs that have not only the same extension, but are also completely the same in meaning, differing only in the sound of their letters. This one point, it is true, did escape me, namely, that in the class of signs which signify mutually, we found none that did not also signify itself among the other things it signified.

I have recalled these points to the best of my ability. I leave it to you to say whether I have arranged them in a good and logical order, for I do not think you said anything in our conversation unless you knew it was certain.

Chapter 8

21. *Aug.* You have done rather well to recall from memory everything that I asked. Furthermore, I must acknowledge to you that these distinctions seem much clearer to me now than they did when we were both bringing them to light from some sort of hidden abode by means of our inquiry and discussion.

But it is hard to say at this point what the objective is that I am trying to reach with you by such roundabout ways. Maybe you think we are being playful and are turning our minds from serious matters by some kind of childish and trifling questions, or that we are only looking for a slight or unimportant result. Or, if you feel that this discussion will result in something important, you want to know right now what it is, or a least to hear what it is. Now I want you to know that I have not injected any worthless comedy[1] into our conversation, though we may perhaps be acting playfully. Yet even this is not to be regarded as child's play, nor are we to suppose that we have only slight or unimportant benefits in mind. And yet, if I assert that there is a happy life, and one that is everlasting, and that I desire that we should be led to it by God, Who is Truth itself,[2] as our Guide, by stages adapted to our faltering steps, I fear I may seem ridiculous for having first embarked upon so long a course with a consideration of signs rather than of the realities they signify. You will pardon me then if I engage in some preliminary play with you, not for the sake of playing, but to exercise and sharpen our mental powers. This will enable us not only to endure, but also to love the warmth and light of that region wherein is found the happy life.[3]

Ad. Do go on as you have begun, for I could never consider as trivial anything which you think is worth saying or doing.

22. *Aug.* Come now, and let us consider the class of signs which signify, not other signs, but the things we call signifiable. And, first of all, tell me whether man is man.

Ad. I cannot tell now whether you are joking.

---

1 *vilia ludicra.* A reference to the previous passage (2.3) where, indulging in a play on words, Augustine remarks that the discussion of "nothing" has resulted in their being detained by "nothing."
2 An excellent presentation of this central theme in Augustine's philosophy is available in C. Boyer, *L'Idée de vérité dans la philosophie de saint Augustin* (2 ed. Paris 1940).
3 The subject of Augustine's early Dialogue, *The Happy Life.* The thought and language of this passage reflect the influence of Plato's dialectic as a necessary preparation for the soul's vision of the truth.

Aug. Why is that?

Ad. Because you think I have to be asked whether man is anything but man.

Aug. So I suppose you would think I was jesting with you if I were also to ask whether the first syllable of this noun man [*homo*] is other than *ho,* and the second other than *mo.*

Ad. I certainly would.

Aug. But would you deny that these two syllables, taken together, make *homo?*

Ad. Who could deny it?

Aug. I ask you, then, whether *you* are these two connected syllables?

Ad. Not at all. But I do see what you are driving at.

Aug. Well then, tell me, so you will not think I am being offensive.

Ad. You think the conclusion is that I am not a man.

Aug. Why should you not think the same, since you grant as true all the previous points from which this conclusion was drawn?

Ad. I will not tell you what I think until I first hear from you whether, in questioning me as to whether man is man, you are asking about those two syllables, or about the reality itself which they signify.

Aug. You tell me, instead, in what sense you have taken my question. For if it is ambiguous, you should have guarded against this before and should not have answered until you were certain in what sense I proposed the question.

Ad. Why should I be hampered by this ambiguity, when I have replied to both senses of the question? The term *homo* [man] is certainly *homo,* since those two syllables are nothing more than those two syllables, and what they signify is none other than the existing reality.

Aug. An ingenious reply, to be sure. But why have you taken only this term "man" in both senses, and not the others that we also mentioned?

Ad. How can you prove that I did not also take the others in the same way?

Aug. To mention only one, if you had understood my first question entirely from the viewpoint of the sound of the syllables, you would have given me no answer, for you could have thought that I had not even asked a question. But now, when I expressed three words, repeating the one in the middle, and asked *utrum homo homo sit* [whether man is man], you understood the first and last words, not as mere signs, but as realities signified by the signs. This was obvious from the mere fact that you were at once so certain and sure of yourself as to feel that my question should be answered.

Ad. What you say is true.

Aug. Why, then, did you see fit to take only the middle word [*homo*] both with respect to the sound and to the reality it signifies?

Ad. Look here, now I am going to take the whole sentence from the viewpoint of what is signified. For I agree with you that we simply cannot engage in conversation unless the mind is directed by the sound of the words to the realities signified by these signs. Now, then, show me how I was deceived by a line of reasoning that resulted in the conclusion that I am not a man.

Aug. No, but I shall repeat the same questions so that you can find out for yourself where you made your mistake.

Ad. You are right.

23. *Aug.* I will not repeat my first question because you have already answered it. See, now, whether the syllable *ho* is anything other than *ho*, and the syllable *mo* anything other than *mo*.

Ad. Really, I can see no difference here.

Aug. See, likewise, whether man [*homo*] results from the combination of these two syllables.

Ad. I could never grant such a thing. We did agree, and rightly so, that whenever a sign is expressed, our attention should be directed to the reality it signifies, and, once we have considered it, we should either affirm or deny what it expressed. Since, however, those two syllables have no meaning when they are pronounced separately, we agreed that they were only sounds.

Aug. Then you agree, and are firmly convinced, that answers to questions should be made only with reference to the things signified by the words.

Ad. I see no reason to disagree, provided that the sounds are words.

Aug. I would like to see how you would refute the man who concluded that a lion came forth from the mouth of his opponent, as is often told in jest. When asked whether the things we say do come forth from our mouth, the other could not deny it. He had no trouble getting the man to say "lion" while he was speaking. When that happened, he began to make fun of him and to press the point that, good man that he was, he had discharged from his mouth so savage a beast; for he had acknowledged that whatever we say comes forth from our mouth, and he could not deny that he had said "lion."

Ad. Really, it would not be difficult at all to refute such a buffoon, because I would not grant that whatever we say goes out of our mouth. We signify the things we speak of, and what comes forth from the speaker's mouth is not the thing signified, but the sign by which it is signified. We make an exception for signs that signify themselves, but we dealt with this class a short time ago.

24. *Aug.* This would certainly make you a match for him. Just the same, what answer would you give me if asked whether "man" is a noun?

Ad. What else, but a noun?

Aug. Well, then, am I seeing a noun when I look at you?

Ad. No.

Aug. Do you want me to say what follows from this?

Ad. Please do not. I can see for myself the inference that I am not a man, since in reply to your question whether man is a noun, I said that it was. We had, in fact, already agreed that when we give or deny assent to what is said, we do so from the side of the reality which is signified.

Aug. But the very fact that you hit upon this reply is, in my opinion, not without significance. For reason's own law, which is implanted in our minds, prevailed over your caution. If I were to ask, for example, what man is, you might answer an "animal." But if I should ask what part of speech is "man," the only correct answer you could give would be a "noun." Consequently, though man is found to be both a noun and an animal, the former designation has to do with signs, the latter, with the thing signified. So when anyone asks whether "man" is a "noun," I can only reply that it is, since he indicates clearly enough that he wants to know what man is precisely as a sign. But if he asks whether man is an animal, I will reply in the affirmative even more promptly. If he does not mention either "noun" or "animal," and merely asks what man [*homo*] is, then, following an approved rule of language, my mind would quickly turn its attention to the reality signified by the two syllables, and answer an "animal"; or I might even state the full definition of man, namely, that he is a mortal rational animal. Do you not think so?

Ad. I do, absolutely. But when we grant that "man" is a noun, how can we escape the highly offensive conclusion that we are not men?

Aug. How do you suppose, if not by showing that this conclusion was not drawn according to the sense of the term agreed upon with the one who asked the question. But if he acknowledges that he drew the conclusion from the other sense of the term, the inference should not frighten us at all. For why should I fear to admit that I am not "man" [*hominem*], namely, that I am not those three syllables?

Ad. Nothing could be truer. Why, then, does the mind take

offense at the inference that you are not "man," since, according to what we have agreed upon, nothing truer could be said?

Aug. Because I cannot help thinking that as soon as the words are expressed, the conclusion has reference to the reality itself signified by these two syllables; and this, by reason of that rule so compelling by nature, namely, that whenever the sounds are heard, our attention is directed towards the things signified.

Ad. I agree.

Chapter 9

25. *Aug.* Now, then, I would have you understand that the realities signified are to be valued more highly than their signs. For whatever exists for the sake of something else must be of less value than that for which it exists. Would you agree?

Ad. I do not think one should assent to this too hastily. When we say "filth" [*coenum*], for example, I think the word far excels the reality it signifies. For that which makes the term offensive to us, whenever we hear it, has nothing to do with the sound of the word. Actually, by changing a single letter, the noun *coenum* [filth] becomes *coelum* [heaven]; and we see how far apart the realities are which these nouns signify. That is why I could never impute to the sign the quality we loathe in the reality which it signifies. I am right, then, in preferring the former to the latter, for we would rather hear the word than experience the reality by any of our senses.

Aug. You are very much on the alert. It is false, then, that all realities are to be valued more highly than their signs?

Ad. It looks that way.

Aug. Tell me, now, what you think those men had in mind when they gave a name to something so foul and revolting as this; also, whether you approve or disapprove what they did.

Ad. For my part, I would not presume to approve or disapprove, nor do I have any idea of what they had in mind.

Aug. Can you at least see what you yourself have in mind when you mention the word?

Ad. I certainly can. My purpose is to use a sign in order to teach or remind the one I am speaking with about this particular reality, because I think that this is something he should know.

Aug. What of the knowledge itself exchanged between you by such teaching and calling to mind, which you aptly express by means of this name? Is it not to be more highly valued than the word itself?

Ad. I grant that the knowledge itself which results from such a sign should be regarded more highly than the sign, but I do think that this is therefore also true of the reality.

26. *Aug.* Although it may be false, in our opinion, that all realities should be valued above their signs, it still remains true that everything that exists for the sake of something else is of less value than that for which it exists. To be sure, the knowledge of filth, for the sake of which the word "filth" has been coined, should be more highly esteemed than the word itself which, in turn, must be preferred, as we have seen, to filth itself. The sole reason why this knowledge has been preferred to the sign now under discussion is that the latter exists for the sake of the former, not the former for the sake of the latter. So it was that a certain glutton, a "worshiper of the belly,"[1] to use the words of the Apostle, declared that he lived to eat. Exasperated by what he heard, a certain temperate man replied: "Would it not be much better to eat in order to live?"[2] It was, nevertheless, because of this very same rule that both had so spoken. The glutton was in disfavor simply because he so underestimated the value of his life as to esteem

---
1 Cf. Rom. 16.18.
2 An ancient maxim of uncertain origin, sometimes attributed to Socrates. Cf. A. Gellius, *Noctes Atticae* 9.2.7; Quintilian, *Institutio oratoria* 9.3.85.

it of less worth than the pleasures of the palate, declaring that he had lived for the sake of feasting. The temperate man deserves to be praised for the single reason that, recognizing which of the two should be done for the sake of the other, subordinate, that is, to the other, he reminded us that we should eat to live rather than live to eat. Again, if some talkative person, with an infatuation for words, should say, "I teach in order to talk," you or any other person capable of discerning the true value of things might well reply: "Dear man, why do you not rather talk in order to teach?"

If all this be true, and you know it is, you must indeed realize how much less value is to be given to words than to the things on account of which we use words. Even our use of words must itself be given priority over words. For words exist to be used, and we make use of them to teach. Teaching, therefore, excels talking just as much as talking excels words. So teaching far excels words. But I am eager to hear any objections that you think might be raised.

27. *Ad.* I certainly agree that teaching is superior to words. But I do not know whether some objection might not be made to that rule which states that everything which exists for the sake of something else is inferior to that for which it exists.

Aug. We shall treat this problem more appropriately and more thoroughly at another time. For the present, the point that you grant is sufficient for what I am trying to prove. You grant, for example, that the knowledge of realities is of greater value than their signs. Consequently, the knowledge of these realities which are signified is to be preferred to the knowledge of their signs. Do you not think so?

Ad. Have I ever granted that the knowledge of realities is superior to a knowledge of their signs, but not superior to the signs themselves? So I am afraid to agree with you on this point. Suppose, for example, that just as the name "filth" is better than what it signifies, so, too, the knowledge of this name is to be preferred to the knowledge of that reality, though the name itself is inferior to this knowledge—then what? We are really dealing with four things here: the name, the reality, knowledge of the name, and knowledge of the reality. Hence, just as the first excels the second, why may the third not excel the fourth? Even if it does not excel, must we also consider it inferior?

28. *Aug.* I see that you have done remarkably well to remember what you have granted, as well as to explain your own views. But you do understand, I suppose, that this three-syllable noun which we express by saying *vitium* [vice] is better than what it signifies, though the knowledge of the noun itself is of far less value than the knowledge of vices. Accordingly, even though you propose those four things and give them your attention—the name, the reality, knowledge of the name, knowledge of the reality—we rightly prefer the first to the second. This name is found, for example, in the poem where Persius says: "This man is stupified by vice,"[3] and not only does it not vitiate the verse, but it even lends embellishment to it. But when the reality signified by the name is found in anyone, it necessarily leaves him vitiated. But then the third thing does not excel the fourth, but the fourth, the third. For the knowledge of this name is of little importance compared to the knowledge of vices.

Ad. Do you think such knowledge is preferable, even when it makes men all the more wretched? For of all the punishments ever devised by cruel tyrants or inflicted by their greed, this same Persius assigns the first place to that which tortures men who are compelled to acknowledge vices which they cannot avoid.

Aug. In the same way, you could also deny that even the knowledge of virtues is preferable to the knowledge of the name "virtue," since to see virtue and not to have it is a torment. And it was the wish of this same satirist that tyrants might be punished this way.[4]

---
3 *Sat.* 3.32.
4 Cf. *ibid.* 35-38.

Ad. God save us from such folly! I see now that when the mind is imbued with knowledge by the noblest of all the branches of learning,[5] it is not the knowledge itself that is to be blamed. I see too that they should be deemed the most wretched of all, as I think Persius himself thought, who suffer from a disorder of this kind which cannot even be relieved by so potent a remedy.

Aug. You are right. But what does it matter to us, whatever Persius thought? In matters of this kind we are not subject to the authority of the poets. Then too, the question of which kind of knowledge is preferable to another cannot be easily explained here. I am satisfied with what we have shown so far, namely, that the knowledge of realities which are signified, even if not superior to the knowledge of signs, is nevertheless superior to the signs themselves. So let us examine more and more thoroughly what kind of realities those are which, as we have said, can be indicated without signs, such as speaking, walking, sitting, lying down, and so on.

Ad. I now recall the problem you mention.

Chapter 10

29. *Aug.* Do you think that all those actions which we can perform as soon as we are asked about them, can be indicated without signs, or would you make some exceptions?

Ad. As I consider over and over again this class of signs as a whole, I still find that nothing can be taught without signs, with the possible exception of speaking, and perhaps teaching, if someone should ask just what teaching itself is. For I see that whatever I do to make him learn, in response to his inquiry, he will not be learning from the action itself which he wants to have shown him. Now if someone should ask me what walking is when, as we said, I am not doing any-

---

5 A reference to the excellence and primacy assigned to moral science by Socrates, Plato, and the Stoics.

thing, or am doing something else, and I should try, without signs, to teach him what he wants to know by starting at once to walk, how shall I keep him from thinking that the distance I walked means the same as walking? He would be mistaken to think so, because he will suppose that someone who walks a longer or shorter distance than I did is not walking. And what I have said about this one word "walking" carries over to all those things which I had agreed could be indicated without signs, apart from the two exceptions we have made.[1]

30. *Aug.* This I accept, of course. But do you not think that speaking is one thing and teaching another?

Ad. It certainly seems so. For if they were the same, no one could teach unless he were speaking. But since we also teach many things by signs other than words, who could doubt that there is a difference?

Aug. What about teaching and signifying? Are they the same, or is there some difference?

Ad. I think they are the same.

Aug. But suppose someone else were to say that we teach in order to use signs? Could he not be easily refuted by applying the rule we mentioned before?

Ad. That is correct.

Aug. So if we use signs to teach, and do not teach in order to use signs, teaching and signifying are not the same thing.

Ad. That is true, and I was wrong when I answered that they were the same.

Aug. Now answer me this: when one is teaching what teaching is, does he do this by using signs, or in some other way?

Ad. I fail to see how he could do it otherwise.

Aug. Then what you said a while ago is untrue, namely, that when one is asked what teaching is, the thing itself can be shown without the use of signs. For we realize now that not even this can be done without signs, seeing that you have

---

[1] Namely, speaking and teaching.

granted that using signs and teaching are not the same. If they are different, as it appears they are, and the latter can only be indicated by the former, then teaching is certainly not made known by itself, as you had thought. So nothing has yet been found that can be made known of itself, except for speaking, which, in addition to other things, also signifies itself. But, since even this is also a sign, there is as yet absolutely no evidence to show that anything can be taught without the use of signs.

Ad. I see no reason to disagree.

31. *Aug.* Then it has been established that nothing can be taught without signs, and that we should value knowledge itself more highly than the signs which lead us to it, though it may be that some of the things signified are not superior to their signs.

Ad. It seems so.

Aug. Please bear in mind, will you, what a small result has come from such a roundabout discussion. Now, from the moment we began this fencing with words, which has been going on for so long, we have done our best to find out three things: whether anything can be taught without signs; whether some signs should be preferred to what they signify; and whether the knowledge of realities themselves is better than their signs. But there is a fourth point that I would like to find out from you in a few words, namely, do you think that things we have already discovered are such that you can no longer doubt about them?

Ad. I would certainly like to think that we have arrived at some certainties by so devious and winding a course. But that question of yours unsettles me for some strange reason, and keeps me from giving assent. For I think you would not ask me this unless you had some objection to make. Besides, the very complexity of these questions does not permit me to get a view of the whole problem and give a safe answer. I fear that amidst such complexity some point will pass unnoticed which my mind may not be sharp enough to bring to light.

Aug. I am glad to put up with your hesitation, for it reveals a cautious habit of mind, and this is the surest safeguard to preserve tranquility. It is very difficult indeed not to be perturbed when the things we held with a ready and eager assent are demolished by opposing arguments, and are wrenched, so to speak, from our hands. Accordingly, just as it is reasonable to yield to arguments that have been carefully weighed and examined, so is it hazardous to mistake what is not known for what is known. When conclusions are frequently undermined, which we thought would hold up and endure, there is danger that we may fall into such a hostile and distrustful attitude towards reason as to make it appear that we should not trust even the clearest evidence of truth.[2]

32. But come, let us quickly reconsider now whether you were right to regard these conclusions as doubtful. Suppose now that someone unfamiliar with the business of snaring birds, which is done with reeds and birdlime, should encounter a bird-catcher fitted out with all his equipment, though he is not snaring birds but simply going on his way. At the sight of him, he quickens his pace and, as is usually the case, reflects and, in amazement, asks himself the meaning of the man's paraphernalia. Suppose, too, that the bird-catcher, aware that the other's attention is fixed upon him, and eager to show off his prowess, releases the reeds and, with his rod and hawk, snares a little bird which he sees nearby which he comes up to and captures. Would he not, I ask you,

---

[2] Augustine may have in mind Socrates' warning to avoid uncritical assent to arguments which later appear inconclusive and thus expose the inquirer to the danger of distrusting the power of reason to discover truth. (Cf. *Phaedo* 80-90c.) More likely, he is recalling his own experience when, following his disillusionment with the Manichaean sect, he inclined for a time towards the kind of skepticism professed by the New Academy. The first work composed after his conversion, *Contra Academicos*, is a lengthy refutation of this doctrine which he regarded as the most pernicious of errors. Cf. *Retract.* 1.1.1.

teach that spectator of his what he was so eager to know, not by any sign, but by the reality itself?

Ad. I am afraid we are confronted here with a situation similar to that where I referred to the man who asks what walking is. Neither do I think that everything about bird-catching has been made known even in the present case.

Aug. It is an easy matter to put your mind at ease. I will make the further qualification, that if the spectator were intelligent enough, he could grasp everything there is to know about the art of bird-catching from what he saw. It is sufficient for our purpose that *some* men can be taught *some* things, though not all, without the use of signs.

Ad. I too could further qualify my remarks by saying that if one is really intelligent, he will learn all about walking as soon as someone indicates it to him, by taking a few steps.

Aug. You may make that qualification as far as I am concerned. I not only have no objection, but am even favorable to it. You see, in fact, that we have both reached the conclusion that some things can be taught without the use of signs, and that we were wrong in thinking a little while ago that nothing at all can be taught without signs. Actually, these examples bring to mind, not one or two, but thousands of things, which are made known by themselves without having to resort to signs. Why, I ask, should we have any doubt of this? For, apart from the numerous plays performed in every theater by actors who play their part by enacting the events themselves, without using signs, does not God, as well as nature, exhibit and manifest to the view of all, and just as they are, the sun and the light which covers and clothes all the things around us, the moon and the other stars, the earth and sea, and all the countless things which they bring forth?

33. Now if we examine the matter more carefully, perhaps you will discover that nothing is learned by means of its signs. For when I am shown a sign, it cannot teach me anything if it finds me ignorant of the reality for which the sign stands; but if it finds me acquainted with the reality, what do I learn from the sign? When I read this, for example: "And their saraballae were not changed,"[3] the word "saraballae" does not convey to me the thing it signifies. If it is some kind of head-covering that goes by this name, did I, upon hearing the word, come to learn either what "head" or "covering" means? These things I knew before, and I came to know them, not when they were called these names by others, but when I saw them by myself. Indeed, when the sound of the two-syllable word *caput* [head] first struck my ears, I was just as ignorant of what it signified as when I first heard or read the word "saraballae." But, after frequent repetitions of the word "head," I discovered, by paying careful attention at the time it was used, that this was the word for something that was well known to me by sight. Before discovering it, the word was only a sound so far as I was concerned. I came to know it as a sign when I discovered the reality of which it is a sign. And I learned what this reality was, not, as I have said, by any sign, but by looking at it. Hence, it is more of a matter of the sign being learned from the thing we know, than it is of knowing the thing itself from the manifestation of its sign.

34. To grasp this point more clearly, let us pretend that we now hear the word "head" for the first time, and, not knowing whether it is merely a vocal sound or whether it also signifies something, we inquire what "head" is. Remember now, we want to become acquainted, not with the thing signified, but with the sign itself, which we actually do not know as long as we do not know the thing it signifies. But if the reality is pointed out to us while we are inquiring about it, it is by seeing this reality that we learn its sign, which we had heard before but had not understood. But since there are two

---

[3] Dan. 3.94. The term *sarabarae*, or as the Vulgate reads, *sarabala*, occurs in the account of the three youths in the fiery furnace. The expression *Et sarabala eorum non fuissent immutata* . . ., is rendered by the Douay version ". . . nor their garments altered . . . ." The obscurity of the term itself only serves to illustrate Augustine's thesis that words of themselves can teach us nothing about things.

things about this sign, namely, the sound and its meaning, we certainly do not perceive the sound because it is a sign, but, by the very fact that it strikes the ear, whereas its meaning is perceived by looking at the reality it signifies. For the pointing of the finger can signify nothing else but the reality to which it is pointed, not towards the sign, but towards a member of the body which we call the head. Consequently, by means of this pointing, I learn neither the reality, which I already knew, nor the sign, towards which the finger was not pointed.

But I am not too much concerned about this matter of pointing the finger since, as I see it, this is more of a sign of what indicating is itself than it is of any of the things being indicated. It is like our use of the adverb *ecce* [look!]. Even when we use this adverb, we usually point our finger too, just in case the one sign is not sufficient to indicate the object. The point I am trying most of all to make you see, if I can, is this, that we learn nothing from signs which we call words. For, as I have pointed out, it is rather a question of learning the sense of the word, that is, the meaning hidden in the sound, from a previous knowledge of the reality signified than it is of perceiving that reality from a sign of this kind.

35. And I might also have said the same thing regarding "coverings" and other countless things as I said about the word "head." Yet, though I already know what these are, I still do not know what those *saraballae* are. If someone were to signify them to me by a gesture, or should draw a picture of them or show me something like them, I will not say that he did not teach me what they were, which I could easily prove if I wanted to speak at somewhat greater length. But I do say what is very much to the point, that he did not teach me this by means of words. But if he happens to be looking at them in my presence, and should call my attention to them by saying: "Look, *saraballae*," I will learn something new, not by my words that were spoken, but by looking at the reality.

And it was this that also enabled me to become acquainted with the word and to remember its meaning. Certainly, when I learned to know the reality, I did not rely upon the words of another, but upon my own eyes, though I did possibly rely upon words to direct my attention, that is, to see what there was to see by looking.

Chapter 11

36. So far, the most I can say for words is that they merely intimate that we should look for realities; they do not present them to us for our knowledge. But the man who teaches me is one who presents to my eyes or to any bodily sense, or even to the mind itself, something that I wish to know. So by means of words we learn only words, or better, the sound and noise of words. For if something cannot be a word unless it is a sign, I still cannot recognize it as a word until I know what it signifies, even though I have heard the word. Accordingly, it is by knowing the realities that we also come to a knowledge of their words, whereas, by the sound of words, we do not even learn the words. For we cannot learn words we already know, and, as for those which we do not know, we cannot profess to have learned them until we have seen their meaning. And this comes about, not by hearing the sounds they make, but from a knowledge of the realities they signify. It is perfectly logical and true to conclude that whenever words are spoken, we either know what they mean or we do not. If we know, they recall rather than teach something to us; if we do not know, they cannot even recall something, though they may lead us to inquire.

37. You may insist that we cannot really know what those head-coverings are except by seeing them, since the name is only a sound for us, and that we can know no more about the name itself unless we know what the realities are. And yet, we do accept as true the story of those boys: how their faith triumphed over the king and the flames, how they sang a hymn of praise to God and were found worthy to receive honors even from their very enemy. Have we learned all this otherwise than by words? I shall reply by noting that we already knew everything that those words signified. What is meant by "three boys," "furnace," "fire," "king," and, finally, "unharmed by fire," as well as the other things signified by those words, this I already knew. On the other hand, the names Ananias, Azarius, and Misael are just as much unknown to me as the *saraballae*. These names did not help me at all to know them, nor could they possibly do so. But that everything recounted in that story occurred at that time exactly as recorded, that, I admit, is something I "believe" rather than "know," and those same men, whose word we believe, were themselves not ignorant of this distinction.[1] For the Prophet says: "Unless you believe, you shall not understand,"[2] which he really could not have said if he thought that there was no difference between the two. Hence, what I understand, that I also believe, although I do not also understand everything I believe. Also, everything I understand, I know, though I do not know everything I believe. Nor do I for that reason fail to see how useful it is also to believe many things which I do not know, including also this account of the three boys. Accordingly, while there are a

---

1 Here the term "know" *(scire)*, as opposed to "believe" *(credere)*, indicates an immediate and certain cognitive awareness of realities present to the knower. In *Letter* 147, Augustine makes a similar distinction between "see" *(videre)* and "believe," as relating to a knowledge of things "present" and "absent," respectively. A further distinction is drawn in *The Trinity* between *scientia*, knowledge of things temporal, and *sapientia*, knowledge of things eternal. For further connotations of these terms, cf. H. I. Marrou, *Saint Augustin et la fin de la culture antique* (Paris 1938) 561-569.

2 Isa. 7.9. The Septuagint rendering of the text is of capital importance for Augustine's teaching on the primacy of faith and on the role of reason to penetrate the meaning of revealed truth. In a letter to Consentius *(Ep.* 120), he presents a summary of the relation between faith and reason.

great many things that I am unable to know, I do nevertheless know how useful it is to believe them.³

38. But as for all those things which we "understand," it is not the outward sound of the speaker's words that we consult, but the truth which presides⁴ over the mind itself from within, though we may have been led to consult it because of the words. Now He who is consulted and who is said to "dwell in the inner man,"⁵ He it is who teaches us, namely, Christ, that is to say, "the unchangeable Power of God and everlasting wisdom."⁶ This is the Wisdom which every rational soul does indeed consult, but it reveals itself to each according to his capacity to grasp it by reason of the good or evil dispositions of his will.⁷ And if the soul is sometimes mistaken, this does not come about because of any defect on the part of the truth it consulted, just as it is not through any defect in the light outside us that our bodily eyes are often deceived. We acknowledge that it is this light which we consult with regard to visible objects so that it may manifest them to us according to our capacity to perceive them.

---

3 Shortly after his ordination to the priesthood in 391, Augustine wrote *The Usefulness of Belief*. It is dedicated to his friend Honoratus whom he had converted from paganism to Manichaeism during his own proselytizing days in the sect. It seems that Augustine was less successful in winning his friend over to the Catholic faith.
4 A favorite expression employed by Augustine to describe the action of the "inner light" upon the soul in its perception of truth.
5 Cf. Eph. 3.14-17.
6 Cf. 1 Cor. 1.23-24.
7 From his reading of the Platonic writers, including Plotinus, and quite probably Porphyry, Augustine had come to understand the role of moral dispositions in the attainment of truth. His earlier enthusiasm for this philosophy occasionally gave rise to such exaggerations as this, that truth can only be seen by the pure of heart (cf. *Solil.* 1.1.21). While this extreme view is expressly repudiated in the *Retractations* (1.4.2), he continued to insist upon moral rectitude as a necessary condition for understanding revealed truth, a position well summarized in his statement that *mores perducunt ad intelligentiam* (*Tractatus in evangelium Ioannis* 18.5.7).

Chapter 12

39. Now if we consult light for colors, and consult the basic elements[1] of the material world which comprise those bodies known by the senses regarding the other sense qualities, and consult the senses themselves which the mind uses as interpreters[2] to know these things; if, again, we use our reason to consult that inner truth for the things that we understand—then what more could be said by way of proof to show that we learn nothing by means of words, except their sound which strikes the ear? For everything we perceive, we perceive either by the bodily sense or by the mind. We call the former, sense objects, the latter, intelligible objects; or, to appropriate the terminology of our own inspired Writers, we call the first carnal, the second, spiritual.[3] When asked about the former, we can reply if what we perceive is present to us, as when

---

1 A reference to the doctrine of the "four elements," earth, air, fire, and water. According to Empedocles, these elements, or "roots," are the eternal and changeless principles which combine and separate to account for the generation and corruption of bodies. Augustine will later make use of this teaching in his doctrine of the "seminal reasons" in an attempt to reconcile the uniqueness of God's creative act with the progressive appearance of new forms of life.

2 Augustine's characterization of the senses as "interpreters" or "messengers" of the mind reflects the Plotinian body-soul relation as conceived within a hierarchically-ordered universe which rigidly excludes any direct causal action of lower things upon those higher. In contrast with the Aristotelico-Thomistic view that *sentire est compositi*, Augustine maintains that the soul alone is the proper cause of sensation: *neque enim corpus sentit, sed anima per corpus, quo velut nuntio utitur ad formandum in seipsa quod extrinsecus nuntiatur (De genesi ad litteram* 12.24.51). For a good exposition of the Augustinian theory of sensation, including several points at variance with Plotinus, cf. M. A. Gannon, "The Active Theory of Sensation in Saint Augustine," *The New Scholasticism* 30 (1956) 154-180.

3 In a work of the same period, Augustine had stated that the Platonists had only to change a few of their expressions and views to become Christians (cf. *The True Religion* 4.7). Here, too, he purports to see only a verbal difference between the Platonists and "our own authors," namely, the inspired writers. Again, in his review of the Dialogue, *On Order*, he insists that there is no real difference between Plato's "intelligible world" and "the eternal and unchangeable Wisdom by which God made the world" (cf. *Retract.* 1.3.2).

someone asks us about the phase and position of the new moon while we are looking at it. If my questioner in this instance does not see the moon, he believes my words, though often he does not. In no case, however, does he really learn unless he sees for himself the thing we are talking about. He learns it then, not indeed by the sound of the spoken words, but by the things themselves and his senses. For the words sound the same to one who sees the object as they do to one who does not see it. But when questions are asked, not about things we perceive while they are present to us, but about those which our senses perceived on former occasions, then our words do not refer to the things themselves, but to the images impressed by them upon the senses and stored away in the memory.[4] And, since we are reflecting upon what is unreal, I fail to see how we can possibly speak of them as true, unless it be for the fact that we are recounting, not what we see and perceive at the moment, but what we have already seen and perceived. So it is that we bear these images in the deep recesses of the memory as witnesses, so to speak, of things previously experienced by the senses. When reflecting upon these images in our mind, we can speak of them in good conscience, without lying. But these images are only witnesses for ourselves. If the one who hears what I am recounting has seen these things for himself and was there on the spot, he does not learn them from my words but recognizes them himself by the images he took away with him from these things. But if he has not experienced them with his senses, then it is clearly a matter of his believing my words rather than of learning.

40. But when it is a question of things which we behold with the mind, namely, with our intellect and reason, we give verbal expression to realities which we directly perceive as

---

[4] Augustine's later treatment of memory in the *Confessions* (10.8-27) represents a notable and original contribution to this area of psychological inquiry. The subject is again discussed in *The Trinity* (11.7-11).

present in that inner light of truth[5] by which the inner man, as he is called, is enlightened and made happy. But, here again, if the one who hears my words sees those things himself with that clear and inner eye of the soul, he knows the things whereof I speak by contemplating them himself, and not by my words. Therefore, even when I say what is true, and he sees what is true, it is not I who teach him. For he is being taught, not by my words, but by the realities themselves made manifest to him by the enlightening action of God from within. Consequently, he could also answer questions about these things if he were asked. What more absurd than the notion that he is being taught by what I say, when he could explain those very things even before I spoke, if only he had been asked about them?

But as for the case frequently encountered where someone replies to a question in the negative and is led on by other questions to answer in the affirmative, this springs from a weakness in one's mental perception which makes it impossible for him to consult that light regarding the matter in its entirety. He is led on to consider it part by part when questioned about those very same parts comprising the whole, which he was unable to perceive in its entirety. If he is brought around to this by the words of his questioner, the words still do not teach him, but only propose questions in a way suited to his capacity to learn from his inner light. For example, if I should ask you about the very matter now under

---

5 This expression of the Saint's teaching on "divine illumination" is notable for the absence of any vestiges of Platonic "reminiscence." In *Question* 46 of the *Eighty-Three Diverse Questions*, composed during this same period, Augustine integrated his teaching on illumination with that on the Divine Ideas as follows: "To the degree that the rational soul is united to Him by charity, by so much does it contemplate these intelligible principles *(rationes)*, through whose vision it is made supremely happy, being bathed, so to speak, and illumined by Him with spiritual light." For several recent interpretations of this difficult doctrine, cf. C. Schützinger, "Die augustinische Erkenntnislehre in Lichte neurer Forschung," *Recherches Augustiniennes* 2 (1962) 177-203; L. Cilleruelo, "Pro memoria Dei," *Revue des études augustiniennes* 12 (1966) 65-84.

consideration, namely, whether anything can be taught by means of words, the question might appear to you absurd at first because you are unable to see the whole problem. Consequently, I would have to frame the question in a way suited to your capacity to hear that Teacher who teaches from within. Where, I might ask, have you learned all those things which you admitted were true as I was speaking, and which you think you now know for sure? You might reply that I was the one who had taught them to you. Suppose then, by way of questioning you further, I were to tell you that I had seen a man flying. Would my words give you the same certainty as if you were to hear me say that wise men are better than fools? You would of course deny this, and answer that you do not believe my first statement, or that even if you do believe it, you do not know it, whereas you know the other statement to be absolutely certain. This would surely enable you to see that you had not learned anything by my words, whether, as in the one instance, where you did not know what I was speaking of, or in the other, where you understood perfectly well. As a matter of fact, if you had been asked about those statements separately, you could have even sworn that you did not know the former and that you did know the latter. Then indeed you would admit as true the proposition in its entirety which you had denied, since you would now have a clear and certain grasp of all that it involves. It is this: Whenever we express anything in words, our hearer either does not know whether it is true, or he knows it is untrue, or he knows it is true. In the first of these three, it is a matter of belief or opinion or doubt; in the second, of opposition and denial; in the third, of attesting to what is true. In none of these cases, therefore, does he learn. It follows, therefore, that one who does not grasp the reality after hearing our words, or who knows that what he heard is untrue, or who could have given the same answer, if asked, has learned nothing by any words of mine.

Chapter 13

41. It further follows that where realities discerned by the mind are concerned, it is of no avail for one who does not perceive them to hear the words of one who does, except when it is useful to believe them so long as he lacks knowledge of them. But anyone who is able to perceive them is an inward disciple of the truth and an outward judge of the speaker, or better, a judge of what he is saying. For he very often understands what was said even when the speaker himself does not. Let us suppose, for example, that someone who takes the word of the Epicureans and judges that the soul is mortal, should expound arguments which have been advanced by the wiser philosophers in favor of its immortality. If someone capable of spiritual discernment happens to hear him, he will judge that what this man says is true, whereas the speaker does not know whether such arguments are true; in fact, he even thinks they are completely false. Are we, then, to think of him as teaching what he does not know? Yet he uses the same words which could also be used by one who understood them.

42. Hence, not even the role of expressing what the speaker has in mind is any longer left to words, since it is not certain that he knows what he is saying. There are, in addition, those who lie and deceive, so that you can readily see from them how words not only do not reveal their thoughts, but even conceal them. I have no doubt whatever that the words of truthful men are an attempt and a sort of pledge to reveal the thoughts of the speaker, and that they would succeed in this, as all agree, if only liars were not allowed to speak.

Yet, we have often observed, both in ourselves and in others, that words are spoken which do not express the thoughts in one's mind. I see two ways that this can happen, either some kind of speech, frequently repeated and memorized, flows out of the speaker's mouth while he is thinking of something else, as often happens to us when we are singing a hymn; or, unintentionally, and by a slip of the tongue, some words are blurted out instead of others, so that in this case too, the words which are heard are not signs of what is in our mind. Liars, of course, also think of what they are saying, so that while we may not know whether what they say is true, we know nevertheless that they are saying what is in their mind, provided that neither of the two things I just mentioned happens to them. If someone contends that these things happen only occasionally and that it is obvious whenever they do, I will not object. Yet they often go unrecognized and have frequently deceived me as I listened to them.

43. But in addition to these cases where words do not convey their meaning, there is another kind, quite widespread, to be sure, and the source of endless bickering and disputes. It happens when the speaker actually says what he is thinking, but often does so only to himself and some others, while he does not convey the same meaning to the person spoken to, or to others as well. Suppose, for example, that someone should say in our hearing that man is surpassed in virtue by certain brute animals. We find ourselves at once unable to countenance such a remark and we spare no effort to refute so false and pernicious a view. The speaker, however, may be using the word "virtue" to signify physical strength to express what he has in mind. He is neither lying nor mistaken about the facts themselves. Neither is he spinning out words committed to memory, while he has his mind on something else, or is saying something different from what is on his mind by a slip of the tongue. He is merely indicating his thoughts by a different name than we do. We would agree with him at once on this point if we could read his thoughts, which he has as yet been unable to reveal to us, even though he has already made use of words to set forth his view.

They tell me that definitions can correct errors of this kind. Accordingly, if the speaker in this instance should define what "virtue" is, it would become apparent, so they say, that the dispute is not over the reality, but over the word. Even granting that this is the case, how many can you find who are good at defining? Besides, many points have been urged against the rules of definition, which it is not opportune to consider here, and with which I do not even entirely agree.

44. I pass over the fact that we fail to hear many words distinctly and enter into extended and heated arguments, just as if we had heard them. A short time ago, for instance, when I remarked that a certain word in the Punic tongue[1] meant "mercy," you stated that you had heard from those better acquainted with that language that it meant "piety." But I disagreed, insisting that you had completely forgotten what you had heard. For I thought you had said not "piety" but "faith," even though you were seated close to me and though these two words do not sound so much alike that they would deceive my hearing. Yet I thought for some time that you did not know what had been said to you, when all the while it was I who did not know what you had said. For if I had heard you correctly, I would never have thought it incongruous that "piety" and "mercy" should be expressed by the one word in the Punic language.

Such cases occur quite frequently, but I will, as I said, pass over them so as not to give the impression that I am censuring words unfairly because of carelessness or even deafness on the part of men who hear them. The cases I cited above are more perplexing, where we cannot know the speaker's thoughts, even though we share the same language and the words spoken in Latin are heard very distinctly.

---

1 Although the Roman conquest of North Africa was completed in 146 B.C., the Punic language survived and continued in usage even in St. Augustine's day. Cf. W. Green, "Augustine's Use of Punic," University of California *Publications in Semitic Philology* 11 (1951) 179-190; J. Lecerf, "Notule sur saint Augustin et les survivances puniques," *Augustinus Magister* (Paris 1954) 1.31-33.

45. See, I am going to yield to a point and grant that when words are heard by one acquainted with them, he can know that the speaker has been thinking about the things they signify. But does he thereby likewise learn that what was said is true, which is the question under discussion?

Chapter 14

Do teachers ever claim that it is their own thoughts that are grasped and retained, rather than the branches of learning themselves which they purport to transmit by their speaking? What foolish curiosity could ever prompt a man to send his child to school in order to have him learn what the teacher thinks? But when teachers have made use of words to explain all those branches of learning which they profess to be teaching, including even those dealing with virtue and wisdom, then those who are known as pupils reflect within themselves whether what has been said is true, contemplating, that is, that inner truth according to their capacity. It is then, therefore, that they learn. And when they discover within themselves that what has been said is true, they praise their teachers, unaware that they are not so much praising the teachers as they are praising those who have been taught, provided, however, that the teachers also know what they are saying. But men make the mistake of calling people "teachers" when they are not that at all, because there is generally no interval of time between the moment of speaking and that of knowing, and because their coming to learn from within follows quickly upon the suggestive force of the speaker's words, they think that they have learned externally from him who spoke those words.

46. We shall, God willing, resume our inquiry on another occasion into the whole question of the usefulness of words,[1] which is one of no small importance if you look into it carefully. For the present, I have cautioned you that we must not ascribe more importance to words than is their due. Accordingly, we should no longer merely believe, but also begin to understand the truth of those words based on divine authority, that we should not call any man on earth a teacher, seeing that "there is One in heaven who is the Teacher of all."[2] What is meant by "in heaven" is something that will be taught us by Him who directs us even through human agencies and external signs to turn inwardly to Him for our instruction. To love Him and to know Him, that is the happy life, which all proclaim they are seeking, but few there are who can rejoice at having really found it. But now I would like you to tell me what you think of this entire discourse of mine. For if you know that what was said is true, then, had you been questioned about each particular point, you would have declared that you know them too. So you can see from Whom it was that you learned these things. It was not from me, for you could have answered to everything I was asking you. But if you did not know that what I said was true, then neither He nor I have taught you. Not I, because I can never teach you; not He, because you are not yet able to learn these things.

Ad. I myself have come to learn through the suggestive power of your words that words merely stimulate a man to learn, and that the words of the speaker seldom reveal his thoughts to any great extent. But as to the truth of what is said, I have also learned that He alone teaches who made

---

[1] The project was never realized, possibly because of Augustine's failure to complete the treatises on the liberal arts which he had planned and begun at Milan while preparing for baptism. Only the works on grammar and music were ever completed, the latter at Tagaste. Nothing of the remaining works on dialectics, rhetoric, geometry and philosophy, not even the completed work on grammar, had survived when the aged Bishop undertook the review of his books about 427. Cf. *Retract.* 1.6.

[2] Matt. 23.9.

use of external words to remind us that He dwells within us. With His help, I shall now love Him all the more ardently as I advance in learning. I am grateful, however, that your remarks have continued without interruption, particularly because they anticipated and answered all the objections I was prepared to raise. You have not neglected a single question that had caused me to doubt, or which has not been answered for me by that inner Oracle[3] exactly as you had expressed it in words.

---

[3] Although generally used by Augustine to indicate the Sacred Scriptures, the term "oracle" in this context seems rather to refer to the "inner Teacher" just identified with the "One in heaven who is the Teacher of all."

THE FREE CHOICE OF THE WILL

(De libero arbitrio)

INTRODUCTION

SAINT AUGUSTINE's *De libero arbitrio* is the last and most important in the series of Dialogues begun after his conversion to the Catholic faith in the late summer of 386. While preparing for baptism at the country villa of Cassiciacum, not far from Milan, the neo-convert conducted discussions of a predominantly philosophical nature in the company of his mother, Monica, his son, Adeodatus, and a few pupils and friends. To this earliest literary period belong the Dialogues, *Contra Academicos, De beata vita,* and *De ordine,* which deal, respectively, with the problem of certitude, human happiness, Divine Providence and the problem of evil. Next in order is the *Soliloquia,*[1] a kind of contrived dialogue between Augustine's reason and himself, in which the two questions basic to Augustinian philosophy are examined, namely, God and the soul.[2] The problem of the immortality of the soul is discussed more fully in his next work, *De immortalitate animae,* composed at Milan, though not in dialogue form, while Augustine was a candidate for baptism. A further study on the soul, *De quantitate animae,* was written the following year at Rome shortly before Augustine's return to Africa. While a member of the small lay-community which he had established in his native town of Tagaste, Augustine composed the well-known dialogue, *De magistro,* which reproduces discussions with his son, Adeodatus, on the function of language and the role of the teacher in learning, including some of his earliest statements on the celebrated

---
1 Augustine himself coined the term *soliloquia.* Cf. *Soliloquia* 2.7.14; *Retract.* 1.4.1.
2 Translations of these four Dialogues are available in Vol. [5] of this series (Writings of St. Augustine I, New York 1948).

doctrine of divine illumination. Although begun at Rome between 387 and 388, the *De libero arbitrio* was not completed until after his ordination to the priesthood at Hippo in 391. With the completion of this work, not later than 395, there comes to an end the so-called philosophical period of Augustine's writings which, for the most part, contain personal reflections upon the great themes of classical philosophy, examined in the light of a reason already illumined by the Christian revelation.

The *De libero arbitrio* is among Augustine's first works against the Manichees in a prolonged polemic extending over a period of almost twenty years. It is not surprising that his first polemic should have been directed against the very system which had won his allegiance for nearly ten years, and which continued to pose a serious threat to the Catholic faith, not only in North Africa, but throughout the whole Roman Empire. In this work, Augustine readily acknowledges that the facile and convenient solution of the problem of evil proposed by the Manichees had been a powerful factor in his decision to join the sect in his twentieth year.[3] According to the metaphysical dualism of Manes, man was composed of two antagonistic elements derived from two eternal and conflicting principles of Light and Darkness, corresponding to Good and Evil respectively. Accordingly, the conflict in man between good and evil represented merely one aspect of the universal conflict between these ultimate cosmic forces which, in effect, exonerated man from any moral responsibility for his conduct.[4] The principal scope of the *De libero arbitrio* is a refutation of this dualistic doctrine, with special reference to the nature and origin of moral evil, and to the created

---

3 1.2.4.
4 The best modern exposition of Manichaeism is that by H. C. Puech, *Le Manichéisme: son fondateur, sa doctrine* (Paris 1949). A good English account, based largely upon the former, is found in the recent biography by G. Bonner, *Saint Augustine of Hippo: Life and Controversies* (London 1963) 157-192. Cf. also J. Ries, "Manichaeism," *New Catholic Encyclopaedia*, 9.153-160.

will as its sole and adequate cause. As early as 386, Augustine had raised the problem of evil from the standpoint of a universal providence in the dialogue, *De ordine,* but had to abandon the original plan of the work almost from the start, owing to the inability of his youthful pupils to cope with so difficult a problem at the time. As a result, these two books deal largely with the proper order to be observed in studies so that the mind may pass more securely from the consideration of things corporeal to the contemplation of incorporeal reality.[5]

When Augustine had completed the *De libero arbitrio,* he little realized that some of his own weapons employed against the Manichees would, ironically, be turned upon him during a later polemic that was to occupy the last twenty years of his life. It was at Rome, about the year 410, that the future heresiarch, Pelagius, first came upon this striking sentence from the tenth book of Augustine's *Confessions:* "Grant what thou dost command, and command what thou wilt." Pelagius, we are told, was infuriated by this implicit denial of man's moral sufficiency and took sharp issue with his companion, a friend of Augustine, who had quoted the passage to him. The whole affair is described in *De dono perseverantiae*[6] by Augustine, who dates the origin of the Pelagian controversy from this episode.

In essence, the doctrine of Pelagius involved a denial of the absolute gratuity and necessity of grace for man's moral perfection, based upon the conviction that man can fulfill the Law perfectly and merit salvation by his own unaided will. As the controversy progressed, Pelagius occasionally made the concession that grace might make it easier for a

---

5 Cf. *Retract.* 1.3.1. The *Retractations,* in two books, present a general review of Augustine's works, excluding the *Letters* and *Sermons.* The true scope of this work, composed between 426 and 427, is more accurately conveyed by the title *De recensione librorum,* indicated by Possidius, Augustine's first biographer; cf. his *Vita* 28 (translated in this series, Vol. 15 [New York 1952] 108).

6 20.53.

man to lead a good life, but this in no way altered his essential position that man alone is the cause of his own salvation.[7] From the notion of moral sufficiency, Pelagius was logically led to a denial of original sin and of the necessity for baptism.

From the very beginning of the controversy, Pelagius strongly insisted that his teaching on man's freedom and natural capacity to merit salvation were in substantial agreement with the views expressed by Augustine in the *De libero arbitrio,* and that Augustine had abandoned these in favor of a later and novel doctrine on grace. To support the charge Pelagius cleverly extracted a number of passages from the Dialogue, which he interpreted in favor of man's moral suffering. In the general review of his books, the *Retractations* (426-427), the aged Bishop insists upon the following points in his defense against this Pelagian accusation. First, there is no doctrinal incompatability between his early teaching on free will and his later and more explicit teaching on grace. And, since he was occupied at the time in refuting the Manichees, it was sufficient to establish that, while God is the sole and supreme Cause of all that exists, He is not the Author of evil, which has its adequate cause in the created will. Secondly, though the emphasis in the Dialogue is on man's free will, there are explicit references to grace, and an even larger number of passages where the doctrine is clearly implied. Augustine further insists that certain passages of the *De libero arbitrio* would appear even to have anticipated the later errors of Pelagius. The Saint's grave concern to vindicate his doctrinal consistency and to exonerate the Dialogue from any Pelagian interpretation, is evidenced by the minute and extensive treatment accorded this work in the *Retractations.*[8]

Several factors may explain the importance and lasting value of this early work on free will. It is not only one of the earliest, but also one of his more definitive refutations of basic Manichaean doctrine. In a letter to Jerome, some twenty years

---
7 Cf. *Ep.* 186.
8 A translation of the relevant chapter is found below, pp. 235-241.

later, Augustine states that the book was widely circulated from the time it appeared, and that it is still read by many.[9] Earlier he had recommended it to his Manichaean adversary, Secundinus, against whom he wrote about the year 406.[10] Again, owing to the comprehensive scope of the subject matter treated in connection with the central theme, the work emerges as a kind of compendium of Augustinian philosophy, which is the main reason why it has survived its usefulness as a mere anti-Manichaean polemic. An eminent French scholar has called it the most mature and solid of all the earlier Dialogues and writings of the Saint.[11]

In addition to its principal theme, freedom of the will and the origin of moral evil, those three books resume and develop more fully a number of philosophical notions found in the earlier Dialogues. As a result, there is scarcely a single topic of major importance for philosophy that is not brought to bear in some way on the central and unifying theme. Subjects discussed include the existence of certitude, the internal and external senses, being and its properties, the theory of illumination, the spirituality and immortality of the soul, beatitude, eternal and natural law, and the virtues. Particularly noteworthy is Augustine's celebrated proof for God's existence in the second book, the most detailed and systematic exposition of the argument to be found in all his works. Finally, there is the characteristic and important teaching on the relation of faith to reason and on the role of faith in the development of what may be termed a Christian philosophy. The Dialogue itself represents an early and faithful illustration of the familiar Augustinian principle "believe that you may understand,"[12] which centuries later would find its definitive and well-known formulation in Anselm's *"Credo ut intelligam."*

---

9 *Ep.* 166.3.7.
10 *Contra Secundinum* 11.
11 C. Boyer, in *Gregorianum* 20 (1939) 449.
12 *Tractatus in evangelium Ioannis* 29.6.

From the testimony of the *Retractations,* it is clear that the three books entitled *De libero arbitrio* resulted from discussions held during Augustine's second sojourn in Rome the year before his final return to North Africa, late in 388.[13] The first book, and quite probably the first part of book two, were completed at Rome; the remaining parts of book two and the third book were not completed until about 395, four years after Augustine's ordination to the priesthood at Hippo Regius in 391. Despite the silence on the part of the manuscript tradition and the *Retractations* concerning the identity of Augustine's interlocutor, his Letter to Evodius, written in 415, seems to leave no reasonable doubt that it was the latter.[14] According to the *Confessions,* our main source for a knowledge of his early years, Evodius was, like Augustine, a native of Tagaste, and had served in the military before his conversion to the Catholic faith in Milan.[15] He accompanied Augustine to Cassiciacum in the late summer of 386, and was present at Monica's death at Ostia the following year.[16] He then returned with Augustine to Rome for a year, where he participated in the two Dialogues, *De quantitate animae* and *De libero arbitrio.* Upon returning to Africa, he lived with Augustine both at Tagaste and at Hippo until his appointment as Bishop of Uzala in 396.

The present translation has been made from the critical text edited by William M. Green, in *Corpus scriptorum ecclesiasticorum latinorum* 74 (Vienna 1956).[17]

---

[13] 1.9.1.
[14] 162.2. The remaining extant correspondence between Augustine and Evodius includes the following: Augustine to Evodius, Letters 159, 164, 169; Evodius to Augustine, Letters 158, 160, 163.
[15] 9.8.17.
[16] 9.12.31.
[17] The traditional division into chapters and sections has been used, however, in preference to Green's new system of sectioning.

SELECT BIBLIOGRAPHY

Text:

Maurist Edition: *Sancti Augustini Hipponensis episcopi Opera* 1 (Paris 1689) 569-642. Reproduced, with some variants, by:
Migne, J. P. *Patrologia Latina* 32 (Paris 1861) 1221-1303.
Green, W. *Corpus scriptorum ecclesiasticorum latinorum* 74 (Vienna 1956).

Translations:

Baravalle, G. *Sant' Agostino: Il libero arbitrio* (Rome 1960).
Benjamin, A., L. Hackstaff. *On Free Choice of the Will* (The Library of Liberal Arts; Indianapolis-New York-Kansas City 1964).
Burleigh, J. H. S. "On Free Will," *Augustine: Earlier Writings* (The Library of Christian Classics 6; Philadelphia 1953) 102-217.
Montanari, P. *Aurelius Augustinus: II "De libero arbitrio"* (Rome 1939).
Perl, C. *Aurelius Augustinus: Der freie Wille* (3 ed. Paderborn 1962).
Pontifex, M. *The Problem of Free Choice* (Ancient Christian Writers 22; Westminster, Md. 1955).
Seijas, E. *Del libre albedrío* (Biblioteca de Autores Cristianos 21: Obras de San Agustín 3 [Madrid 1947] 235-521).
Sparrow, C. *Saint Augustine on Free Will* (Richmond, Va. 1947).
Thimme, W. *Augustinus, Theologische Frühschriften: Vom freien Willen, Von der wahren Religion* (Bibliothek der Alten Welt, Reihe Antike und Christentum; Zürich-Stuttgart 1962).
Thonnard, J. *Du libre arbitre* (Bibliothèque Augustinienne: Oeuvres de saint Augustin 6.3 [2 ed. Paris 1952] 123-481).
Tourscher, F. *The Free Choice of the Will* (Philadelphia 1937).

Secondary Works:

Clark, M. *Saint Augustine, Philosopher of Freedom* (New York 1958).
Cotta, S. "Droit et justice dans le *De libero arbitrio* de saint Augustin," *Archiv für Rechts- und Sozialphilosophie* 47 (1961) 159-172.
De Lubac, H. "Note sur saint Augustin: *De libero arbitrio* 3.20.56," *Augustinus Magister* (Paris 1954) 3.279-286.
La Bonnardière, A. M. "Évodius, évêque d'Uzale," in A. Baudrillart (ed.), *Dictionnaire d'histoire et de géographie ecclésiastiques* 16 (1964) 133-135.
Rowe, W. "Augustine on Foreknowledge and Free Will," *Review of Metaphysics* 18 (1964-1965) 356-363.

THE FREE CHOICE OF THE WILL

BOOK ONE

Chapter 1

1. *Evodius.* Tell me, please, whether God is not the cause of evil.[1]

Augustine. I will tell you if you make it clear what kind of evil you are inquiring about, for we usually speak of evil in two ways: first, when we say that someone has done evil; second, when someone has suffered something evil.

Ev. I am eager to know about both kinds.

Aug. But if you know or take it on faith that God is good (and it would be irreligious to think differently), then He does no evil. Again, if we acknowledge that God is just (and to deny this would be sacrilegious), then, as He bestows rewards upon the good, so does He mete out punishments to the wicked. To those who suffer them, such punishments are of course evil. Accordingly, if no one suffers penalties unjustly (and this we must believe since we believe that the universe is ruled by Divine Providence), God is not at all the Cause of the first kind of evil, though He is of the second.

Ev. Is there not, therefore, some other cause of that evil which we have found cannot be God?

Aug. There certainly is, for, without a cause, it could not come to exist. But if you ask me who that cause is, no answer

---

[1] The opening words of the Dialogue are suggestive of a variant title of the work supported by early manuscripts and by the designation given by Possidius in his *Indiculum*, namely, *Unde malum et de libero arbitrio tres libri*.

is possible, for it is no one person but rather each evil man that is the author of his own misdeeds. If you have any doubt of this, take note of our earlier remark that evil deeds are punished by God's justice. For unless they were committed voluntarily, their punishment would not be just.[2]

2. *Ev.* I fail to see how anyone can sin who has not learned to do so. If this is true, I want to know who that someone is from whom we have learned to sin.

Aug. Do you look upon learning as something good?

Ev. Who would dare say that learning is something evil?

Aug. What if it is neither good nor evil?

Ev. I think it is good.

Aug. It certainly is, since, in fact, knowledge is imparted or awakened in us by learning, and it is only in this way that something is learned.[3] Or do you have a different idea?

Ev. I think that only good things come to us by learning.

Aug. See to it then that you do not say that evil is learned, for the word "learning" derives solely from the verb "to learn."

Ev. If evil things are not learned, then how is it that man can do them?

Aug. Possibly, evil comes about from the fact that man turns his back upon learning and estranges himself from it. But whether this, or something else, is the reason, this much is certainly clear, that since learning is something good, and "learning" comes from "to learn," it is altogether impossible to learn things evil. For, if evil is learned, it is included in learning and thus, learning will not be something good. But learning is, according to your own admission, something good. Consequently, evil is not something learned, and it is pointless for you to ask who it is that teaches us wrongdoing. But if evil is something learned, we learn how to avoid it, not

---

[2] This is the first of many passages found in the *Retractations* (1.9.3) quoted by Pelagius in favor of his teaching on grace. The entire chapter from the *Retractations* (1.9) is translated below (pp. 235-241).
[3] A passing reference to the theory of "illumination" already suggested in the *Soliloquia* and stated for the first time in the *De magistro*.

how to do it. Hence, to do evil is nothing else than to stray from the path of learning.

3. *Ev.* I really think there are two kinds of learning: one, teaching us to do good; the other, to do evil. But when you asked whether learning was something good, I replied that it was, for the love of this very good had taken such hold on my mind that I was thinking of that kind of learning which concerns good conduct. But now I realize that there is another kind of learning which I declare, beyond any shadow of doubt, to be something evil, and I am looking for its author.

Aug. Do you at least think that understanding is something that can only be good?

Ev. So good, in fact, that I fail to see how anything else in man can be better, and I could not possibly say that any kind of understanding is evil.

Aug. Suppose the person being taught does not understand. Can you think of him as having learned?

Ev. Not at all.

Aug. If, then, every kind of understanding is good and no one learns who does not understand, then whoever is learning is doing good. For everyone who learns, understands, and everyone who understands is doing good. Consequently, whoever is looking for the author through whom we learn something is really looking for the author of our good actions. Put an end, therefore, to your wish to find an evil teacher of some kind or other. For if he is evil, he is not a teacher; if he is a teacher, he is not evil.

Chapter 2

4. *Ev.* Now that you force me to admit that we do not learn how to do evil, go on and tell me the reason why we do evil.

Aug. You raise a question which sorely perplexed me while yet a young man, and one which in my weariness drove me into the company of heretics and resulted in my fall.[1] I was so injured by this fall, so weighed down by the vast accumulation of nonsensical fables that, had not the love of finding the truth obtained divine aid for me, I would have been unable to rise from this fall and to breathe again in the former atmosphere of free inquiry. And as I took great pains to extricate myself from this perplexity, so I will follow the same procedure with you that led to my liberation. For God will be at hand and will enable us to understand what we have believed. We know well that we are following the course enjoined by the Prophet who says: "Unless you believe, you shall not understand."[2] We believe that all things in existence are from the one God, though He is not the author of sin. But this problem confronts the mind: if sins come from souls created by God, while these souls in turn come from God, how is it that sins are not at once chargeable to God?

5. *Ev.* You have just stated very clearly the problem which plagued my mind so much and which forcibly drew me into this inquiry.

Aug. Take courage, and go on believing what you believe, for there is no better belief even though the reason for it is hidden from me. To hold God in the highest esteem is most truly the beginning of all piety. Anyone who does not believe that God is Almighty or absolutely unchangeable, or that He is the Creator of all things good, though surpassing them in excellence, or that He is also a most just Ruler of all that He has created, or that He had need of no other

---

[1] Although the dualistic solution of the problem of evil figured largely in his decision to embrace Manichaeism, Augustine acknowledges that he was also influenced by the professed rationalism of the system and by its claim to a knowledge of the secrets of physical nature. Cf. *De utilitate credendi* 2.
[2] Isa. 7.9 [LXX]. This Septuagint rendering of the text is of capital importance for a proper understanding of the spirit of Augustine's philosophy.

nature in creating, as if He were not sufficient unto Himself—such a one does not hold God in the highest esteem.

It follows, therefore, that God created all things from nothing. But Him who is equal to the Father, and whom we call the Only Son of God, He did not create but begot Him from His own substance. When we try to represent Him more clearly, we call Him the Power and Wisdom of God through whom He made all that He created from nothing.

Having set down these points, let us strive with the help of God to understand the problem you raise in the following manner.

Chapter 3

6. Since your question has to do with the cause of our doing evil, we must first have a discussion on the nature of evil. State your opinion on this matter. If you cannot express it fully, all at once and in a few words, let me at least know what you think by mentioning, in particular, some evil deeds themselves.

Ev. Adultery, murder, and sacrilege, to say nothing of others which time and my memory do not allow me to mention. Can anyone think that these are not evil?

Aug. Tell me first, then, why you think it is wrong to commit adultery? Is it because the law forbids it?

Ev. It is not wrong just because the law forbids it; rather, the law forbids it because it is wrong.

Aug. What if someone with an exaggerated idea of the delights of adultery should press us further and ask us why we judge it wrong and reprehensible? Do you think that, for men who are eager not only to believe but also to understand, we must fall back on the authority of the law? I am one with you in this belief, and I do firmly believe and I call upon all peoples and nations to believe that adultery is wrong. But right now we are trying to acquire a rational understanding and a firm grasp of something that we have accepted on faith. Think it over, then, as best you can, and tell me the reason why you think adultery is wrong.

Ev. I know it is wrong for the very reason that I myself would be unwilling to tolerate it in my own wife. But anyone who does to another what he is unwilling to have done to himself is certainly doing wrong.

Aug. What if a man's lust leads him to offer his wife to another to have her willingly violated by him, and he, in turn, desires the same liberty with the other's wife? Do you think he is doing nothing wrong?

Ev. On the contrary. He is doing great wrong.

Aug. But, according to that rule of yours, such a man commits no sin, for he is doing nothing that he is unwilling to have done to him. Accordingly, you must find another reason to show why adultery is wrong.

7. *Ev.* I think it is wrong for the reason that I have often seen men condemned for such a crime.

Aug. What of the fact that men have often been condemned for good deeds? Without sending you to other books, examine that history which owes its excellence to divine authority. You will find what a bad opinion we should have of the Apostles and all the martyrs if we agree that being condemned is a sure indication of wrongdoing, for they were all judged as deserving of condemnation for having confessed their faith. Consequently, if whatever is condemned is evil, then it was evil at that time to believe in Christ and to confess the faith itself. On the other hand, if not everything that is condemned is evil, you must look for another reason for teaching that adultery is wrong.

Ev. I cannot find any answer to give you.

8. *Aug.* Perhaps it is passion that is evil in adultery. But as long as you look for the evil in the outward act itself, which can be seen, you will run into difficulties. To give you an idea how the evil of adultery is passion, let us suppose that

there is no opportunity for intercourse with another man's wife, though it is somehow evident that one has the desire and would do the act if he could. In this case, he is no less guilty than if he were caught in the act.

Ev. Nothing could be clearer. I see now that there is no need for a long discussion to convince me of this in the case of murder and sacrilege, and, in fact, for all kinds of sin. It is now clear that passion[1] alone is the ruling factor in every kind of wrongdoing.

Chapter 4

9. *Aug.* Do you know too that another name for passion is desire?

Ev. I do.

Aug. Do you think there is any difference between this and fear?

Ev. Indeed. I think there is a great difference between them.

Aug. I believe you think so for the reason that desire seeks its object, while fear avoids it.

Ev. It is just as you say.

Aug. But suppose someone kills a man, not out of desire to gain possession of something, but because he fears that some evil may befall him—will he not be a murderer?

Ev. He will, indeed. Yet his act is not thereby free of the ruling passion of desire, because whoever kills a man out of fear, certainly desires to live free of fear.

Aug. Do you think it is a small good to live free of fear?

Ev. It is a great good, but it cannot possibly come to the murderer through his crime.

Aug. I am not asking you what can come to him but what

---

[1] *Libido* indicates the disorderly and perverse tendency in man's lower nature resulting from original sin and inclining him to evil. Against the Stoics, however, Augustine defends the view that the passions *in se* are both good and necessary for man. Cf. *De civitate Dei* 14.8-9. For a clarification of the terms *concupiscentia* and *libido,* cf. Bonner, *op. cit.* 398-401.

it is that he himself desires. Whoever desires a life free of fear certainly desires a good and, consequently, the desire is not blameworthy; otherwise we shall be placing blame upon all who love what is good. Hence we are forced to admit that there can be murder where we are unable to discover evil desire as the dominant factor, and it will no longer be true that the malice in all sins stems from the dominant influence of passion; otherwise there will be some form of murder that cannot possibly be sinful.

Ev. If murder means taking the life of a man, this can sometimes happen without any sin. When a soldier slays the enemy, when a judge, or his deputy, executes a criminal, when, by chance, a deadly weapon leaves someone's hand unintentionally or thoughtlessly, I do not think that these are guilty of sin in killing a man.

Aug. I agree, but such men are not usually called murderers. Answer me this question. If a slave kills his master from whom he was in fear of grave torture, do you think we should include him among those who take a man's life in a way that does not warrant their being called murderers?

Ev. I see a great difference between the two. The first are acting either according to the law or in a way not opposed to the law. But there is no law to sanction this man's crime.

10. *Aug.* You are bringing me back to authority again. But you must keep in mind that we have presently undertaken to understand what we believe. We take the laws on faith, and therefore, we must try to understand, if this is at all possible, whether the law may not be doing wrong in punishing such an act.

Ev. It is not wrong at all when it punishes a man who knowingly and willingly slays his master, which is something that none of the others did.

Aug. Do you recall having said a while ago that in every evil deed passion is the dominant factor whereby an act is made evil?

Ev. Yes, I do.

Aug. Well, did you not also grant that a man who desires to live free from fear is not harboring an evil desire?

Ev. I remember that too.

Aug. Therefore, when a master is slain by his servant from this kind of desire, it is not done by a desire that is blameworthy. Consequently, we have not yet found out why this deed is evil. For we agree that all wrongdoing becomes such only by passion, namely, by a desire that is blameworthy.

Ev. It now seems to me that this servant was condemned unjustly. I would not venture this opinion if I could think of something else to say.

Aug. Have you then convinced yourself that such a serious crime should go unpunished before you stop to consider whether that servant desired to be free from fear of his master in order to gratify his passions? The desire to live free from fear is characteristic not only of the good but also of evil men, with this difference, that good men desire it by turning their love from whatever cannot be possessed without fear of loss, while evil men, bent upon enjoying such things securely, try to remove whatever hindrances stand in their way. As a result, they lead a life of crime and wickedness which should be called death rather than life.

Ev. I have come to my senses, and am very glad to have a clear understanding of the nature of that blameworthy desire called passion. I now see that it is the love of things which each one can lose against his will.

Chapter 5

11. Let us now inquire, if you will, whether passion is also the dominant factor in acts of sacrilege which we see frequently committed out of superstition.[1]

---

1 No further mention of this problem occurs in the dialogue.

Aug. Take note whether this question be not premature. I think we should first inquire whether an on-rushing enemy or a stealthy assassin may be slain, in the absence of passion, to defend one's life or liberty or virtue.

Ev. How am I to judge that these men are free of passion who take up the sword in defense of things that can be lost against their will? On the other hand, if they cannot lose them, what need is there to go to the extreme of killing a man to defend them?

Aug. Then the law is not just which gives a traveler the right to kill a robber to avoid being killed himself, or the right to any man or woman to destroy, if they can, an assailant about to attack with violence before the injury is inflicted. Soldiers, too, are commanded by law to kill the enemy, and if a soldier refrains from doing this, he is punished by the commander. Can we be rash enough to assert that these laws are unjust, or rather that they are no laws at all? For an unjust law, it seems to me, is no law.

12. *Ev.* I think the law is well protected against any such accusation since, for those people whom it governs, the law allows for minor transgressions to prevent the commission of more serious crimes. It is a far lesser evil that one who plots another's death should be slain rather than the person who is protecting his own life. And it is a much greater crime that a man should be the victim of a violent attack than that the attacker should be killed by the victim of the attempted attack. In the slaying of any enemy, the soldier is an agent of the law and consequently readily discharges his duty apart from any passion. A law which itself has been enacted for the protection of the people, cannot be charged with passion. Actually, if the lawgiver enacts a law, and does so at God's command, namely, in compliance with eternal justice, he may have done so completely free of passion. But if he did enact this law under the influence of passion, it does not follow that compliance with the law must be accompanied by passion, since a good law can be enacted by a lawgiver who is not good. If, for example, a ruler who has seized tyrannical power should accept a bribe from an interested party to issue a decree making it unlawful to carry off a woman forcibly, even for the purpose of marriage, the law is not evil just because it was made by an unjust and corrupt lawmaker. One can, therefore, without passion, obey a law enacted for the protection of its citizens when it commands that an enemy force be met by the same kind of force. The same may be said of all public servants who are subject to the ruling powers according to the existing law and established order.

But I fail to see how these men mentioned before can be without blame, though they are blameless in the sight of the law. For the law does not compel them to kill, but leaves it within their power. Consequently, they are not at liberty to kill anyone to defend those things which can be lost against their will and which, on this account, ought not be loved at all. As for life, there may be a doubt on the part of some as to whether it can be taken away from the soul at all when the body is destroyed. But if it can be taken away, it is worthless; if not, there is nothing to fear. But as for chastity, who could doubt that it is rooted in the soul itself, seeing that it is a virtue? It cannot, therefore, be snatched away by the violence of an assailant. Whatever the slain attacker was going to snatch from us is something not entirely within our power and, consequently, I fail to see how we can call it our own. Accordingly, I certainly am not blaming the law which permits such assailants to be slain, yet I can find no way to defend those who kill them.

13. *Aug.* I can find far less reason for your trying to defend men who are not guilty in the eyes of the law.

Ev. Perhaps guilty by no law, but only if these are laws which men can see and read. I am not sure that they are not bound by some more compelling and entirely unseen law if we suppose that there is nothing in nature over which Divine

Providence does not rule. How, in the light of this law, are they without sin who defile themselves by human slaughter for the sake of things which ought to be despised? It seems to me that the law drafted for governing people legally permits such things, while Divine Providence punishes them. A law enacted for the governing of people is concerned with upholding whatever is enough to maintain peace among unenlightened men so far as this is possible by man-made laws. But transgressions against the divine law have other appropriate penalties from which, as I see it, wisdom alone can set them free.

Aug. I commend and approve this distinction of yours. Though it is only a beginning and not fully developed, it nevertheless gives promise of leading us on to higher things. You are of the opinion that laws enacted for the government of cities make many concessions and leave unpunished many crimes which are nevertheless punished by Divine Providence, and rightly so. And we should not reproach what a law fails to accomplish simply because it does not do everything.

Chapter 6

14. Let us examine, if you will, how far evil deeds are punishable by that kind of law which restrains people in this present life and then see what remains for the hidden and inescapable punishment meted out by Divine Providence.

Ev. I am eager to do so, if only we can come to a conclusion on so important a matter, for I think the subject is inexhaustible.

Aug. Rather take courage and, placing your trust in God, enter upon the path of reason. For there is nothing so obscure and difficult that cannot, with God's help, become perfectly clear and easy. Therefore, with reliance upon God and with a prayer for His help, let us investigate the question we have raised. First of all, tell me whether laws promulgated in written form are a help to men living in the present life.

Ev. Obviously they are, for surely states and nations are made up of these men.

Aug. What of men themselves, and peoples? Do they belong to that class of reality where they cannot perish or change, or are they subject to change and to the conditions of time?

Ev. Could anyone doubt that human nature is obviously subject to change and time?

Aug. If, therefore, people are found possessed of moderation and prudence, vigilant for the common good wherein each one esteems his own private interest of less importance than the public good, is it not right to enact a law permitting such people to set up for themselves magistrates to provide for their welfare, that is, for the public welfare?

Ev. It is absolutely right.

Aug. If, after having gradually grown corrupt, these same people should afterward prefer the individual to the common good, should offer their vote for sale and, bribed by those who covet honor, should entrust the government to wicked and disreputable men, would it not also be right, provided some honest man of great ability was found at the time, to strip these people of the power to elect public officials and to subject them to the rule of a few good men, or even to that of one man?

Ev. That would also be right.

Aug. Since these two laws then appear to be contradictory, insofar as one grants the people the power to elect public officials while the other takes it away and, since the second law was enacted in such a way that both cannot be in force at once in the same city, are we to say that one of them is unjust and should never have been made?

Ev. Not at all.

Aug. Let us then call that law "temporal" which, though just, can yet be justly changed in the course of time.

Ev. Let us give it that name.

15. *Aug.* What of that law called supreme reason,[1] which must always be obeyed, whereby the wicked merit an unhappy life and the virtuous a happy life and by which, ultimately, that law which we called "temporal" can be justly enacted and justly changed? Can any thinking person fail to see that this law is changeless and eternal? Could it ever be unjust that the wicked should be unhappy, while the good are happy; or that people possessed of moderation and prudence should elect their own rulers, while a depraved and good for nothing people should be without such freedom?

Ev. I see that this law is eternal and changeless.

Aug. I think that you also see that it is from this eternal law that men have derived whatever is just and lawful in the temporal law. For if those people elect officials at one time and at another time do not, each motivated by justice, this alteration of the temporal law derives its character of justice from that eternal law whereby it is always just for responsible people to elect their officials, but not for irresponsible people. Or do you have a different view?

Ev. I agree.

Aug. Therefore, let me explain briefly, as well as I can put it in words, the notion of that eternal law which is impressed upon our nature:[2] "It is that law in virtue of which it is just that all things exist in perfect order." If you think differently, just say so.

Ev. When you say what is true, there is nothing for me to contradict.

Aug. Since this law, therefore, is the one law which is the source for all the variations in those temporal laws for governing men, is the eternal law itself capable of any variation?

---

[1] Mainly under the influence of Christian revelation, the Ciceronian formula is transformed by Augustine to express the notion of divine exemplarism and that of the eternal law, which it implies.
[2] Another passing reference to the Augustinian doctrine of illumination.

Ev. I see that this is absolutely impossible, for there is no force, no chance-occurrence, no natural upheaval that could ever bring it about that justice would no longer mean the perfect ordering of all things.

Chapter 7

16. *Aug.* Come now, and let us see how man himself realizes perfect order within himself, for a people is made up of men united under one law, and this, as we said, is the temporal law. Tell me, now, whether you are absolutely certain that you are alive.

Ev. Where could I ever have found anything more certain by way of an answer?

Aug. Can you see the difference between being alive and knowing that one is alive?

Ev. I realize, of course, that no one can know he is living unless he is alive, but I do not know whether everything living knows that it is alive.

Aug. I only wish that, as you already believe, so too, you might come to know that animals are without reason. Then our discussion might pass on quickly from the present subject. But since you say you do not know, you are stirring up a lengthy discussion. The point is not one that can be passed over while we still go on to our conclusion with the kind of strict logic that I feel is necessary. Now, then, tell me this. We often observe how wild beasts are tamed by men, that is, made subject to man, not only in body but also in spirit, so they obey man's will by a kind of instinct and habit. Do you think it could possibly happen that some beast of great ferocity or physical strength, endowed also with sharp cunning, might try in turn to subdue a man, though many beasts can destroy his body either by sheer force or by stealth?

Ev. I do not agree that this could possibly happen.

Aug. Very good. Now tell me this too. Since it is obvious that man is easily surpassed by many brute animals in physical strength and in other bodily functions, what is it in which man so excels that no beast can master him, while he can master many beasts? May it not be that very thing that is usually called reason or understanding?

Ev. I cannot discover anything else, since that is the one thing in the soul by which we excel the beast. If animals did not have souls, I would say that we excel them by the very fact that we have a soul. But, since they have souls, there is something wanting in their souls, making them subject to us, which is found in ours, making us superior to them. And since, as anyone can see, it is something of no little importance, what better name can we give it than reason?

Aug. Now you see how something which men find very difficult can become easy, when God comes to our aid. For I acknowledge that I thought that this question, which I now see we have concluded, would have detained us for as long a time as for all the other subjects covered since the start of our discussion. Keep this point in mind so that our subsequent discussion may proceed in a logical fashion. Now I believe you understand that what we call knowledge is the same thing as what we perceive by our reason.

Ev. That follows.

Aug. Therefore a man who knows he is living is not without reason.

Ev. That is evident.

Aug. Now beasts have life, although they are without reason, as was brought out above.

Ev. That is clear.

Aug. See, now you know what you answered you did not know, namely, that not everything living knows that it is living, although everything that knows it is living has to be living.

17. *Ev.* I have no further doubt of it. Continue now with

what you have in mind, for I have learned well enough that it is one thing to live, another, to know that one is living.

Aug. Which of these two, then, is the more excellent in your opinion?

Ev. What else but the knowledge of life?

Aug. Do you think the knowledge of life is better than life itself? Or do you feel perhaps that knowledge is a higher and truer form of life since no one can know who does not understand. What does it mean to understand, if not to live a more enlightened and perfect life by the very light of the mind? That, if I am not mistaken, is why you have not preferred anything else to life, but have placed the better life above just any form of life at all.

Ev. You have grasped and expounded my own view perfectly, provided, however, that knowledge can never be evil.

Aug. I do not think this is possible unless we use the term "understanding" in a transferred sense, meaning "personal experience." Experience is not always something good, as is the case when we experience punishment. But how can knowledge, understood in the strict and proper sense, ever be evil, since we acquire it by reason and intelligence?

Ev. I see that distinction too. Continue now with the remaining points.

Chapter 8

18. *Aug.* Here is what I am trying to say: Whatever sets man above the beast, whether we call it "mind" or "spirit"[1] or, more correctly both, since we find both terms in the Scriptures, if this rules over and commands the other parts that make up man, then man's life is in perfect order. We see how many things we share in common not only with brute animals but

---

[1] Augustine's terminology for the soul is not strictly fixed. The various terms employed, such as *anima, animus, spiritus, mens, ratio, intelligentia,* and *intellectus* have been elucidated as far as possible by E. Gilson, *The Christian Philosophy of Saint Augustine,* trans. L. Lynch (New York 1960) 269-271.

also with trees and plants, for we observe that bodily nutrition, growth, reproduction, and health are also proper to trees, which make up the lowest level of life. We also notice, and admit the fact, that brute animals see and hear and have the power to perceive corporeal qualities by smell, taste, and touch, and that frequently their perceptions are keener than ours. Add to all this, the physical strength and power of their limbs, the swiftness and agility of their bodily movements. We excel some animals in all these respects, in others, we are their equal, while in others, we are even surpassed by some animals. Certainly, qualities of this kind are possessed by us in common with brute animals. Actually all animal activity consists in the pursuit of bodily pleasures and in the avoidance of what is disagreeable.

But there are other things which apparently do not pertain to animal life though even in man they are not his highest endowments, such as the power to jest and laugh. Anyone with a true discernment of human nature will say that this is a human quality, though of a lower order. Again, there is the love of praise and glory, and the lust for power which, though absent in the beasts, must not make us think that we are better than beasts because of our desire for such things. When this desire is not subject to reason, it makes men unhappy, and no one has ever thought that unhappiness should make him better than someone else. We are to think of a man as well-ordered, therefore, when his reason rules over these movements of the soul, for we must not speak of right order, or of order at all, when the more perfect is made subject to the less perfect. Do you not think so?

Ev. That is obvious.

Aug. It follows, therefore, that when reason, or mind, or spirit, rules over the irrational movements of the soul, then that is in control in man which ought to be, by virtue of that law which we found to be eternal.

Ev. I understand and agree with you.

Chapter 9

19. *Aug.* Do you think then that a man is wise when his life is organized and ordered in this way?

Ev. If we do not think that he is wise, I fail to see how anyone else could be.

Aug. I believe you also realize that most men are unwise.

Ev. That, too, is obvious enough.

Aug. If wise is the opposite of unwise, and we already know what a wise man is, then you also know who the unwise man is.

Ev. Anyone can see that he is a man whose mind is not in perfect control.

Aug. Should we say, then, that such a man has no mind at all, or rather, that even though it is present, his mind is not in control?

Ev. It is a case of the latter.

Aug. I would especially like to know what grounds you have for knowing that there is a mind in men when it fails to exercise its mastery.

Ev. I wish you would do this yourself, for it is not easy for me to shoulder this task.

Aug. It should at least be easy for you to recall what we said a short time ago, namely, that when beasts are tamed and trained, they serve man's purposes, and that men, in turn, would be subjected to the same treatment from beasts were they not superior to them in some way, as we have already shown. Now it was not in the body that we discovered this superiority, and when it became clear that it was found in the soul, we could find no other name for it but reason. Later on, we remembered that is also called mind and spirit. But if reason and mind are not the same, it is certain at least that only the mind can make use of reason. Hence the conclusion that whoever has reason cannot be without mind.

Ev. I remember this very well and agree with it.

Aug. Well then, do you think that only men who are wise can tame animals? I call wise only those men whose life is controlled by the mind and who are at peace with themselves by their complete mastery over every unlawful desire.

Ev. It is ridiculous to regard as wise those men who are commonly referred to as animal trainers, or even shepherds or herdsmen or charioteers. We see how all of them have control over animals that are tame and what pains they take to train the untamed.

Aug. See, now you have patent proof to make it clear that mind can be found in a man and still not have the mastery. It is certainly present in such men, for they act in a way that would be impossible without having a mind. But the mind does not have this mastery because they are unwise, and, as we know very well, this mastery on the part of the mind is found only in those who are wise.

Ev. I am amazed that we should have already reached this conclusion earlier, and that I was still unable to think of an answer.

Chapter 10

20. But we are now speaking of other matters, for it has already been shown that wisdom in man consists in this mastery on the part of his mind and also that it is possible for the mind to lack such mastery.

Aug. Do you think that the power of passion is greater than the mind, which we know has been given mastery over the passions? Personally, I do not think so. For there could be no perfect order if the weaker should lord it over the stronger. Consequently, I feel that the power of the mind must be greater than desire for the very reason that it is only right and just that it should hold sway over desire.

Ev. I feel the same way, too.

Aug. We can have no hesitation, then, in preferring every

virtue to all vices, so that a virtue is more perfect and sublime to the extent that it becomes stronger and more invincible?

Ev. Unquestionably.

Aug. It follows that a soul infected with vice cannot overcome one fortified by virtue.

Ev. Very true.

Aug. I think you will not deny that any kind of soul at all is better and stronger than any body.

Ev. No one denies this who understands (and it is readily understandable) that a living substance should be more highly valued than a non-living substance, or that what imparts life should be esteemed more than that which receives it.

Aug. It is then far less possible for any kind of body at all to overcome a soul endowed with virtue.

Ev. That is perfectly evident.

Aug. What of a just soul and mind that keeps its natural right to rule? Could it ever dethrone some other mind possessed of equal power and virtue, and make it subject to desire?

Ev. This is impossible, not merely because both souls have the same degree of excellence but also because, in its attempt to degrade the other soul, the first will defect from its just state and become a wicked mind, thereby becoming the weaker of the two.

21. *Aug.* You have grasped this point very well. Consequently, you have only to tell me, if you can, whether you think there is anything more excellent than a mind endowed with reason and wisdom.

Ev. Nothing, I think, apart from God.

Aug. I think so too. But the question is a difficult one, and this is not the opportune time to seek a proper understanding of it. And, though we accept this matter with a firm faith, a full discussion of this problem must be undertaken by us with care and diligence.

Chapter 11

For the time being we can be sure that whatever that nature is which rightfully excels a mind adorned with virtue, it cannot possibly be unjust. Consequently, though it were within its power to do so, not even this nature will force the mind to become a slave to passion.

Ev. Anyone could see that right away.

Aug. Whatever, therefore, is the equal of mind, or superior to it, will not make it a slave to lust because of its own justice, provided the mind is in control and is strong in virtue. On the other hand, anything inferior to the mind cannot do so because of its own weakness, as we have learned from what we already agreed upon. We are faced with the conclusion, then, that nothing else can make the mind the companion of evil desire except its own will and free choice.

Ev. Nothing, I see, could be more logical.

22. *Aug.* It follows that you feel it is only just that such a mind should suffer punishment for so great a sin.

Ev. I cannot deny it.

Aug. Well, then, are we to take lightly a punishment entailing such consequences as these, where passion lords it over the mind, dragging it about, poor and needy, in different directions, stripped of its wealth of virtue, now mistaking the false for the true, even defending something vigorously at one time only to reject at another what it had previously demonstrated, while all the while it rushes headlong into other false judgments; now withholding all assent, while fearful for the most part of the clearest demonstrations; now in despair of the whole business of finding the truth while it clings tenaciously to the darkness of its folly; now at pains to see the light and understand, and again falling back out of weariness to the darkness? And all the while, the cruel tyranny of evil desire holds sway, disrupting the entire soul and life of man by various and conflicting surges of passion;

here by fear, there by desire; here by anxiety, there by empty and spurious delights; here by torment over the loss of a loved object, there by a burning desire to acquire something not possessed; here by pain for an injury received, there by the urge to revenge an injury. On every possible side, the mind is shriveled up by greed, wasted away by sensuality, a slave to ambition, is inflated by pride, tortured by envy, deadened by sloth, kept in turmoil by obstinacy, and distressed by its condition of subjection. And so with other countless impulses that surround and plague the rule of passion. How could we ever think that this is not a punishment when, as you see, it is something that all have to suffer who do not hold fast to wisdom?

23. *Ev.* I do indeed consider this a heavy penalty and one that is absolutely just, if a man, who once occupied the summit of wisdom, should choose to descend therefrom and become the slave of passion. But it is doubtful whether anyone could be found who has either made such a choice, or who would make it now. We believe that man was so perfectly created by God and established in happiness that it was only by his own will that he fell from this state into the miseries of this mortal life. Nevertheless, while I accept this firmly on faith, I have as yet not grasped it by my understanding. If you think we should put off a careful inquiry into this matter for the present, you do so against my will.

Chapter 12

24. But the problem that troubles me most is why we suffer these very severe penalties when, to be sure, we are not wise and have never been wise before, or why it would be right to say that we suffer them because we abandoned the heights of virtue and chose to be enslaved by passion. If you can clear up this point by discussion, I would not agree at all that you should postpone the question.

Aug. You speak as if you knew for sure that we have never been wise, for you have in mind the period of time beginning with our birth into this life. But wisdom resides in the soul, and whether the soul lived another kind of life before its union with the body and one time lived a life of wisdom is a great question, a great mystery, which will have to be examined in its proper place.[1] But there is no reason why this should keep us from elucidating as far as possible the subject at hand.

25. I am asking you whether we have a will.

Ev. I do not know.

Aug. Do you want to know?

Ev. Even that I do not know.

Aug. Then do not ask me any more questions.

Ev. Why?

Aug. Because I do not have to answer your questions unless you want to know what you are asking. Furthermore, if you have no desire to attain wisdom, there should be no discussion with you about such matters. Finally, you can be no friend of mine unless you wish me well. Furthermore, look into yourself and see whether you do not will a happy life for yourself.

Ev. I acknowledge there can be no denying that we have a will. Go on now, and let us see what you are going to conclude from this.

Aug. I shall, but tell me first whether you think you also have a good will.

Ev. What is a good will?

Aug. It is a will by which we seek to live a good and upright life and to attain unto perfect wisdom. See now whether you are not seeking after a good and upright life and whether you do not have a strong desire to be wise, or whether, in any case, you can dare deny that we have a good will when we choose these things.

---

[1] In Book Three, Augustine reviews for the first time the four views proposed to explain the origin of the soul (20.56-58; 21.59).

Ev. I do not deny any of this, and I agree, therefore, not only that I have a will but also that it is now a good will.

Aug. Please tell me what value you set on this will. Do you think that riches or honors or bodily pleasures, or all three together, can be compared in any way with the will?

Ev. God forbid such wicked folly!

Aug. Should we not then rejoice a little that we have something in the soul—I am referring to this good will itself—in comparison with which all the things we mentioned are worthless, though we see how men in great numbers spare no effort or risk to acquire them?

Ev. Rejoice we should, indeed, and very much so.

Aug. Do you think that those who fail to experience this joy suffer only a small loss when they are deprived of so great a good?

Ev. On the contrary, they suffer a very great loss.

26. *Aug.* I believe you see then that it lies within our will either to enjoy or to lack so great and true a good as this.[2] For what is more within the power of the will than the will itself? When anyone has a good will, he really possesses something which ought to be esteemed far above all earthly kingdoms and all the delights of the body. On the other hand, if he does not have a good will, he is truly deprived of something which the will alone can of itself bestow upon him and which is more excellent than all those goods which lie beyond our control. Accordingly, when he thinks himself most unhappy if he loses his fine name, vast wealth, and various kinds of bodily goods, will you not rather think him most unhappy for clinging to goods he can lose so easily and which he cannot have when he wants them, even though he possesses all these things in abundance? For he lacks a good will which should not even be compared with these, and though it is so great a good, one has only to will it in order to possess it.

Ev. Very true.

---

[2] Also adduced by Pelagius against Augustine's teaching on the necessity of grace. Cf. *Retract.* 1.9.3.

Aug. It is, therefore, only right and just that foolish men should suffer such misery, even though there was never a time when they were wise—and this is an uncertain and baffling question.

Ev. I agree.

Chapter 13

27. *Aug.* Now consider whether you think that prudence is the knowledge of things that we should desire and avoid.

Ev. I think it is.

Aug. What of fortitude? Is it not that disposition of soul whereby we despise all misfortune and the loss of things that are not within our control?

Ev. I think so.

Aug. And is not temperance also that disposition which restrains and checks our desire for those things which it is shameful for us to desire? Or do you disagree?

Ev. On the contrary, you are saying just what I think.

Aug. And how shall we define justice except to say that it is a virtue whereby each one is given what is his own?

Ev. My own idea of justice is no different.

Aug. The man of good will (and we have been discussing its excellence at length) will consequently embrace this alone with a love that knows nothing better. Let him find his delight therein and make it the object of his joy and delight, while he examines and appraises its value, aware that it cannot be snatched from him or stolen against his will. Can we doubt that this man will be opposed to everything that is hostile to this one good?

Ev. He would simply have to be opposed.

Aug. Do we think that he is devoid of all prudence if he sees that he should seek this good and avoid whatever is opposed to it?

Ev. I do not think that anyone could possibly do this without prudence.

Aug. Right. But do we not also ascribe fortitude to this man? He cannot really love or esteem highly all the things that lie outside our control, for these are loved by a perverse will which he must oppose as inimical to his most cherished good. But since he has no love for them, he does not grieve over their loss but is rather disdainful of them, and this, as we have already seen and agreed, is the task of fortitude.

Ev. Let us certainly ascribe fortitude to him. I do not see how I could possibly apply this term more properly than to a man who bears with calm equanimity the absence of those goods which we are unable either to acquire or retain by the sheer powers of our nature. And we have seen how the man with fortitude must do this very thing.

Aug. Now see whether we may deprive him of temperance, since this is the virtue which keeps our passions in check. And what is so harmful to a good will as passion? Consequently, you will readily understand why a man who values his good will resists the passions in every way possible and is at war with them, and therefore has a right to be called a temperate man.

Ev. Go ahead. I am in agreement.

Aug. There remains the virtue of justice which, as I see it, cannot possibly be wanting in such a man. For a man who has a good will and values it, resisting, as we said, whatever is contrary to it, cannot bear ill-will towards anyone. It follows that he will not injure anyone, which is only possible when a man gives to each one his due. I believe you recall that you were in agreement when I stated that this was the function of justice.

Ev. I do indeed, and I acknowledge that in a man who esteems highly his own good will and loves it, all those four virtues are found which you defined a short time ago to my satisfaction.

28. *Aug.* What, then, can keep us from acknowledging that the life of this man is praiseworthy?

Ev. Nothing at all. In fact, everything inclines, and even compels us to do so.

Aug. Well, then, can you possibly think that an unhappy life should not be avoided?

Ev. I am very much of the same opinion, and believe that there is nothing else for us to do but to avoid it.

Aug. But you certainly do not think that a praiseworthy life should be avoided.

Ev. I think that it should rather be sought after earnestly.

Aug. A praiseworthy life, therefore, is not an unhappy life.

Ev. That follows, of course.

Aug. You have no further difficulty, as far as I can see, in agreeing with this conclusion, namely, that the life that is not unhappy is the happy life.

Ev. That is obvious.

Aug. Then we agree that the happy man is one who values his own good will, in comparison with which he despises whatever else may be called good, which can be lost even when the will to retain it remains.

Ev. Why should we not agree to a conclusion that follows logically from points already agreed upon?

Aug. You have a good grasp of the matter. But tell me now, if you will, whether having a love for one's good will and a high esteem of it, as we said, is itself a good will?

Ev. What you say is true.

Aug. But if we rightly judge this man to be happy, shall we not also be right in judging as unhappy a man whose will is of a contrary nature?

Ev. Absolutely right.

Aug. How are we justified then in regarding as doubtful the fact that it is by the will that we merit and live a good and praiseworthy life, and, by the same will, a life that is shameful and unhappy,[1] even though formerly we were never wise?

---

[1] Cited by Pelagius in support of his teaching on free will. Cf. *Retract.* 1.9.3.

Ev. I admit that we arrived at this conclusion by arguments that are certain and undeniable.

29. *Aug.* Consider this point too. I think you will recall how we defined a good will, where I believe we said it was that by which we seek to live a good and upright life.

Ev. That is my recollection.

Aug. If, then, it is by a good will that we love and embrace this good will, preferring it to all those things that we are unable to retain by our sheer volition, then it follows, as our reasoning has shown, that those four virtues reside in the soul and that possessing them is the same as living a good and upright life. Accordingly, any man with the will to lead a good and upright life, provided he prefers this will to all fleeting goods, will acquire so great a possession with such great ease that to have what he wills is the same thing as to will it.[2]

Ev. Honestly, I can hardly restrain myself from shouting for joy at the sudden appearance of a good at once so great and so easy to acquire.

Aug. When this very joy deriving from the possession of this good uplifts the soul peacefully, quietly, and steadfastly, it is called the happy life. Or do you think that living the happy life is something other than finding delight in goods that are true and certain?

Ev. I feel as you do.

Chapter 14

30. *Aug.* That is right. But do you not think that every man wills and desires the happy life in every way possible?

Ev. Undoubtedly.

Aug. Then why do they not all attain it? We had agreed in our discussion that men merit a happy life by their will

---

[2] Also employed by Pelagius to defend man's moral sufficiency. *Ibid.*

and an unhappy life also by their will, so that they deserve what they get. But now a kind of contradiction suddenly appears, which, unless we examine it carefully, threatens to upset our previous careful and clear line of reasoning. How, for example, can anyone endure an unhappy life because of his own will when there is no one at all who wills to live unhappily? Or how does man by his will attain the happy life when there are so many unhappy, and yet they all will to be happy?

Does it come about because it is one thing to will what is good or bad, but another to merit something in virtue of a good or bad will? For those who are happy—and they must also be good—are not happy simply because they willed to live the happy life, for bad men do this too, but because they wished to live upright lives, which bad men are unwilling to do. It is little wonder, therefore, that unhappy men do not attain what they want, namely, the happy life, for they do not also will what must be its companion, and without which no one can deserve to attain it, namely, an upright life. Certainly, the eternal law, which it is now time to consider again, has unalterably decreed that merit is in the will,[1] whereas reward and punishment are identified with happiness and unhappiness. Hence, when we say that men are unhappy by their own choice, we are not saying they want to be unhappy but that their will is such that unhappiness results of necessity and even against their will. Hence this does not go counter to our earlier conclusion that all men want to be happy, though not all succeed because they do not all have the will to lead an upright life, and it is this will which alone can merit the happy life. Do you have any objections to raise here?

Ev. No, I have none.

---

[1] Another passage adduced by Pelagius to show that man can merit eternal happiness by his own unaided will. Cf. *Retract.* 1.9.3.

Chapter 15

31. But let us see now how all this is related to the question we raised about the two kinds of law.

Aug. Just as you say. But first tell me whether the man who loves an upright life and takes such delight in it that it becomes for him not only something righteous but also a pleasure and a joy—tell me whether he loves and cherishes this law when he sees that it bestows a happy life upon a good will, and an unhappy life upon a bad will.

Ev. He loves it with a strong and perfect love, for it is in following it that he lives as he does.

Aug. In loving this law then, is he loving something changeable and temporal, or something fixed and lasting?

Ev. Something everlasting of course, and changeless.

Aug. And what of those who persist in their evil will and yet desire to be happy? Is it possible for them to love that law whereby unhappiness is their first recompense?

Ev. Not at all, it seems to me.

Aug. Is there anything else that they love?

Ev. Yes, there are many, namely, those things which their persistent bad will prompts them to acquire or to retain.

Aug. I take it that you are speaking of wealth, honors, bodily delights, and beauty, and all the rest that they cannot acquire when they want them and which they can lose against their will.

Ev. Those are the very things.

Aug. Can you think that these are everlasting when you see how subject they are to the vicissitudes of time?

Ev. Only a fool could think so.

Aug. Obviously, then, there are men who love things eternal, and others who love things temporal, and we have already agreed that there are two laws, one eternal and the other temporal. Now if you have any idea of justice, which of these men, in your opinion, should be subject to the eternal law, and which to the temporal law?

Ev. I think the answer to your question is easy. I think that men whose happiness derives from their love of things eternal come under the eternal law, whereas the temporal law is laid upon the unhappy.

Aug. Your judgment is correct provided you hold fast to the conclusion which our reasoning proved so clearly, namely, that those subject to the temporal law cannot be immune from the eternal law. For we have already determined that it is the source of whatever is just and of whatever may undergo just alteration. You apparently understand well enough that men who adhere to the eternal law by a good will have no need of the temporal law.

Ev. I see what you mean.

32. *Aug.* So the eternal law commands us to turn our love from temporal things and to direct it, once purified, to things eternal.

Ev. Yes, it does.

Aug. Next, what would you say is commanded by the temporal law? Only this, that men inordinately attached to those goods which we can call our own for a time, should possess them by virtue of that very right which preserves peace and human society, so far as is possible in such affairs. These temporal goods include, first of all, the body and what are called goods of the body, such as sound body, keenness of sense, strength, beauty, and any others there may happen to be. Some are necessary for the useful arts and must therefore be valued more highly; others are of less value. Next comes freedom, which is not true freedom except for those who are happy and who adhere to the eternal law. But I am presently speaking of that freedom which makes men think they are free when they have no masters, or which is desired by those who want to be set free from any human masters. Then come parents, brothers, wife, children, kindred, relatives, friends, and those who are joined to us by ties of intimacy. Then there is the state itself which is commonly regarded as holding the place of a parent. Also, honors and praise, and what is called popular favor. Last of all, there is money, a single term including all things of which we are the rightful owners, and which we seem to have the power to dispose of by sale or donation.

To explain just how the temporal law assigns each man his share of these things would be a difficult and lengthy matter, and one that is clearly unnecessary for the question at hand. It suffices to understand how, in the meting out of punishment, the power of the law does not go beyond depriving those punished of these goods, or of a portion of them. Consequently, it imposes restraint through fear and accomplishes its purpose by constantly harassing the souls of unhappy men for whose government it has been designed. As long as they fear to lose these goods, they practice a kind of moderation in their use capable of holding together a society that can be formed from men of this stamp. The law does not punish the sin committed by loving these things, but the crime of taking them from others unjustly.

See, therefore, whether we have now reached the end of a discussion which you thought was interminable, for we had undertaken to inquire how far the temporal law governing peoples and states of this world can go in inflicting punishment.

Ev. I see we have finished this question.

33. *Aug.* Then do you also see that if men did not love those things which can be taken away against their will, there would be no question of any punishment, either in the form of an injustice done them or by way of a just penalty inflicted upon them?

Ev. I see that too.

Aug. Accordingly, with respect to the same things, one man makes good use of them, another, bad use. The man who makes bad use of them is captivated by his love for them and is entangled by them. In other words, he becomes subject to things which should be subject to him, making these goods his goal when, really, his true good should consist in assigning them their proper place and use. On the other hand, the man who uses them rightly shows that these things are really good but that they are not his true good; for they do not make him a good or better man, rather, they become so because of him. Consequently, he is not held fast by their love and does not make them, so to speak, members of his own soul (which would result from loving them), lest, when they come to be amputated, they afflict the soul with excruciating pain and corruption. He rises completely above these things, ever ready, as the occasion requires, to possess and control them, and even more ready to lose them and be without them.

In view of all this, do you think it is right to blame silver and gold because of greedy men, or food and wine because of gluttons and drunkards, or the feminine form because of fornicators and adulterers, and so on, particularly, when you see the physician puts fire to a good use while the poisoner uses bread for his wicked purposes?

Ev. It is perfectly true that we should not blame the things themselves but men who put them to a bad use.

Chapter 16

34. *Aug.* Very well. I believe we have now begun to see the force of the eternal law and have discovered just how far the temporal law may go in meting out punishment. We have also made a clear enough distinction between two classes of things, eternal and temporal, and again between two classes of men, those who pursue and love things eternal, and those who pursue and love temporal things. But we also agreed that what each man chooses to pursue and embrace is within the power of the will to determine, and that it is only the will that can dethrone the mind from its citadel and despoil it of its right order.[1] It is also clear that when someone puts a thing to bad use, we are not to blame the thing itself but the one who makes bad use of it. Let us go back, if you will, to the question proposed at the start of this discussion and see whether it has been solved. We had set out to inquire about the nature of wrongdoing and our entire discussion has been directed to this end.

We may now, then, turn our attention to this question and inquire whether wrongdoing is anything else than the pursuit of temporal things to the neglect of things eternal, namely, the pursuit of things, as if they were great and wonderful, which are perceived by the lowest part of man, his body, and which we can never be sure of, and the neglect of those things which the mind enjoys and perceives of itself, and which cannot be lost to the man who loves them. For every kind of wrongdoing, namely, sin, is included, it seems to me, under this one class. But I am waiting to find out what you think.

35. *Ev.* It is just as you say, and I agree that all sins fall under this one class and occur when a man turns away from what is divine and truly abiding and turns to what is changing and uncertain. And though these latter have been assigned their rightful place and achieve a kind of beauty all their own, nevertheless, it is the mark of a wicked and perverse soul to become a slave to the pursuit of those things which should rather be regulated according to the good pleasure of the soul whose right to rule derives from divine order and law. I think we have at the same time found a solution to the problem of why we do evil, which we proposed to examine after the question on the nature of wrongdoing. For, unless I am mistaken, we do evil from the free choice of the will, as was shown by the argument already advanced.

---

[1] Quoted by Pelagius in favor of man's moral autonomy.

But now I am asking whether He who created us should have given us that very freedom of choice by which it has been shown that we have the power to sin. For, without this power, we apparently would not have been capable of sinning, and there is thus reason to fear that God will be adjudged the cause even of our evil deeds.

Aug. Have no fear of this. But we will have to find another time to examine this matter more carefully since the discussion at hand needs to be kept within limits and brought to an end. I would have you believe that we have, so to speak, knocked at the door of great and abstruse questions that warrant our inquiry. When we have begun, with God's help, to penetrate their inner recesses, you will certainly recognize what a difference there is between our present discussion and those that are to follow, and how these latter excel, not only in the mental discernment required for their inquiry, but also in the lofty character and resplendent light of their truth. Only let us be religiously motivated so that God in His Providence may allow us to hold fast to the end the course we have embarked upon.

Ev. I accede to your will, and willingly concur with your judgment and wishes.

BOOK TWO

Chapter 1

1. *Ev.* Now explain to me, if that is possible, why God gave man free choice of the will since, if he had not received it, man would certainly be unable to sin.

Aug. Do you know for sure that God has given man something which you think should not have been given him?

Ev. From what I seem to gather from the previous book, we do have free choice of the will and this alone enables us to sin.

Aug. I also recall that this point was made clear. But I have asked you just now whether you know that it was God who gave us that very thing which we obviously possess and which enables us to sin.

Ev. I think it is none other, for it is from Him that we have our being and from Him that we merit reward or punishment, according as we live good or sinful lives.

Aug. I am also eager to know whether you see this clearly or whether you are willing to believe it on authority, even though you do not understand it.

Ev. I assure you that I first accepted this on authority; yet what could be truer than that everything good comes from God, that everything just is good, and that it is just that there should be punishment for sinners and rewards for the righteous? Hence the conclusion that God makes sinners unhappy and the righteous happy.

2. *Aug.* I agree, but I would raise this other question as to how you know that we have our being from God. For you did not now explain this, but only that it is from Him that we merit either punishment or reward.

Ev. I see that the only evidence for this point stems from our earlier conclusion that God punishes sins, since, in fact, all justice comes from Him. For while it is a mark of goodness to bestow benefits upon strangers, it is not in keeping with justice to inflict punishments upon them. Clearly, therefore, we belong to God, not only because He is most generous to us with His gifts, but also because He is most just in meting out punishment. Again, from the fact that every good comes from God, and here you agreed with my contention, we can understand that man too comes from God. For man himself, insofar as he is man, is something good because he can live an upright life whenever he so wishes.[1]

3. *Aug.* Obviously, if this is so, the question you raised is already answered. If, indeed, man is something good and cannot do what is right unless he wills to, then he must have free will, without which he cannot do what is right. For we must not suppose that because a man can also sin by his free will that God gave it to him for this purpose. The fact that man cannot lead an upright life without it is sufficient reason why God should have given it. That it was given for this purpose can be seen from this, that when he has used it to commit sin, he is subject to divine punishment, which would be unjust if free will had been given him not only to live uprightly but also to commit sin. How could punishment be justly visited upon a man who used his will for the very purpose for which it was given him? But when God punishes a sinner, what does He seem to say but: "Why did you not use your free will for the purpose for which I gave it to you, namely, to do what is right?" Besides, if man were without free choice of the will, what would become of the good called justice whereby sins are punished and good deeds are honored? For, unless something is done by the will, it can be neither a

---

[1] The first of two sentences from this Book quoted by Pelagius for his teaching on free will. Cf. *Retract.* 1.9.3.

sin nor a good deed. Consequently, punishments and rewards would be unjust if man did not possess free will. Moreover, there must be a place for justice both in punishments and rewards because it is one of those goods that come from God. It follows, therefore, that God should have given man free will.

Chapter 2

4. *Ev.* I admit now that God gave it. But let me ask you this: if it was given to do good, do you not think it should have been impossible to turn it to a sinful purpose? As with justice itself, which is given man to lead a good life, how could anyone lead a bad life by reason of his being just? So, too, if the will were given to do good, no one would be able to sin by his will.

Aug. I hope God will enable me to answer your question, or better, that He will enable you to answer it yourself, when you are enlightened by that truth within you, which is the greatest teacher of all.[1] I wish you would tell me shortly—provided you know for sure that God gave us free will, which was what I asked you—whether we should say that something should not have been given when we acknowledge that it was God who gave it. For, if it is not certain that He gave it, it is right for us to ask whether it was a good gift, so that if we find that it was, we will also have found that it was given by Him who has given all good things to man. Now if we find

---

1 A summary of conclusions already reached in the *De magistro* on the doctrine of illumination and its logical counterpart of the teacher's role in learning. Though inspired by both Neoplatonic and biblical sources, Augustine's doctrine possesses an originality that cannot be reduced to any of the classical epistemologies of Greek philosophy. For a summary of the theory and its interpretation, including that of the author himself, cf. Gilson, *The Christian Philosophy of St. Augustine* 77-96. Several new interpretations have been more recently advanced. Cf. J. Morán, *La teoría del conocimiento en san Agustín* (Valladolid 1961); C. E. Schuetzinger, *German Controversy on Saint Augustine's Illumination Theory* (New York: Pageant Press 1960).

that it was not a good gift, we will realize that God did not give it, since it is blasphemous to charge Him with wrongdoing. But if it is certain that He Himself gave it, then, no matter how it was given, we must acknowledge that there is no reason why it either should not have been given or been given differently than it was given. For He gave it, who may never be rightly blamed for what He has done.

5. *Ev.* While I accept all this with a firm faith, yet, since I have no intellectual grasp of it, let us so conduct our inquiry as if it were all uncertain. As I see it, our uncertainty as to whether free will was given us to do good, since we can also sin by it, gives rise to the further uncertainty as to whether it should have been given at all. If it is uncertain that free will was given to do good, it is also uncertain whether it should have been given, and, consequently, also uncertain that God gave it to us. For, if it is uncertain whether it should have been given, it is uncertain that it was given by God since it would be impious to suppose that He has given anything which he should not have given.

Aug. You are certain, at least, that God exists.

Ev. This too I hold firmly, not from direct knowledge, but by faith.

Aug. Suppose, then, that one of these fools of whom it is related in the Scripture, "the fool has said in his heart, there is no God,"[2] should say this to you, and should be unwilling to go along with what you believe, but want to know whether what you believe is true. Would you abandon this man or would you think that he should somehow be convinced of what is a matter of firm belief for you, especially if he was not stubborn in his opposition but was eager in his desire to know?

Ev. What you just said clearly suggests how I should answer him. Even though he were utterly unreasonable, he would at least admit that no one should enter into a discussion on any

---

2 Ps. 13.1.

subject at all with a man who is insincere and obstinate, and, most of all, on a subject of such importance. Once this was admitted, he would first prevail upon me to believe that he is making this inquiry in good faith and that as far as the present problem is concerned, he harbors no hidden guile or obstinacy. I would then point out (and I think this would be a simple matter for anyone) that since he wishes another to believe the hidden thoughts of his own mind, thoughts known to him but unknown to the one who believes them, it is much more reasonable for him to believe in God's existence on the authority of the books of those great men who have left a written record testifying that they lived with the Son of God. They have also recorded certain things they witnessed which could not possibly have happened if there were no God. And it would be very foolish of him to reproach me for believing these men since he wished me to believe him. Now certainly he could find no good reason for not wanting to imitate what he is unable to reproach.

Aug. Now if you think it is enough to accept God's existence on the word of such great men without being rash, then what of those other questions which we undertook to explore, as if they were uncertain and completely unknown? Why, I ask, do you do not likewise think that we should also believe these things on the authority of these men to the extent that we need expend no further effort in investigating them?

Ev. But we are eager to know and understand what we believe.

6. *Aug.* Your memory serves you well, and there is no denying that this was the position we took at the opening of our earlier discussion.[3] For, unless believing and understanding were different, and unless we were first to believe those important and heavenly truths which we are eager to understand, there would be no point in the prophet's saying: "Un-

---

3 Cf. 1.2.4.

less you believe, you shall not understand."[4] Our Lord, too, both by word and deed, exhorted those whom He called to be saved that they should first believe. Later, when He referred to the gift He would bestow upon those who believed, He did not say, "This is eternal life that they may *believe*," but, "This is eternal life that they may *know* Thee, the one true God, and Him whom Thou hast sent, Jesus Christ."[5] Then, to those who already believed, He said: "Seek and you shall find."[6] Now we cannot say that we have "found" something which is believed but not known, nor can anyone become fit to find God unless he has first believed what he will afterwards come to understand. Let us, therefore, in obedience to the Lord's command, carry on our inquiry earnestly. For what we are seeking at His behest, that we shall find upon His manifesting it to us Himself, so far as these things can be found in this life and by men like ourselves. We must believe that they are perceived and grasped more clearly and perfectly by more virtuous men, even while they dwell on this earth, and certainly by all good and religious men after their present life. We must make this our hope too, and, despising all that is worldly and human, we must desire and love the higher things in every way possible.

Chapter 3

7. Let us pursue our inquiry, if you will, according to this order: first, what evidence is there that God exists;[1] next,

---

4 Isa. 7.9. In the *De doctrina christiana* (1.2.17), Augustine mentions the alternative reading suggested by the Hebrew text but interprets it according to the sense of the Septuagint version.
5 John 17.3.
6 Matt. 7.7.

1 The beginning of Augustine's rational dialectic to prove God's existence from the existence and nature of truth. Nowhere else in his writings is the problem dealt with *ex professo* or in such detail. The connection between the problem of certitude and God's existence, as here evidenced, strongly supports Gilson's observation ". . . that in

do all things, insofar as they are good, come from God; lastly, should free will be numbered among things good. Once these questions have been answered, I think it will become clear enough whether it was right to give free will to man.

Hence, to begin with what is most evident, I will ask you whether you yourself exist. Possibly, you are afraid of being mistaken by this kind of a question when, actually, you could not be mistaken at all if you did not exist?[2]

Ev. Go on instead to the other questions.

Aug. Then, since it is evident that you exist, and that this could not be so unless you were living, then the fact that you are living is also evident. Do you understand that these two points are absolutely true?

Ev. I understand that perfectly well.

Aug. Then this third point is also evident, namely, that you understand.

Ev. It is evident.

Aug. Which of these three, in your opinion, is the most excellent?

Ev. Understanding.

Aug. Why do you think so?

Ev. Because, while these are three in number, existence, life, and understanding, and though the stone exists and the animal lives, yet I do not think that the stone lives or that the animal understands, whereas it is absolutely certain that whoever understands also exists and is living. That is why I have no hesitation in concluding that the one which contains

---

Saint Augustine the problem of God's existence cannot be distinguished from the problem of knowledge; knowing how we apprehend truth and knowing the existence of Truth are one and the same thing" *(The Christian Philosophy of Saint Augustine* 18).

2 Although suggested as early as the Cassiciacum period in *De beata vita* (2.7) and the *Soliloquia* (2.1.1), this is the first formal statement of Augustine's own argument against the Skeptics based on the immediate evidence of personal existence. Similar formulations appear later in *De vera religione* (39.73), *De Trinitate* (15.12.21), and *De civitate Dei* (11.26). For a comparison with the "cogito" of Descartes, cf. G. Lewis, "Augustinisme et Cartésianisme," *Augustinus Magister* (Paris 1954) 2.1087-1104.

all three is more excellent than that which is lacking in one or both of these. Now whatever is living is certainly also existing, but it does not follow that it also understands. This kind of life, I think, is proper to animals. But it certainly does not follow that what exists must also live and understand, for I can admit that a corpse exists, but no one would say it lives. And still less can something understand if it is not living.

Aug. We maintain, then, that two of these three are lacking in a corpse, one in the animal, and none in man.

Ev. That is true.

Aug. We likewise maintain that the most excellent among the three is what man possesses together with the other two, namely, understanding, and that having this, he must also exist and live.

Ev. We do, indeed.

8. *Aug.* Now tell me whether you know you have these well known senses of the body, sight, hearing, smell, taste, and touch.

Ev. I do.

Aug. What do you think is the function of sight, that is, what do we perceive when we see?

Ev. Anything corporeal.

Aug. When we see, we do not likewise perceive what is hard and soft, do we?

Ev. No.

Aug. What then is the proper function of the eyes, that is, what do we perceive with them?

Ev. Color.

Aug. Of the ears?

Ev. Sound.

Aug. Of smell?

Ev. Odors.

Aug. Of taste?

Ev. Flavor.

Aug. Of touch?

Ev. Soft or hard, smooth or rough, and many such qualities.

Aug. And what of the shapes of bodies? Do we not perceive that they are large, small, square, round, and so on, both by touch and sight? Consequently, these qualities are not proper either to sight or vision alone, but belong to both.

Ev. I understand.

Aug. Then you further understand that each sense has its own proper object to report while some senses have certain objects in common.

Ev. I understand that also.

Aug. Can we, therefore, determine by any of these senses what is the proper object of each sense or what those objects are which some or all of them have in common?

Ev. Not at all. This is discerned by some power within.

Aug. Might not this be the reason itself, which is wanting in beasts? For, in my opinion, reason enables us to grasp these and to know just what they are.

Ev. I think it is rather reason that enables us to know that there is a kind of internal sense to which everything is referred by those well-known five senses. Now the power enabling the animal to see is one thing, that by which it shuns or seeks what it perceives by seeing is something else. The former is located in the eye, the latter within, in the soul itself. The inner sense enables the animal to seek and acquire things that delight and to repel and avoid things that are obnoxious, not only those that are perceived by sight and hearing, but all those which are grasped by the other bodily senses. But this power cannot be called either sight or hearing or smell or taste or touch, but is some other kind of power that presides over all of them together. Although, as I mentioned, we do grasp this power by our reason, yet we may not call it reason, since it is obviously present in beasts.

9. *Aug.* I acknowledge that this power, whatever it is, does exist, and I do not hesitate to call it the inner sense. But

unless the impressions brought to us by the bodily senses pass beyond even this inner sense, they cannot result in knowledge. For it is by reason that we grasp whatever we know. To mention but a few instances, we know that color cannot be perceived by hearing nor sound by sight. And this is something that we do not know by sight or hearing or by that inner sense which is not lacking in beasts. We are not to suppose that beasts know that light is not perceived by the ear or sound by the eye, since we discern this only by rational reflection and thought.

Ev. I could not say that I have grasped this point. Suppose that beasts do discern that color cannot be perceived by hearing or sound by sight by means of that inner sense which you admit they do possess.

Aug. You do not suppose, do you, that animals can distinguish one from another the color they perceive, the power of sense in the eye, the inner sense within the soul, and reason by which all these are enumerated and defined, one by one?

Ev. Not at all.

Aug. But could reason distinguish these four things one from another and assign their limits by definition unless color was referred to it by the sense of sight, and this sense, in turn, by that inner sense which presides over it, and this inner sense, in turn, by its direct action upon reason, provided, however, that there is no other power interposed?

Ev. I fail to see how it could be otherwise.

Aug. Are you aware of this, that color is perceived by the sense of sight, whereas this sense of sight is not perceived by sight itself? For you do not see the act of seeing itself by the same sense by which you see color.

Ev. Absolutely not.

Aug. Try now to make these further distinctions. You will not deny, I think, that color and seeing color are different, and also that the power is different by which color can be perceived in its absence as if it were present.

Ev. I draw a distinction between these two, and admit that they are distinct from one another.

Aug. Except for color, you do not see any of these three with the eyes, do you?

Ev. Nothing else but color.

Aug. Tell me then what it is that enables you to see the other two, for you could not distinguish them if they were not seen.

Ev. I do not know the nature of that other power. I know it exists but nothing more.

Aug. Then you do not know whether it is reason itself or that vital power, called the inner sense, which presides over the bodily senses, or something else?

Ev. I do not know.

Aug. But this much you do know, that reason alone can define these powers and that it can only do so with what is presented for its scrutiny.

Ev. That is certain.

Aug. It follows that this other power, whatever it is, which enables us to perceive all that we know, is the servant of reason. It presents and reports to reason whatever has come within its reach so that the objects of sense perception can be assigned their proper limits and be grasped not only by sensation but also by knowledge.

Ev. That is right.

Aug. Reason itself distinguishes between its servants and the impressions they convey to it, and likewise recognizes what a difference there is between these and itself and asserts its primacy over them. Now does reason know reason in any other way than by reason itself? Or how would you otherwise know that you had reason unless you perceived it by reason?

Ev. That is very true.

Aug. Consequently, in perceiving color, we do not perceive by the same sense our act of seeing; in hearing we do not hear our act of hearing; in smelling a rose, the act itself of smelling imparts no fragrance to us; in tasting a flavor, the act itself has no taste in our mouth, and in touching something, we cannot touch the act itself of touching. It is evident that those five senses cannot be perceived by any one of them, though all corporeal qualities can be perceived by them.

Ev. It is evident.

Chapter 4

10. *Aug.* I think it is likewise clear that the inner sense perceives not only what it receives from the five bodily senses but also the senses themselves. For if the beast were not aware of its act of perception, it could not otherwise direct its movements toward something, or away from it. This awareness is not ordered towards knowledge, which is the function of reason, but towards movement which it does not perceive by any of the five senses.

If this is still obscure, it may become clear if you note the single example of what occurs in any one of the senses, such as sight. The beast could not open its eyes at all or turn its gaze towards the thing it wants to see were it not for the fact that while its eyes were closed or not fixed upon the object, it perceived that it was not seeing. But if it is conscious of its not seeing when in fact it does not see, it must also be aware of its seeing when it does see. The fact that, while seeing, the beast does not alter its gaze by that desire which moves it to turn its gaze when it does not see something, shows that it is aware of both states.

But whether this vital power, which is aware of its perceiving corporeal things, also perceives itself, is not so clear, except for the fact that when a person raises the question in his own mind, he comes to see that all living things shun death. Since death is the contrary of life, we must infer that the vital power is aware of itself since it shuns what is contrary to it. But if this point is still not clear, then disregard it, so that our effort to reach the desired conclusion will be based solely on clear and evident proofs.

These points are clear: corporeal qualities are perceived by the bodily senses; one and the same sense cannot perceive itself; the inner sense perceives that corporeal qualities are perceived by the bodily sense and also the bodily sense itself; all these things of sense, as well as reason itself, are known by reason and come under the heading of knowledge. Do you not think so?

Ev. I do indeed.

Aug. Come, tell me how this question arose, for we have been pursuing this avenue of inquiry a long time in our desire to reach a solution.

Chapter 5

11. *Ev.* So far as I recall, we are now dealing with the first of those three questions which we proposed a while ago when we arranged a plan for this discussion, namely, how the existence of God can be made evident, though we must believe it with a strong and persevering faith.

Aug. You have recalled this very well. But I want you also to keep carefully in mind that when I asked whether you were existing, it was made clear that you knew not only this but also two other things.

Ev. I remember that too.

Aug. Now see which one of these three you think is that one to which pertains everything perceived by the bodily senses, that is, in what class of things you think we should locate whatever is perceived by our senses, by the eyes or by any other organ of the body. Should it be with things that merely exist, with those that also live, or with those that also understand?

Ev. With those that merely exist.

Aug. In which of the three classes do you think the sense power itself should be placed?

Ev. In the class of things living.

Aug. Which of these two do you think is better, the sense itself or its object?

Ev. The sense, of course.

Aug. Why is that?

Ev. Because whatever also has life is better than something which merely exists.

12. *Aug.* And what of that inner sense which we found was inferior to reason and which we still share in common with beasts? Would you hesitate to rank this sense above that by which we perceive a body, which you said should be ranked above the body itself?

Ev. I would have no hesitation whatever.

Aug. I should like you to tell me why you have no hesitation on this point. For you cannot say that this inner sense should be placed in that one of the three classes which also includes understanding, but rather in the class of things which exist and live, although they lack understanding. This inner sense is found also in beasts which are without understanding. If this is so, I would like to know why you rank the inner sense above that which perceives corporeal qualities, since both are found in the class of things that live. You ranked the sense which perceives bodies above bodies because the latter are in the class of things which only exist, while the former are in the class of things that also live. Since the inner sense is also found in this class, tell me why you think it is better.

If you say it is because the inner sense perceives the bodily sense, I do not believe you will find any rule that we could rely upon for holding that the subject perceiving is better than what it perceives. Otherwise, we might also be forced to conclude that the person understanding is better than what he understands. This, of course, is untrue because man understands wisdom but he is not better than wisdom itself. Consider, then, why you thought that the inner sense should be ranked above the sense by which we perceive things corporeal.

Ev. It is because I look upon the inner sense as a ruler and kind of judge of the latter. For if there is any shortcoming in the discharge of their function, the inner sense demands this service from the bodily senses as a kind of debt owed by its servant, as was pointed out a short time ago. The sense of sight does not see that it is seeing or not seeing and, failing to do so, it cannot judge what is missing or what is sufficient. This is done by the inner sense which directs the soul of the beast to open its eyes when they are closed and to supply what it perceives is missing. There can be no doubt in anyone's mind that what judges is better than what is judged.

Aug. Do you understand then that even the bodily senses pass a kind of judgment on bodies? Pleasure and pain are theirs to experience whenever they come in contact gently or roughly with a body. Just as the inner sense judges as to what is missing or what is sufficient in visual perception, so the eyes themselves judge as to what is deficient or sufficient in the matter of color. So too in the case of hearing, just as the inner sense judges whether or not it is attentive enough, so the auditory sense judges concerning sounds, discerning those which either flow gently into the ear or which produce a harsh dissonance.

There is no need to continue with the rest of the bodily senses. I think you know already what I am trying to say, namely, that just as the inner sense judges the bodily senses, approving what is complete in them and requiring what is deficient, so too the bodily senses themselves judge bodies, admitting pleasurable sensations of touch found in them, while rejecting the opposite.

Ev. I see these points clearly and agree that they are perfectly true.

Chapter 6

13. *Aug.* See now whether reason also judges the inner sense. I am not asking whether you have any doubt that reason is better than the inner sense because I am sure that this is your judgment. Yet I feel that now we should not even have to ask whether reason passes judgment on the inner sense. For in the case of things inferior to it, namely, bodies, the bodily senses, and the inner sense, is it not, after all, reason itself that tells us how one is better than the other and how far superior reason itself is to all of them? This would not be possible at all unless reason were to judge them.

Ev. Obviously.

Aug. Consequently, that nature which not only exists but also lives, though it does not understand, such as the soul of beasts, is superior to one that merely exists and neither lives nor understands, such as the inanimate body. Again, that nature which at once exists and lives and understands, such as the rational mind in man, is superior to the animal nature. Do you think that anything can be found in us, namely, something among those elements which complete our nature and make us men, that is more excellent than that very thing which we made the third in those three classes of things? It is clear that we have a body and a kind of living principle which quickens the body itself and makes it grow, and we recognize that these two are also found in beasts. And it is also clear that there is a third something, the apex, so to speak, or eye of the soul, or whatever more appropriate term may be employed to designate reason and understanding, which the animal nature does not possess. So I ask you to consider whether there is anything in man's nature more excellent than reason.

Ev. I see nothing at all that is better.

14. *Aug.* But suppose we could find something which you are certain not only exists but is also superior to our reason, would you hesitate to call this reality, whatever it is, God?

Ev. If I were able to find something which is better than what is best in my nature, I would not immediately call it God. I do not like to call something God because my reason is inferior to it, but rather to call that reality God which has nothing superior to it.

Aug. That is perfectly true. For God Himself has given this reason of yours the power to think of Him with such reverence and truth. But I will ask you this: if you should find that there is nothing above our reason but an eternal and changeless reality, would you hesitate to say that this is God? You notice how bodies are subject to change, and it is clear that the living principle animating the body is not free from change but passes through various states. And reason itself is clearly shown to be changeable, seeing that at one time it endeavors to reach the truth, and at another time it does not, sometimes it arrives at the truth, sometimes it does not. If reason sees something eternal and changeless not by any bodily organ, neither by touch nor taste nor smell nor hearing nor sight, nor by any sense inferior to it, but sees this of itself, and sees at the same time its own inferiority, it will have to acknowledge that this being is its God.

Ev. I will openly acknowledge that to be God, if, as all agree, there is nothing higher existing.

Aug. Good! It will be enough for me to show that something of this kind exists. Either you will admit that *this* is God or, if there is something higher, you will admit that *it* is God. Accordingly, whether there exists something higher or not, it will become clear that God exists, when, with His assistance, I shall prove, as I promised, that there exists something above reason.

Ev. Prove then what you are promising.

Chapter 7

15. *Aug.* I shall do so. But first I shall ask you whether my bodily senses are the same as yours, or whether mine are mine alone and yours are yours alone. If this latter were not so, I would be unable to see anything with my eyes which you would not see.

Ev. I fully agree that though the senses are of the same nature, yet each one of us has his own sense of sight or hearing, and so forth. One man cannot only see but also hear something that another man does not hear, and one man can perceive by any one of the senses something different from what another perceives. So it is obvious that your senses are yours alone and mine are mine alone.

Aug. Would you give the same or a different answer concerning the inner sense?

Ev. Not a different answer, certainly. My inner sense perceives my bodily sensations and your inner sense perceives yours. I am often asked by a man who sees something whether I also see it, simply because I am conscious of seeing or not seeing it, while he is not.

Aug. What of reason itself? Does not each one of us have his own since, actually, it can happen that I understand something while you do not, and you may be unable to know whether I do understand, although I do know.

Ev. It is also clear that each one of us has his own rational mind.

16. *Aug.* You could not possibly say, could you, that we possess individually our own sun or moon, or morning star, or other such things that we see, though each one of us sees these things with his own sense?

Ev. I could never say such a thing.

Aug. So it is possible for many of us to see some one thing at one and the same time, though each of us has his own individual senses with which he perceives the same thing which we all see at the same time. Consequently, though my senses are distinct from yours, it may happen that what we see is not something different for both, but the one thing which is present to each of us and which is seen by both of us at the same time.

Ev. That is perfectly clear.

Aug. We can also hear the same voice at the same time so that, while my hearing is distinct from yours, yet it is not a different voice that we are hearing at the same time. Neither is one part of the voice heard by me and another part by you, but whatever sound is made is within the hearing of both of us, perceived as one sound in its entirety.

Ev. That too is clear.

17. *Aug.* With regard to the other senses, you must now take note that what we have to say in this connection holds for them in a way neither entirely the same nor entirely different from what was said about the two senses of sight and hearing. You and I can inhale the same air and perceive the quality of the air by its odor. Again, we can both taste the same honey, or any other kind of food and drink, and perceive its quality from the taste. Although the taste is the same, yet our senses are individual to us, yours belong to you, and mine to me. So when both perceive the one odor or taste, you do not perceive it with my sense nor do I perceive it with yours. Neither do I perceive it by a single sense which we can share in common, but my sense is mine entirely and so is yours, though it is the one odor or taste that is perceived by both of us.

Accordingly, these two senses of smell and taste are found to have something similar to the two senses of sight and hearing. But they differ in a way which has a bearing on the subject we are presently considering. For, though we both inhale the same air with our nostrils or taste the same food that we take, I do not breathe in that part of the air which you do, or eat the same portion of food that you eat, but I take one part, and you, another. Therefore, when I breathe, I inhale as much of all the air as I need, and you do the same. And though the same food is all eaten by both of us, yet it cannot be taken wholly by both of us in the way that we both hear a whole word at the same time and both see the same sight equally well. But in the case of food and drink, different portions have to pass into each of us. Do you have some faint understanding of all this?

Ev. On the contrary, I agree that it is perfectly clear and certain.

18. *Aug.* You would not say, would you, that we should compare the sense of touch with those of sight and hearing with reference to the point now under discussion? We can both perceive by the sense of touch not only the same body, but also the same part of the body. It is different with food, for each one of us cannot take all the food placed before us when we are both eating it. But you and I can touch the same body in its entirety, not just different parts of it, but the whole body.

Ev. I admit that in this respect the sense of touch is very much like the two previous senses. But I see it differs in this, that both of us can see and hear all of the same thing together, that is, at the same time. Now both of us can touch a whole body at one time, but only in different parts, and only the same part at different times. I cannot apply my sense of touch to the part you are touching unless you remove yours.

19. *Aug.* A very astute answer! But you should note this point too, that though some objects perceived by us are perceived together and others separately, yet each of us has an individual awareness of his own sense perceptions of the objects he perceives through the bodily sense. I am neither aware of your sensations nor are you aware of mine. In other words, with regard to things corporeal, what we can perceive individually but not together is that alone which so becomes part of us that we can change and transform it into ourselves. So it is with food and drink where both of us cannot taste the same portion. Although nurses actually serve food already masticated to infants, yet the portion which is taken to be tasted and is assimilated into the body of the nurse chewing it cannot be returned and given back as food for the infant. When the palate tastes something pleasant, no matter how small a portion it is, it claims this for itself once and for all, and makes it become part of the body's nature. If this were not the case, no taste could remain in the mouth after masticated food was rejected from the mouth. We may say the same of the parts of the air we breathe. Though you can inhale some of the air which I exhale, you cannot do so with that part which has become nourishment for me because it cannot be returned. Physicians point out that we take in nourishment even with our nostrils. When I breathe, I am the only one who can perceive this nourishment and I cannot return it by exhaling it for you to inhale it again and perceive it with your nostrils.

Although we perceive other sense objects, our perception of them does not destroy their nature and change them into our bodily substance. We can both perceive them either together or at different times, so that what I perceive, either in whole or in part, can also be perceived by you. Light, sound, and bodily objects are examples of things with which we can come in contact, but without altering their nature.

Ev. I understand.

Aug. It is clear, therefore, that those things which are not changed by us, though we perceive them with our bodily senses, are not the property of our senses and hence are all the more common to us, seeing that they are not changed or converted into our own individual or, so to speak, private property.

Ev. I am in full agreement.

Aug. We are to understand by individual and, so to speak,

private property, that which is identified with each one of us and which each one alone can perceive within himself as belonging properly to his own nature. By common and, so to speak, public, we understand that which is experienced by all who perceive something, without any deterioration or change in the thing itself.

Ev. That is correct.

Chapter 8

20. *Aug.* Come now, and let me have your attention. Tell me whether anything can be found which all thinking men perceive in common, each one making use of his own mind and reason. Something which is seen is present to everybody and is not changed into something else useful for those to whom it is present, like food and drink, but remains whole and entire, whether it is seen or not. Or do you think that perhaps no such thing exists?

Ev. On the contrary, I see there are many, but it is sufficient to single out one of them, the nature and truth of number which are present to all who make use of reason. Everyone engaged in computing them strives to grasp their nature with his own reason and intelligence. Some do this rather easily, others with more difficulty, while others cannot do it at all, though the truth makes itself equally available to all who can grasp it. And whenever someone experiences this, it is not altered or changed into a kind of nourishment for the one who perceives it. When anyone errs in judgment about it, the reality itself, which remains true and intact, is not at fault; rather, his own error is measured by his failure to behold the reality itself.

21. *Aug.* That is certainly true. I see you were quick to find an answer as becomes a man not unfamiliar with such matters. But suppose I were to tell you that these numbers have not been impressed upon our mind by any nature of their own but come from things which we grasp with the bodily senses and are a kind of sense-image of things visible, how would you reply? Or would you also be of the same opinion?

Ev. I could never think of such a thing. Even if I could perceive numbers by the bodily senses, I could not on this account also perceive the nature of numerical division and addition by the bodily sense. It is by the light of the mind that I show a man to be wrong whose computation indicates an incorrect total either in addition or subtraction. Besides, I cannot tell how long anything will endure which comes in contact with my bodily senses, such as the heavens and the earth, and all the other bodies which I see are contained in them. But seven and three are ten, not only now, but forever. And there has never been, nor will there ever be a time when seven and three were not ten. This is why I have said that the indestructible truth of number is common to me and to anyone at all who uses his reason.

22. *Aug.* I cannot gainsay the absolute truth and certainty of your answer. But you will readily see that even the numbers themselves have not been brought in through the bodily senses if you realize that all numbers are designated as multiples of the number one. For example, twice one is two, one tripled is three, and ten times one is ten. No matter what the number, it is so designated according to the number of times it contains the number one. But anyone with a true notion of "one" will doubtless discover that it cannot be perceived by the bodily senses. Whatever comes in contact with the bodily senses can be shown to be many, and not one, since, being a body, it also has numberless parts. To say nothing of the minute and barely discernible particles, no matter how small the tiny body, it has one part on the right, another on the left, one above and another below, one to the far side and another on the near side, parts at the extremes and parts in between. We have to admit that such parts are found in any body, no matter how small it is. Accordingly, we acknowledge that no bodily reality is one, truly and simply, and yet it would be impossible to enumerate so many parts within the body unless these were differentiated by the concept of one.

Whenever I look for this "one" in a body, though I am sure I will not find it, I certainly know what I am looking for and what it is that I do not find there. I know it cannot be found, or better, that it is not present there at all. Consequently, when I recognize that a bodily reality is not one, I know the meaning of one; otherwise, I could not number the many parts in the body. Wherever it is that I come to know one, I certainly do not know it by the bodily senses, for by these I know only bodies, which, as we have shown, are not one, truly and simply. Furthermore, if we have not perceived one by the bodily sense, then neither have we perceived any number by them, none at least of those numbers which we can discern with the understanding. For there is not one of them that does not get its name from its being a given multiple of one, which is not perceived by the bodily senses. The half of any small body has itself its own half, although the whole body is made up of two halves. Hence those two parts of the body are such that even they are not simply two. But the number we call two, because it is twice that which is simply one, has one for its half, namely, that which is simply one, and this in turn cannot have a half or a third, or any other fraction, because it lacks parts and is truly one.

23. Since we are following numerical order, we see next that two follows one and that it is related to one as its double. The double of two does not follow at once, but three, and then four, which is the double of two. And this ordered sequence extends to all the remaining numbers according to a fixed and changeless law. Thus, after one, the first of all numbers, the first number, apart from one, which follows next is two, the double of one. After this second number, namely, two, the second number, apart from the number two, is the double of two, since the first number after two is three, while the second after two is four, the double of two. After the third number, apart from three, is the double of three, since after three, the first number is four, the second is five, and the third is six, which is the double of three. So too, after number four, the fourth number, apart from four, is the double of four, since following the fourth number, namely, after four, the first number is five, the second is six, the third is seven, and the fourth is eight, which is the double of four. You will also find that the same thing holds for all the other numbers, which we discovered when we combined the first two, that is, numbers one and two, namely, that the double of any number is as many times removed from that number as the number doubled is removed from the beginning of number.

How, then, do we discern that this numerical relationship, which we observe to prevail throughout the whole range of numbers, is changeless, fixed, and indestructible? No one perceives all numbers by any bodily sense, for they are innumerable. I say, then, how do we know that this holds true for all numbers? What idea or image enables us to see with such assurance that this fixed law governing number holds throughout innumerable instances, unless it be that inner light of which the senses have no knowledge?

24. Men endowed with the God-given ability to reason and not blinded by stubbornness, are constrained by these and many other such proofs to acknowledge that the law and truth of numbers do not pertain to the bodily sense, that they remain changeless and incorruptible, and belong to all who use their reason to perceive them. Many other things possibly come to mind which, as the common and, as it were, public possession of all who use reason, are there to be seen by the mind and reason of each one who perceives them, though the realities themselves remain intact and unchanging. However,

I was delighted to hear that the law and truth of numbers came especially to your mind when you wanted to give an answer to my question. It is not without some intent that number and wisdom are brought together in the Sacred Scriptures, where it is said: "I have gone round—I and my heart—to know and to consider, and to search out wisdom and number."[1]

Chapter 9

25. But let me ask you this: What, in your opinion, should be our view of wisdom itself? Do you think that each man has his own individual wisdom, or that there is one wisdom present to all alike, and that a man becomes wiser the more he shares in it?

Ev. I do not yet know to what wisdom you refer, for I notice that wise actions and words are looked at differently by men. Those who wage war think they are acting wisely, while those who spurn war to devote care and effort to tilling the soil, prefer to extol this activity and to regard it as wisdom. Those shrewd enough to devise schemes for acquiring money are wise in their own eyes. Those uninterested in such things and who renounce them and all such temporal goods, to direct all their effort to the search for truth so as to know themselves and God, judge that this is the one great task of wisdom. Those who are unwilling to allow themselves such leisure for the quest and contemplation of truth, preferring to work for the welfare of men amidst burdensome cares and duties and are occupied with the task of providing just rule and government for human affairs, think that they are wise. And those who combine both of these, living part of their life in the contemplation of truth and part in the discharge of official duties, which they feel are owing to human society, think they have won the prize for wisdom. I

---
[1] Eccles. 7.26.

make no mention of the countless sects where each one sets its own followers above the rest and would have it that they alone are wise.

Consequently, since the answer to our present problem must not be what we believe but what we grasp with a clear understanding, I cannot possibly reply to your question about the nature of wisdom unless I know by reflection and rational discernment what I already hold on faith.

26. *Aug.* Do you think there can be any wisdom but the truth wherein the highest good is seen and possessed? Now those men whom you mentioned as pursuing different goals, all seek good and shun evil, but they pursue different goals because they have different ideas about the good. Any man, then, who seeks what should not be sought is still in error, even though he would not be seeking it unless he thought it was good. A man who seeks nothing, or who seeks what ought to be sought, is not in error.

Insofar, therefore, as all men seek the happy life, they are not in error. But to the extent that a man fails to hold to that way of life which leads to happiness, by so much is he in error, though he avows and professes that he is seeking only happiness. For there is error whenever we follow something which does not lead us where we want to go. And the more one errs in his way of life, the less wise he is, for he is all the farther from the truth wherein the highest good is seen and possessed. It is by attaining to the possession of the highest good that a man becomes happy, which is unquestionably what all of us desire.

Just as we agree that we want to be happy, so do we agree that we want to be wise since, without wisdom, no one is happy. For no one is happy except by the highest good which is found in the contemplation and possession of that truth which we call wisdom. So, just as the notion of happiness is impressed on our minds even before we are happy—this enables us to have the assurance and to state unhesitatingly that we want to be happy—so too, even before we are wise, we have the notion of wisdom impressed on our minds. And if any one of us is asked whether he wants to be happy, it is this notion that enables him to reply that he does, beyond any shadow of doubt.

27. We agree then about the nature of wisdom, though you were not able to put it in words. For if you did not perceive it at all in your mind, you simply could not know that you want to be wise or that this was your duty, which I do not think you will deny. If, then, we are in agreement about wisdom, I want you to tell me whether, as in the case of the law and truth of numbers, you think that wisdom too is present to all alike who use their reason, or whether you feel there are as many wisdoms as there are men capable of becoming wise. For there are as many minds as there are men, so that we do not perceive anything with one another's mind.

Ev. If the highest good is one for all men, then that truth wherein we can contemplate and possess it, namely, wisdom, must also be common to all.

Aug. Do you doubt that the highest good, whatever it is, is the same for all men?

Ev. I really do, because I notice that different men take delight in different things as their highest good.

Aug. I only wish that no one had any doubt about the highest good, just as no one doubts that it is only by the possession of this good, whatever it is, that man can become happy. But as this is an important question and may require a lengthy discussion, let us go all the way and suppose that there are just as many highest goods as there are different classes of things which different men seek as their highest good. It does not follow, does it, that wisdom itself is not something one and common to all alike, simply because those goods which they see and choose in the light of this wisdom are many and varied? If you think it does, you could also doubt that the sunlight is something one, since the objects we see in it are many and varied. From among these objects each one freely chooses something to enjoy through his sense of sight. One man likes to look at a mountain height and finds delight in such a view; another, at the level expanse of a meadow; another, at the slope of a valley; another, at the green forest; another, at the undulating surface of the sea; another gathers in all or several of these at once for the sheer delight of looking at them.

The things which men see in the light of the sun and which they choose for their enjoyment are many and varied, yet there is the one sunlight in which each viewer sees and takes hold of an object for his enjoyment. Similarly, the goods are many and varied from which each one chooses what he wants, and it is by contemplating and taking hold of this object of his choice that each one really and truly makes this the highest good wherein to find his enjoyment. It is still possible that the light of wisdom itself, in which these things are seen and grasped, may be one and shared by all alike who are wise.

Ev. I acknowledge that this is possible and that there is nothing to prevent the one wisdom from being common to all, even though the highest goods are many and varied. But I would like to know whether this is the case, since, by granting that it is possible, it does not necessarily follow that it is so.

Aug. We know for now that wisdom does exist. But whether there is one wisdom common to all, or whether each wise man has his own wisdom in the way that he has his own soul or mind, is something that we do not yet comprehend.

Ev. That is true.

Chapter 10

28. *Aug.* Well then, where do we see the truth of what we now know, namely, that wisdom or wise men exist, and that all men want to be happy? I certainly have no doubt whatever that you do see this and that it is true. Do you see then that this is true just as you see your own thoughts which are completely unknown to me unless you disclose them to me? Or do you see it in such a way as to understand that it can also be seen as true by me, though you did not tell it to me?

Ev. I have no doubt indeed that you could also see it, even against my will.

Aug. Is not this one truth, then, which we both see with our individual minds, common to both of us.

Ev. Quite evidently.

Aug. I also believe you will not deny that we should have a zeal for wisdom and will agree that this in fact is true.

Ev. I do not deny this at all.

Aug. Can we possibly deny that this truth is likewise one and that it is something to be seen by all alike who know it? Yet each one sees it with his own mind, not with mine or yours, or with anyone else's mind, since what is seen is present to all alike who behold it.

Ev. We could never deny that.

Aug. Will you not also admit that these statements have an absolute truth which is present and common to you as well as to me, and to all who see it, namely: we ought to live justly, the less perfect should be subordinated to the more perfect, like things should be equally esteemed, each one should be given his due?

Ev. I agree.

Aug. Can you deny that something incorrupt is better than the corrupt, the eternal better than the temporal, the inviolable better than what is subject to injury?

Ev. Who could possibly deny it?

Aug. Can anyone say, therefore, that this truth belongs to him alone when its changeless character is there to be seen by all who have the power to behold it?

Ev. No one could truly say that this truth belongs to him alone, since it is just as much one and common to all as it is true.

Aug. Who, again, is there to deny that the soul should turn from what is corrupt to the incorrupt, and should love, not the corrupt, but the incorrupt? Or how can anyone, once he acknowledges that something is true, fail to understand its changeless character or to see that it is present to all alike who are able to behold it?

Ev. That is perfectly true.

Aug. Well then, will anyone doubt that a life which does not turn away from its firm and moral convictions by any adversity is better than one which is easily broken and overcome by temporal misfortune?

Ev. Who could doubt it?

29. *Aug.* I will look for no further examples of this kind. It is enough that together we see and admit as an absolute certainty that those truths are so many rules and beacons of virtue, that they are true and changeless, and, whether taken singly or collectively, that they are present in common for all to see who can do so, each one viewing them with his own mind and reason. But what I am really asking is whether you think that these truths pertain to wisdom. I believe that in your opinion a man is wise who has acquired wisdom.

Ev. I certainly think so.

Aug. Could a man who lives justly live this way unless he knew which are the lower things that he subordinates to the higher, which the things of equal rank that he brings together, and what things he assigns as appropriate to each class?

Ev. He could not.

Aug. Then you will not deny, will you, that a man who sees these things does so wisely?

Ev. I do not deny it.

Aug. Does not the man who lives prudently choose the incorrupt and judge that it should be preferred to the corrupt?

Ev. Quite clearly.

Aug. Then when a man chooses to turn his soul to what

everybody admits should be chosen, can we deny that he is making a wise choice?

Ev. I could never deny that.

Aug. Therefore, when he turns his soul to what was a wise choice, he does so wisely.

Ev. Most certainly.

Aug. And the man who is undeterred by fear or punishment from what he has wisely chosen, and to which it was wise of him to turn, is undoubtedly acting wisely.

Ev. Beyond any doubt.

Aug. It is perfectly clear then that all those truths which we call rules and beacons pertain to wisdom. The more a man uses them in the conduct of his life and lives in conformity with them, the more wisely does he live and act. And we cannot really say that what is done wisely is found apart from wisdom.

Ev. That is absolutely true.

Aug. Accordingly, just as there are true and changeless rules governing numbers whose law and truth are, as you said, unalterably present and common to all who see them, so, too, are the rules of wisdom likewise true and changeless. When you were asked just now about a few of them, one by one, you replied that they were true and evident and admitted that they are common for all to see who are capable of beholding them.

Chapter 11

30. *Ev.* I cannot doubt it. But I would very much like to know whether these two, namely, wisdom and number, fall under some one class since you mentioned that they are placed together even in the Sacred Scriptures. Is one derived from the other, or is it contained in the other; does number, for example, derive from wisdom, or is it contained in wisdom? For I would not dare assert that wisdom derives from number or is contained in it. I do not see how I could do so because I am acquainted with many mathematicians or accountants, or whatever else they may be called, who work out perfectly accurate and remarkable calculations. But of wise men, I either know very few, or possibly none at all. Wisdom, it strikes me, is far nobler than number.

Aug. You mention a subject at which I am also wont to marvel. For whenever I go over in my mind the unchanging truth of number, and consider, so to speak, its abode or sanctuary or sphere, or however else we may suitably indicate somehow the seat and dwelling-place of number, I am far removed from the body.[1] And when I chance to find something that I can think of, but not something that I can adequately express in words, I return wearily to the familiar things about us in order to be able to speak, and I speak in the usual way of things that confront our gaze. This happens to me even when I do all I can to think carefully and intently about wisdom. That is why I marvel exceedingly at the fact that, while wisdom and number occupy a hidden and certain abode in Truth, and while there is also the additional scriptural testimony which I cited, linking them together—I marvel exceedingly, as I said, why number is of little value for most men, while wisdom is dear to them.

But it doubtless comes down to this, that they are one and the same thing. Yet, since the Sacred Scripture has this to say of wisdom that "it reaches from end to end strongly and orders all things gently,"[2] then, possibly, the power whereby "it reaches from end to end strongly," is called number, while

---

[1] The Pythagorean influence on Augustine's treatment of number is apparent in the early dialogue *De ordine,* where the "science of number" is assigned a kind of primacy in the order of knowledge (2.18.47). His sermons and scriptural commentaries often reflect the attitude of an age fascinated by the sacramental aspect of number and occasion ingenious pieces of exegesis which at times appear fanciful and extravagant to men of a later day. On the scriptural influence on Augustine's notion of number, cf. W. Most, "The Scriptural Basis of Saint Augustine's Arithmology," *The Catholic Biblical Quarterly* 13 (1951) 284-295.
[2] Wis. 8.1.

that whereby "it orders all things gently" is here called wisdom, though both belong to one and the same wisdom.

31. Wisdom has endowed all things with number, even the least and those at the lowest confines of the universe. Though they hold the lowest place in existence, bodies all possess these numbers. But the capacity for wisdom has not been given to bodily things or to every kind of soul, but only to rational souls. It is there that wisdom has, so to speak, taken up its abode and from where it orders all things it has endowed with number, even the lowest. Since it is easy for us to judge about bodily things, occupying, as they do, a place beneath us, and to see that they have numbers impressed on them which we also judge to be below us, we therefore set a lower value upon numbers.

But once we begin to change our course, as it were, to an upward direction, we discover that number transcends even our minds and abides unchangingly in truth itself. But since few men are capable of wisdom, whereas the ability to count has been given even to fools, men admire wisdom and have little regard for number. There are, on the other hand, men learned and devoted to study, and the more these withdraw from the taint of earthly things, the more clearly they behold in the truth itself both number and wisdom and hold both in high esteem. And when they compare truth with gold and silver and the other things for which men struggle, then not only these, but even they themselves, appear vile in their sight.

32. It should not surprise you that men have belittled number and set a high value on wisdom simply because it is easier for them to count than to acquire wisdom, when you stop to consider how much more they value gold than the light of a lamp, compared to which gold is something trivial. But greater honor is given something far inferior simply because even a beggar can light himself a candle, whereas only a few can possess gold. This is far from implying that, in comparison with number, wisdom is found inferior, since it is the same; but it must find an eye capable of discerning this identity.

Light and heat are perceived coexistent, so to speak, in the one fire and cannot be separated from each other. Yet, the heat reaches objects placed near it, while the light is spread even over a larger area. In like manner, the power of understanding, present in wisdom, warms what is near it, such as rational souls, whereas, for things farther removed, such as bodies, it does not reach them with the warmth of its wisdom, but permeates them with the light of number. Perhaps you find this obscure, for no analogy drawn from visible things to illustrate an invisible reality can be made to fit perfectly.

Only take note of this point which is enough for our problem at hand and is clear even to more lowly minds, such as ours. Though we are unable to see clearly whether number is contained in wisdom, or is derived from it, or whether wisdom itself derives from number, and is contained in it, or whether it can be shown that both are names of the same thing, this much at least is clear, that both are true and are unchangeably true.

Chapter 12

33. You would in no way deny, then, that there exists unchangeable truth that embraces all things that are immutably true. You cannot call this truth mine or yours, or anyone else's. Rather, it is there to manifest itself as something common to all who behold immutable truths, as a light that in wondrous ways is both hidden and public. But how could anyone say that anything which is present in common to all endowed with reason and understanding is something that belongs to the nature of any one of these in particular? You recall, I believe, the result of our discussion a short time ago concerning the bodily senses,[1] namely, that the objects perceived by us in common by sight and hearing, such as color and sound, which you and I see and hear together, are not identified with the nature of our eyes or ears, but are common objects of our perception. So too, you would never say that the things each one of us perceives in common with his own mind, belong to the nature of either of our minds. You cannot say that what two people perceive at the same time with their eyes is identified with the eyes of either one; it is a third something toward which the view of both is directed.

Ev. That is perfectly clear and true.

34. *Aug.* This truth, therefore, which we have discussed at length and in which, though it is one, we perceive so many things—do you think that compared to our minds it is more excellent, equally excellent, or inferior? Now if it were inferior, we would not be making judgments according to it, but about it. We do make judgments, for example, about bodies because they are lower, and we often state not only that they exist or do not exist this way, but also that they ought or ought not so to exist. So too with our souls; we not only know that our soul is in a certain state, but often know besides that this is the way it ought to be. We also make similar judgments about bodies, as when we say that a body is not so bright or so square as it ought to be, and so on, and also of souls, when we say the soul is not so well disposed as it ought to be, or that it is not so gentle or not so forceful, according to the dictates of our moral norms.

We make these judgments according to those rules of truth within us which we see in common, but no one ever passes judgment on the rules themselves. For whenever anyone affirms that the eternal ought to be valued above the things of time, or that seven and three are ten, no one judges that it ought to be so, but merely recognizes that it is so. He is not

---

[1] Cf. 2.7.

an examiner making corrections, but merely a discoverer, rejoicing over his discovery.

But if this truth were of equal standing with our minds, it would itself also be changeable. At times our minds see more of it, at other times less, thereby acknowledging that they are subject to change. But the truth which abides in itself, does not increase or decrease by our seeing more or less of it, but, remaining whole or inviolable, its light brings delight to those who have turned to it, and punishes with blindness those who have turned from it.

And what of the fact that we judge about our own minds in the light of this truth, though we are unable to judge at all about the truth itself? We say that our mind does not understand as well as it ought, or that it understands as much as it ought. But the mind's understanding should be in proportion to its ability to be drawn more closely and to cling to the unchangeable truth. Consequently, if truth is neither inferior nor equal to our minds, it has to be higher and more excellent.

Chapter 13

35. I had promised to show you, if you recall, that there is something higher than our mind and reason. There you have it—truth itself! Embrace it, if you can, and enjoy it; "find delight in the Lord and He will grant you the petitions of your heart."[1] For what more do you desire than to be happy? And who is happier than the man who finds joy in the firm, changeless, and most excellent truth?

Men proclaim they are happy when they embrace the beautiful bodies of their wives and even of harlots, which they desire so passionately, and shall we doubt that we are happy in the embrace of truth? Men proclaim they are happy when,

---
1 Ps. 36.4.

suffering from parched throats, they come to a copious spring of healthful waters, or, when hungry, they come upon a big dinner or supper sumptuously prepared. Shall we deny we are happy when we are refreshed and nourished by truth? We often hear men proclaim they are happy if they recline amid roses and other flowers, or delight in the fragrance of ointments. But what is more fragrant, what more delightful, than the breath of truth? And shall we hesitate to say we are happy when we are filled with the breath of truth? Many decide that for them the happy life is found in vocal music and in the sounds of string instruments and flutes. Whenever these are absent, they account themselves unhappy, whereas when they are at hand, they are thrilled with joy. When truth steals into our minds with a kind of eloquent silence without, as it were, the noisy intrusion of words, shall we look for another happy life and not enjoy that which is so sure and intimately present to us? Men delight in the glitter of gold and silver, in the lustre of gems, and are delighted by the charm and splendor of light, whether it be the light in our own eyes, or that of fires on earth, or the light in the stars, the moon, or the sun. And they think themselves happy when they are not withdrawn from these enjoyments by some kind of trouble or penury, and they would like to go on living forever for the sake of those delights. And shall we be afraid to find our happiness in the light of truth?

36. Quite the contrary. Since it is in truth that we know and possess the highest good, and since that truth is wisdom, let us see in wisdom our highest good. Let us make it our aim to enjoy fully, for happy indeed is the man whose delight is in the highest good.

It is this truth which throws light on all things that are truly good and which men choose according to their mental capacity, either singly or severally, for their enjoyment. By the light of the sun men choose what they like to look at and find delight in it. If some of them are perchance endowed with a sound, healthy, and powerful vision, they will like nothing better than to gaze at the sun itself which also sheds its light on other things in which weaker eyes find delight. Similarly, when the sharp and strong vision of the mind beholds a number of immutable truths known with certainty, it directs its gaze to truth itself, which illumines all that is true.[2] As if unmindful of all else, it clings to this truth and, in enjoying it, enjoys everything else at the same time. For whatever is delightful in other truths is made delightful by the truth itself.

37. Our freedom is found in submission to this truth. And it is our God Himself who frees us from death, namely, from our sinful condition. It is the Truth Himself, speaking also as a man with men, who says to those believing in him: "If you remain in my word, you are indeed my disciples, and you shall know the truth and the truth shall make you free."[3] But the soul is not free in the enjoyment of anything unless it is secure in that enjoyment.

Chapter 14

Now no one is secure in the possession of goods which can be lost against his will. But no one loses truth or wisdom against his will, for he cannot be separated from them by spatial distances. What we call separation from truth and wisdom is a perverse will which makes inferior things the object of its love. But no one wills anything unwillingly.

In possessing truth, therefore, we have something which all of us can equally enjoy in common, for there is nothing want-

---

[2] Augustine's earlier effort to prove the existence of God by rational argument would seem to exclude an Ontologistic interpretation of this passage. For if man's intellect enjoys in this life a natural and intuitive vision of God, then His existence can be neither an object of faith nor of rational demonstration. In the *De Genesi ad litteram* (12.27-28, 55-56), he had allowed the vision of God to Moses and St. Paul, but later rejected this view entirely. Cf. *De Trinitate* 2.16.27.

[3] John 8.31-32.

ing or defective in it. It welcomes all its lovers without any envy on their part; it is available to all, yet chaste with each. No one of them says to another: step back so I too may come close; take your hands away so I may also embrace it. All cling to it; all touch the selfsame thing. It is a food never divided into portions; you drink nothing from it that I cannot drink. By sharing in it, you make no part of it your personal possession. I do not have to wait for you to exhale its fragrance so that I too may draw it in. No part of it ever becomes the exclusive possession of any one man, or of a few, but is common to all at the same time in its entirety.[1]

38. Consequently, the objects we touch or taste or smell bear less resemblance to such truth than those which we perceive by hearing and sight. Every word is fully heard by all who hear it and by each one at the same time; every visible object before our eyes is seen at the same time as much by one as by another.

But these analogies are quite remote. No spoken word, for instance, emits all its sound at the same time, since its sound is prolonged over intervals of time, one part coming before another. And every visible object protrudes, so to speak, through space and is not wholly present everywhere. In any case, these things can all be taken from us against our will, and there are obstacles which stand in the way of our being able to enjoy them.

And even if the beautiful singing of a vocalist were to last forever, his admirers would vie with one another to come to hear him; they would press about each other, and, as the crowd became larger, would fight over seats so that each might be closer to the singer. And as they listened, they could not take any of the sound to keep for themselves but could only be caressed by all the fleeting sounds. And if I should

---

[1] The theoretic principles for Augustine's view of Christian humanism, expounded in *De doctrina christiana* (2.40), stem in part from this conception of truth, which belongs to all because it belongs to none. *Rationem autem veritatis quae nec mea nec tua est sed utrique nostrum ad contemplandum proposita* . . . (*C. Secundinum Manichaeum* 2).

wish to gaze at the sun, and were able to do so uninterruptedly, it would leave me at sunset and could be covered over by a cloud, and I could be forced to give up the pleasure of seeing it because of many other hindrances. Finally, even if the delights attached to seeing light and hearing sound were to be ever present, what great advantage would be mine since I share this in common with brute animals?

But the beauty of truth and wisdom does not turn away any who come because the audience is already overcrowded, provided only that there is a steadfast will to enjoy them. This beauty does not pass with time or move from place to place; it is not interrupted by nightfall or concealed by shadows, and is not at the mercy of the bodily senses. It is near to all throughout the world who have made it the object of their love, and belongs to them forever. It occupies no one place and is nowhere absent; outwardly, it admonishes us, inwardly, it teaches us.[2] All who behold it are changed for the better, and no one can change it for the worse. No one passes judgment on it, and without it no one can judge aright. Hence it is clear, beyond doubt, that truth is superior to our minds, each one of which is made wise by it alone, and is made a judge, not of truth itself, but of all other things in the light of truth.

Chapter 15

39. You granted that if I could prove that there was something above our minds, you would admit it was God, provided that there was still nothing higher. I agreed and stated that it would be enough for me to prove this point. For if there is anything more excellent, then this is God; if not, then truth itself is God. In either case, you cannot deny that God exists,

---

[2] The same theme is developed in *De magistro,* a dialogue between Augustine and his son, Adeodatus, composed about the year 389; translated in the opening pages of this volume.

which was the question we proposed to examine in our discussion. If you are uneasy because of what we have received on faith through the hallowed teaching of Christ, namely, that there is a Father of Wisdom, then remember that we have accepted this also on faith, namely, that the Wisdom begotten of the eternal Father is equal to Him. We are not to inquire further about this just now, but only to accept it with an unshaken faith.

God exists indeed, and He exists truly and most perfectly. As I see it, we not only hold this as certain by our faith, but we also arrive at it by a sure, though, as yet, very inadequate form of knowledge. But this is sufficient for the matter at hand and will enable us to explain the other points that have a bearing on the subject, unless, of course, you have some objections to raise.

Ev. I accept all this, overwhelmed as I am with an incredible joy which I am unable to express to you in words. I declare that it is absolutely certain. I do so, prompted by that inner voice which makes me want to hear the truth itself and to cling to it. I not only grant that this is good, but also that it is the highest good and the source of happiness.

40. *Aug.* You are certainly right. I too rejoice exceedingly. But I will ask you whether we are already wise and happy, or whether we are still striving to make this our goal.

Ev. I think rather we are striving toward it.

Aug. How then do you grasp those things which you rejoice in as being true and certain? You do grant that an understanding of them pertains to wisdom. Can a foolish man know wisdom?

Ev. Not while he remains foolish.

Aug. Then you must now be wise, or else you do not yet know wisdom.

Ev. I am, to be sure, not yet wise, but, insofar as I do know wisdom, I would say that I am not foolish. For I cannot deny that the things I know are certain, and that this is wisdom.

Aug. Please answer me this question: will you not grant that a man who is not just is unjust, and the man who is not prudent is imprudent, and the man who is not temperate is intemperate? Can there be any doubt about it?

Ev. I grant that when a man is not just, he is unjust, and I would give the same answer regarding the prudent and temperate man.

Aug. Why, then, is a man not foolish when he is not wise?

Ev. This I will also admit, that when a man is not wise, he is foolish.

Aug. Now which one of the two are you?

Ev. Whichever one you want to call me, for I dare not say that I am wise. Yet, I see how it follows from what I have admitted that I should not hesitate to say I am foolish.

Aug. Then the foolish man knows wisdom. For, as we have stated, he would not be sure he wanted to be wise, and that he ought to be so, unless the notion of wisdom were fixed in his mind; fixed in his mind, as are those things pertaining to wisdom itself about which, when questioned one by one, you replied, and in the knowledge of which you found delight.

Ev. It is just as you say.

Chapter 16

41. *Aug.* In our effort to be wise as quickly as possible, what else do we do but concentrate our soul wholly upon what the mind has discovered, and make this its permanent abode? As a result, the soul will no longer take delight in any individual good of its own that entangles it in things of a transitory nature but, once stripped of its attachment for the things of time and place, it will take hold of that which is forever one and the same. Just as the soul is the total source of life for the body, so is God the source of happiness for the soul. While we are engaged in this task, and until we have finished it, we are wayfarers. And if it is now granted us to enjoy those true and certain goods which cast their light along our darksome journey, take note whether this be not the very thing which Scripture says about the way Wisdom acts towards its lovers when they come in search of it: "She shows herself to them cheerfully in the ways, and meets them with all providence."[1]

Turn where you will, wisdom speaks to you by the imprint it has left on its works, and, when you are slipping back into what is outward, it entices you to return within by the beauty of those very forms found in things external. This is done so you may recognize that whatever delights you in a body and attracts you by the bodily senses is imbued with number. Thus, you must search for its source and return within yourself and come to see that it is not possible to pass judgment, favorable or unfavorable, on things known by the bodily senses unless you have at your disposal a knowledge of certain laws governing beauty to which you refer whatever objects you perceive outwardly.[2]

42. Look at the heavens and the earth and the sea, and at all the things they contain. Whether these shine from above or crawl on the earth below, or fly or swim, they all have forms because they possess number. Take away number from them, and they are nothing. What then, is the source of their existence but that same source where number derives, since, in fact, they enjoy existence only insofar as they are possessed of number?

Even men who create beauty in working with bodily materials make use of numbers in their art and fashion their products in accordance with them. While producing their work, they manipulate their hands and tools until what

---

[1] Wis. 6.13.
[2] While a Manichaean, Augustine had composed a work on esthetics, *De pulchro et apto*, which was no longer extant at the time he wrote the *Confessions* (4.13.20). The present discussion reveals a marked dependence upon Plotinus' treatise *On the Beautiful*. Cf. *Enneads* (1.6.9).

is being formed externally is made as perfectly as possible to conform with the inward light of number. Then, through the senses as intermediaries, it wins the approval of the mind which judges within, as it contemplates the higher realm of numbers. Ask me next what it is that moves the bodily members of the artisan and it will be found to be number, for even they move in a measured rhythm. If you take from his hand what he is making, and from his mind the intention to make something, then that bodily movement is calculated to give delight, and is called pantomime. Ask what there is in pantomime to cause delight, and number will answer that it is present there.

Now examine the beauty of a graceful body, and number will be found at work in space. Examine beauty in bodily movement, and you will see how number plays a role in the proper timing. Enter into the realm of art where number has its origin, and try to find time and place there. You will find there neither place nor time, and yet it is there that number has its abode. This realm of number is devoid of spaces, nor is its duration measured in terms of days. Yet, when men desirous of becoming artists set about the task of learning this art, they are moving their bodies in space and time, but their soul they move only in time; and with the passing of time they become more proficient in their art.

Now go beyond even the soul of the artist to get a view of the eternal realm of number. Wisdom will now shine upon you from its inner abode and from the very sanctuary of truth. If your gaze, as yet weak, recoils from this light, turn the mind's eye back along the way where "wisdom showed herself cheerfully." Only remember that you have put off for a time a vision which you will seek again when you are stronger and sounder.

43. O Wisdom, O Light most pleasing to a mind made pure! Woe to those who forsake your guidance and grope about among your shadowy imitations and, more enamored of your signs than of you, are forgetful of what you wish to intimate. For you never cease to intimate your nature and excellence to us, and the entire beauty of created things consists in these signs. The artist, too, through the beauty of his work, intimates in a way to the viewer of it that he should not fasten his attention there completely but should so scan the beauty of the artistic work that he will turn his thoughts back fondly upon him who made it. Those who love the things you make instead of yourself are like men who listen to the eloquence of a wise man. In their overeagerness to hear his beautiful voice and the skillful cadence of his words, they neglect the primary importance of his thoughts for which the spoken words were to serve as signs.

Woe to those who turn away from your light and are delighted to cling to their own darkness. Turning their back, so to speak, upon you, they are enchained by works of the flesh as by their own shadow,[3] and yet, even such delight as they experience there, comes to them from the encompassing rays of your light. But while love of the shadow continues, it makes the mind's eye weaker and less able to endure the sight of your presence. Hence, so long as a man prefers to pursue whatever is easier for his weakened condition to endure, the more is he encompassed in darkness. This is the beginning of his inability to see that which exists most perfectly, and he begins to judge as evil whatever deceives him through want of foresight, or appeals to his impoverished condition, or torments him in his state of captivity. Yet he is justly suffering these penalties for having turned from wisdom; and what is just cannot be evil.

44. Hence, if you take a look at any changeable reality, you will be unable to grasp it either by the bodily senses or by mental reflection unless it is held together by some numerical determinant, without which it will fall back into nothing. Have no doubt that there exists an eternal and changeless

---
[3] A clear allusion to Plato's allegory of the "cave" in Book Seven of the *Republic*.

form which keeps such changeable things from losing their existence and enables them to pass, as it were, through the phases of their temporal duration by the regularity of their movements and their separate and varied forms. Such a form is neither circumscribed by place nor spread, as it were, through space; nor is it extended or changed in the course of time. In virtue of this form, all changeable realities are able to receive their forms, each according to its nature, and to realize fully their numerical perfection in place and time.

Chapter 17

45. Every changeable reality must also be capable of receiving form. Just as we call something changeable which is capable of undergoing change, so I would call "formable," whatever is capable of receiving form.[1] But nothing can impart form to itself, because nothing can give itself what it does not have, and, surely, a thing is given form so that it may have form. So if anything possesses form, there is no need for it to receive what it has. But if it does not have form, it cannot receive from itself what it does not have. Nothing, therefore, as we have said, can give itself form. Now what more can we say about the changing nature of body and soul, since enough has been said previously? We may conclude, then, that body and soul both receive forms from an immutable and everlasting form, with reference to which it was said: "Thou shalt change them and they shall be changed, but Thou art forever the same and thy years fail not."[2] The Prophet spoke of years that do not fail to indicate eternity.

---

[1] In the third of his commentaries on the Book of Genesis, *De Genesi ad litteram*, Augustine states that by one single act God produced simultaneously both "unformed matter" and "form," and that the former is prior only by the priority of nature and not of time (1.15.29).
[2] Ps. 51.27.

Of the same form it is likewise said that "abiding in itself, it renews all things."[3]

By this we may also understand that all things are ruled by providence. If everything in existence would become nothing, once form was entirely taken away, then this unchangeable form is itself their providence. Through it all changing realities subsist so as to achieve their perfection and movements by the numerical principles belonging to their forms. If this form did not exist, these would have no being. Accordingly, the man who is making his way toward wisdom will see, as he gazes thoughtfully upon the whole of creation, how wisdom reveals itself cheerfully to him along the way and comes to meet him with all providential care. And he will yearn all the more eagerly to complete this journey as the path itself is made more beautiful by that wisdom which he so ardently desires to reach.

46. If you are able to find some other class of creature besides that which exists without life, and that which exists with life but without understanding, and that which exists with life and understanding, then you might venture to affirm that there is something good which does not come from God. These three classes may even be expressed by two words, if we call them body and life. For that which has only life and no understanding, as animals, and that which has understanding, as man, are rightly said to have life. Now these two, namely, body and life, are reckoned among things created, since we also speak of life of the Creator Himself, and this is the highest form of life. Since these two, namely, body and life, are capable of receiving form, as our earlier remarks have shown, and since they would fall back into nothingness were all form to be taken away, they give sufficient indication that they owe their existence to that form which is always the same.

Consequently, all good things, however great or small, can

---

[3] Wis. 7.27.

only come from God. What can be greater among creatures than life endowed with understanding, or what can be less than body? No matter how far these deteriorate and tend towards nothingness, something of form remains in them to give them such existence as they have. Whatever form is left in anything undergoing such deterioration, comes to it from that form which knows no deterioration and which does not permit even the movements of things, whether towards progress or deterioration, to go beyond the limits imposed by their numbers. Consequently, whatever we find praiseworthy in nature, whether it be deemed worthy of great or of slight praise, must be referred to the highest and unspeakable praise of the Creator. But you may have something further to add.

Chapter 18

47. *Ev.* I am, I admit, sufficiently convinced that God exists and that all goods come from God, so far as such evidence is possible in the present life and for men like ourselves. All existing things come from God, whether they have understanding and life and existence, or have only life and existence, or have only existence. Now let us examine the third question to see whether it can be shown that free will should be reckoned among things that are good. Once this is proven, I will have no hesitation in granting that God gave it to us and that it is something that should have been given.

Aug. You recall very well the questions proposed, and you were quick to notice that the second question has already been cleared up. But you should have seen that the third was also settled. You gave it as your opinion that free will should not have been given because people commit sin by it. In opposition to your view, I retorted that moral conduct is only possible by free will and went on to assert that God had given it for this purpose.¹ You replied that free will should have been given us in the same way as justice, which one can only use rightly. This reply of yours compelled us to embark upon these roundabout discussions to prove that good things, great and small, come from God alone. This point could only be clarified after we had refuted the wicked folly expressed by the fool who said in his heart, "there is no God."² Some kind of reasoning, suited to our feeble mentality, was undertaken on this important matter in order to give us something certain by way of conclusion, while God Himself was helping us along so perilous a course. Although these two truths, namely, that God exists, and that all good things come from Him, were at first held firmly by faith, they have now been examined in such a way that this third truth is manifestly evident, namely, that free will must be numbered among things that are good.

48. In an earlier discussion it was proven and agreed upon by us that a corporeal nature occupies a lower place in existence than does the nature of the soul, and that the soul is therefore a greater good than the body. If, then, among goods of the body we find some which man can misuse, we do not say that they should not therefore have been given, since we do acknowledge that these are good. We should not be surprised then if we also find in the soul some goods which we can also misuse. But because they are good, they could only be given by Him from whom all good things come.

You can see how a great good is wanting in a body having no hands; yet a man who perpetrates cruel and shameful deeds with them makes bad use of his hands. If you were to see someone with no feet, you would admit that an important good is wanting to the body's integrity, and yet you could not deny that a man who uses his feet to injure someone or to disgrace himself is making bad use of his feet.

---
1 A passage exploited by Pelagius in his attack upon Augustine's teaching on grace.
2 Ps. 13.1.

With our eyes we can perceive light and distinguish bodily forms one from another. This power of sight is the noblest endowment of our body and for this reason these organs have been given a kind of exalted place of honor in our body. Our eyes also serve to protect health and furnish many other benefits to life. Yet, many men do much that is shameful with their eyes and enlist them to serve the cause of lust. You can see what a great good is wanting to a face having no eyes, but when we possess them, who else has given them but God, the Giver of all goods?

Just as you look favorably upon these goods in the body and praise Him who gave them, without regard to those who misuse them, so you should also grant that free will, without which no one can live right, is good and is given by God. You should further acknowledge that those who misuse this good should be condemned rather than admit that He who gave free will should not have given it.

49. *Ev.* I would like you to prove for me first that free will is a good, and then I would grant that God gave it to us, because I acknowledge that all things good come from God.

Aug. Have I failed then to prove this to you after so much effort in our earlier discussion? You granted at the time that the beauty and form of a body are wholly derived from the supreme form of all things, namely, the truth, and that these are good. Truth itself says in the Gospel that even the hairs of our head are numbered.[3] Have you forgotten what we said about the supremacy of number and how its power extends from end to end? What perversity to count the hairs of our head, small and lowly as they are, among things good, and fail to discover their cause and to see that God alone is the Creator of everything good, since all good things, great and small, derive from Him, from whom comes every good. Again, what perversity to doubt about free will, without which it is impossible to lead an upright life, as even they acknowledge who live wickedly.

---
3 Cf. Matt. 10.30.

In any case, please tell me now which you think is the higher good in us. Is it that without which we can live rightly, or that without which we cannot live rightly?

Ev. Please go easy on me, for I am ashamed that I could not see this. How could anyone doubt that that without which there can be no right living is the more excellent good by far?

Aug. Would you deny then that a man with one eye can live rightly?

Ev. May I never be guilty of such colossal folly!

Aug. Since you grant, then, that the eye is something good in the body, even though its loss is no hindrance to leading a good life, will you take the view that free will is not a good, when no one can live rightly without it?

50. Think of justice, which no one can put to bad use. It is reckoned among the greatest goods found in man and among all the virtues of the soul which make for a good and upright life. Nor does anyone put to bad use the virtues of prudence or courage or temperance. In all these virtues, as well as in justice itself, which you mentioned, it is right reason that prevails, and without it the virtues cannot exist. But no one can put right reason to a bad use.

Chapter 19

These virtues are, therefore, great goods. But you must remember that not only the great but even the least goods exist through Him alone from whom all good things come, namely, from God. Our earlier discussion led to this conclusion, to which you gladly gave assent time after time.

As I was saying, these virtues which enable us to live rightly are great goods, whereas all forms of bodily beauty are the least goods, since we can live rightly without them. But the powers of the soul, without which there can be no right living, are intermediate goods. No one puts virtues to a bad use, but anyone can put the other goods, namely, the intermediate and least, not only to good, but also to bad use. So no one puts virtues to bad use, since the function of virtue is the good use of those things which we can also put to bad use. No one makes bad use of what he puts to good use. Accordingly, the vast liberality of God's goodness has brought into existence not only the great, but also the intermediate and least goods. His goodness is more to be praised for the great than for the intermediate goods, and more for the intermediate than for the least goods, but still to be praised more for all of them than if He had not given existence to them all.

51. *Ev.* I agree. But, since in our discussion of free will we see that it can make either good or bad use of other things, I am perplexed as to how free will is to be numbered among the things which we use.

Aug. In the same way that our reason gives us certain knowledge of all that we know, though reason itself is numbered among the things we know by reason. Have you forgotten that when we were inquiring as to what reason could know, you admitted that reason too is known by reason? If we make use of other things by our free will, you must not therefore think it strange that we can also make use of free will by free will itself. As in using other things, the will is making use of itself, so in knowing other things, reason also knows itself. Memory, too, embraces not only all the other things we remember, but, by our not forgetting that we have a memory, it also remains somehow within us. It remembers not only other things but also itself; or better yet, it is by memory that we remember ourselves, other things, and memory itself.

52. Consequently, a man possesses the happy life when his will, an intermediate good, clings to the changeless good. This is not his own good exclusively but is common to all, like truth, which we discussed at length without doing it justice. And this happy life, namely, the state of the soul in union with the changeless good, is man's proper and principal good. In this good, too, are found all the virtues which no one can put to bad use. And while these are important and principal goods in man, we understand well enough that they belong to each man and are not the common possession of all.

Men become wise and happy by clinging to truth and wisdom, which are common to all. But one man does not become happy by the happiness of another. Even when he emulates the happy man in order to be happy himself, he seeks happiness from the same source which he knows made the first man happy, namely, the truth, which is changeless and common to all. Nor does one man become prudent or courageous or temperate or just by the presence of these virtues in another. But he acquires these by conforming his soul to the changeless norms and beacons of the virtues, which abide indestructibly in truth itself and in wisdom, which are common to all. The man whose soul is conformed and fixed to these principles is endowed with such virtues and is set up as an example for one's imitation.

53. By adhering to the changeless good, which is common to all, the will acquires the principal and important goods, though the will is itself an intermediate good. But when it turns away from the changeless good, common to all, and turns towards a good of its own, or to an external or lower good, then the will sins. It turns towards a good of its own whenever it wants to be its own master; to an external good, when it is eager to know the personal affairs of others, or whatever is none of its own business; to a lower good, when it loves the pleasures of the body. Thus, a man who becomes proud, curious, and sensuous is delivered over to another kind of life which, in comparison with the higher life, is a death. And yet, this life is subject to the rule of

Divine Providence, which assigns everything to its proper place and gives to each one his due.

As a consequence, neither those goods sought after by sinners are in any way evil, nor free will itself, which we found was to be counted among the intermediate goods. Evil consists rather in the will's turning away from the changeless good and in its turning to goods that are changeable. Since this turning from one thing to another is not done from necessity, but freely, the unhappiness which results is justly deserved.

Chapter 20

54. Since the will undergoes movement when it turns from the unchangeable to the changeable good, you may perhaps ask how this movement originates. It is really evil, though free will must be reckoned as a good, since it is impossible to live rightly without it. For if this movement, namely, the turning away of the will from the Lord, is unquestionably sinful, we could not say, could we, that God is the cause of sin? If this movement, therefore, does not come from God, then where does it come from?

If I reply to your question by saying that I do not know, you may be distressed all the more. Yet, I would be answering you correctly, because what is nothing, cannot be known. Only make sure to hold firm to your religious conviction that you know of no good, either by the senses, or by the intellect, or in any other way, that does not come from God. Hence, no kind of nature will be found that does not come from God. Wherever you find things possessed of measure, number, and order, have no hesitation in ascribing them all to God their Maker. Remove these three from things entirely, and nothing at all will be left. Even were some vestige of an inchoative form to remain where you see no measure or number or order (since wherever these exist, form is complete), you would have to disallow even this inchoative form, since this seems to serve as material which the maker must bring to perfection. For, if the full perfection of form is a good, the beginning of form is something good. Hence, if all good is taken away entirely, there will remain not something, but nothing at all. All good is from God and, consequently, there is no nature that is not from God. Hence, that movement of the soul's turning away, which we admitted was sinful, is a defective movement, and every defect arises from non-being. Look for the source of this movement and be sure that it does not come from God.

Yet, since it is voluntary, this defect lies within our power. If you are fearful of it, then your will is against it, and unless you will it, it will not exist. What could be more secure than to live a life where nothing can happen to you which you do not will? But, since man cannot rise of his own will as he fell of his own will, the right hand of God, namely, our Lord Jesus Christ, is outstretched to us from above.[1] Let us embrace Him with a strong faith, await Him with a sure hope, and love Him with an ardent charity.

If you think there is something further that we should investigate more carefully on the origin of sin—I see no need for it at all—but if you think there is, it will have to be put off for another discussion.

Ev. I will certainly comply with your wish to put off for another time the problems arising from our discussion. For I cannot agree with your view that this matter has already been sufficiently investigated.

---

[1] This clear and explicit statement on the necessity of grace is one of several referred to in the *Retractations* as anticipating the errors of Pelagius (1.9.4-6).

BOOK THREE

Chapter 1

1. *Ev.* Since it is clear enough to me now that free will must be reckoned among things good, and not among the least of them, to be sure, we are therefore forced to admit that it was given by God and that it should have been given. If you deem the question opportune, I would like to find out from you the cause of that movement by which the will itself turns from the unchangeable good, common to all, and turns towards individual goods, either those of others or the lowest goods, and why, for that matter, it turns to all kinds of transitory goods.

Aug. Why do we have to know this?

Ev. Because if the free will given to us is such that this movement comes from its nature, then it turns to these goods of necessity, and where nature and necessity rule, there is no culpability.

Aug. Do you approve of this movement or not?

Ev. I disapprove.

Aug. Then you think it is blameworthy?

Ev. Yes, I do.

Aug. Then you are blaming a movement of the soul that is blameless.

Ev. I am not laying blame on any movement of the soul that is blameless. I simply do not know whether a fault is committed when one abandons the unchangeable good and turns towards goods that are changeable.

Aug. Then you are blaming something you do not know.

Ev. Do not press me over the use of words. I did not know

whether there is any fault committed. I meant to say that
there certainly is a fault and when I said I did not know,
I really meant to ridicule any doubt concerning something so
obvious.

Aug. See just what that very obvious truth is which made
you forget what you said a short while ago. If that movement
of the soul arises from nature or necessity, it can in no way
be blameworthy. But now you are maintaining that it is
blameworthy so tenaciously that you think any doubt about
so obvious a matter deserves to be ridiculed. Why, then, have
you seen fit to assert, or at least to propose as somewhat
doubtful, something which you yourself now show to be manifestly untrue? You said: "If the free will given to us is such
that this movement comes from its nature, then it turns to
these goods of necessity, and where nature and necessity rule,
there is no culpability." Since you have no doubt that this
movement is blameworthy, you should have had no doubt
at all that this was not the kind of will given to us.

Ev. I termed this movement blameworthy, and therefore
stated that I disapproved of it and could not doubt that it
is blameworthy.[1] But I do deny that the soul is culpable when
it is drawn by this movement from the unchangeable good
to changeable goods, if its nature is such that it is drawn
there by necessity.

2. *Aug.* Whose movement is it that you admit is really
blameworthy?

Ev. I see now it is in the soul, but I do not know whose it is.

Aug. Do you deny that the soul moves by this movement?

Ev. I do not.

Aug. Then do you deny that a movement which moves a
stone belongs to the stone? I am not speaking of that motion
by which we move a stone, or where it is moved by some ex-

---

[1] The problem of the origin of evil is crucial to Augustine's refutation of Manichaean dualism. While indebted to Plotinus for the notion of evil as privation, he could not accept the further view that evil is necessary or that matter itself is essentially evil.

ternal force, as when it is thrown up in the air, but of the movement by which a stone tends downward of its own force and falls to the ground.

Ev. I do not deny, of course, that the movement by which a stone, as you say, changes its direction to return to the earth belongs to the stone, but I do say that this movement comes from its nature. Now if the soul also has this kind of movement, then it too is determined by nature and cannot be blamed since its movement is fixed by nature. Even if this movement should bring the soul to ruin, it is driven there by a necessity of its nature. Since, on the contrary, we are certain that this movement is voluntary, we must simply deny that it is determined by nature. Consequently, it is unlike the movement which moves the stone by a natural necessity.

Aug. Have we accomplished anything in our two previous discussions?

Ev. We have, indeed.

Aug. I believe you recall that in our first discussion it was shown to our satisfaction that the mind becomes a slave of sinful desire only by its own will.[2] For it cannot be forced into such a shameful condition by anything superior or equal to it, which would be unjust, or by anything beneath it, which is impossible. We must conclude that the movement by which the soul turns for its delight away from God towards the creature is its own movement. If this movement is looked upon as culpable—and you thought it was ridiculous for anyone to doubt it—then it is not determined by nature, but is voluntary. It resembles in this respect the movement of the stone in its downward course, since one movement belongs to the soul just as the other belongs to the stone. But it is unlike it in another respect, namely, that it is not within the power of the stone to check its downward movement, whereas, while the soul is unwilling, its movement does not make it love lesser goods by forsaking those that are higher. Hence, the

---

2 1.11.21.

movement for the stone is fixed by nature, while that of the soul is voluntary. So if anyone says that the stone sins because it tends downward by its own weight, I will not say he has less sense than the stone, but he is certainly thought to be out of his mind. But we charge the soul with sin when we find it guilty of having forsaken what is higher to find its enjoyment in what is lower.

What need, then, is there to look for a cause of that movement by which the soul turns from the unchangeable to a changeable good? We agree that it belongs to the soul alone and is voluntary, and, consequently, culpable. Furthermore, all practical instruction in this matter has this for its aim, that, renouncing and restraining this kind of movement, we turn our will from the instability of temporal things to the enjoyment of the everlasting good.[3]

3. *Ev.* I see and can almost touch and grasp the truth of what you say. There is nothing I perceive so surely and intimately as the fact that I have a will which moves me to find delight in anything. But if this power which enables me to will or not to will is not mine, then I cannot readily find anything to call my own. So if I do wrong by my will, to what can I impute the act, if not to myself? Since it is the good God who made me, and I can do good only by my will, it is clear enough that the good God gave it to me for this purpose.

But if the movement by which the will can turn in different directions were not voluntary and subject to our control, a man ought not to be praised or blamed when, so to speak, he turns the hinge of his will in the opposite directions of higher and lower goods. And there would be no need at all to admonish him to neglect things temporal and to strive for the possessions of the eternal, or to try to lead a good rather than a bad life. But anyone who would think that man should not be so admonished, should be banished from the company of men.

---

[3] Another passage appropriated by Pelagius to support his teaching on the freedom of the will.

Chapter 2

4. This being the case, I am perplexed beyond words as to how God can have foreknowledge of all things future and yet we are not compelled by any necessity to sin. Were anyone to assert that something can take place otherwise than God foreknew it, he would attempt to destroy God's foreknowledge by the wildest kind of blasphemy.

God foreknew, then, that the first man would sin, which anyone will have to admit who agrees with me that God knows all future events. If this therefore is true, I do not say that God should not have made him, for He made him good, or that the sin of him, whom God made good, could cause any injury to God. In fact, in making man, God manifested His goodness, and in punishing him, He also manifests His justice, and in redeeming him, manifests His mercy. So I do not say that God should not have made him, but I will say that, insofar as God foreknew that man was going to sin, that had to take place which God foreknew was going to happen. How, therefore, is the will free where there appears to be such inevitable necessity?

5. *Aug.* You have been knocking hard at the door of God's mercy. May He come to our help and open it to those who stand knocking. I do think, however, that men for the most part are tormented by this problem only because they fail to pursue their inquiry in a religious spirit and are quicker to excuse their sins than they are to confess them. Or they prefer to think that divine providence does not rule over human affairs, and, surrendering body and soul to blind chance, they give themselves over to lust, to be battered and torn asunder. By denying God's judgments and evading the judgment of men, they fancy they can ward off their accusers through protection from the goddess Fortune. Yet, they usually depict her in statues and paintings as blind, so that they may be better off than Fortune, by which they think they are ruled, or may acknowledge that this same blindness prompts them to think and say such things. It would not be preposterous to admit that such men do everything by the falling out of chance, since their every action is a sort of fall. But I feel we have said enough in our second discussion against this opinion, which is replete with the most foolish and senseless kind of error.[1]

But there are others who, while not daring to deny that God's providence rules over men's lives, prefer to subscribe to the wicked and erroneous belief that this providence is weak or unjust or evil, rather than to confess their sins in a spirit of humble piety. Whenever these conceive of that Being who is most good, just, and powerful, they should all be open to the conviction that God's goodness and justice and power are far greater and higher than anything they conceive in their mind. And they should further understand, if they examine themselves, that they would have a duty to give thanks to God even if He had willed to make them something less perfect than they are, and they should exclaim with all their heart and from the depths of their soul, "I have said: Lord, have mercy on me, heal my soul because I have sinned against thee."[2] Thus they would be led to wisdom along the sure path of divine mercy; they would neither be proud over what they had discovered, nor disheartened about what remains to be discovered; their knowledge would make them more fit for contemplation, while their ignorance would make them pursue their inquiry with great humility. I have no doubt that you are convinced of this, but you must see now how easy it was for me to answer such an important question once you had replied to a few questions of my own.

Chapter 3

6. You are undoubtedly perplexed and puzzled by the prob-

---
[1] Cf. 2.17.45.
[2] Ps. 40.5.

lem as to how these two positions are not mutually opposed and incompatible, namely, that God foreknows all future events and yet we sin freely and not of necessity. If God foreknows that man will sin, then you will say that he must sin, and if this has to happen, there is no freedom of the will in the act of sinning, but rather an inevitable and unbending necessity. You are afraid that our reasoning will lead either to the impious denial of God's foreknowledge, or, if that is impossible, to our having to admit that we do not sin freely, but of necessity. Is there something else troubling you?

Ev. Nothing else just now.

Aug. So it is your opinion that everything foreknown by God takes place of necessity, and not freely.

Ev. I certainly think so.

Aug. Pay attention for heaven's sake! Examine yourself for a moment, if you can, and tell me whether you are going to will something sinful tomorrow or something good?

Ev. I do not know.

Aug. Do you think that God does not know it either?

Ev. I could never believe that.

Aug. If God knows what you are going to will tomorrow, and if He foresees what every man now and in the future is going to will, then all the more does He foresee how He will deal with the just and the wicked.

Ev. Obviously, if I say that God has foreknowledge of my actions, I must say with much greater assurance that He foreknows His own and foresees with absolute certainty what He is going to do.

Aug. If everything which God foreknows happens of necessity and not freely, are you not afraid that someone may counter by saying that God will also do whatever He is going to do, not freely, but of necessity?

Ev. When I stated that those things happen of necessity which God foreknows, I had in mind only those which occur in His creation, but not those which take place within Him; actually, these do not come into existence, but are eternally present in Him.

Aug. Then God does nothing in His creation?

Ev. God has decreed once and for all that order is to be achieved in the universe which He created, and He does not govern anything by a new decree of His will.

Aug. Does not God make anyone happy?

Ev. He does indeed.

Aug. When a man is made happy, God is certainly acting at that time.

Ev. That is true.

Aug. If, for example, you are going to be happy a year from now, God will make you happy a year from now.

Ev. Yes.

Aug. Then He has foreknowledge today of what He will do a year from now.

Ev. He always had foreknowledge of it. I agree once more that He foreknows this, if this is what is going to happen.

7. *Aug.* Please tell me whether you are His creature, and whether your happiness is something that will be realized within you.

Ev. Of course I am His creature and my future happiness will come about within me.

Aug. So your happiness will be realized in you, not freely, but from necessity, through God's action.

Ev. God's will is necessity for me.

Aug. So you will be happy against your will?

Ev. If the power to be happy were mine, I would certainly be happy already. I want to be happy even now, and I am not because it is not I but God who makes me happy.

Aug. The voice of truth is making itself heard very well in you. If our very act of willing is not in our power, then you could not be conscious of anything else that is. Hence nothing is so much in our power as the will itself,[1] for it is there at hand the very instant that we will something. Thus, we may truly say that we do not age freely, but of necessity, or that we do not fall ill freely, but of necessity, or that we do not die freely, but of necessity, and so on. But not even a madman would venture to assert that we do not will by our will.

Consequently, though God foreknows what we are going to will in the future, it does not thereby follow that we are not willing something freely. As for happiness, you stated that you could not become happy of yourself, as if I had denied it. I do maintain that when you come to be happy, you will become so, not against your will, but willingly. Since God has foreknowledge of your future happiness, and since nothing can happen differently than He has foreknown it, or there would be no foreknowledge, we do not have to suppose on this account that you will be happy without willing it. Such a supposition would be absurd and far from the truth. Just as God's foreknowledge of your happiness, which He knows for certain even today, does not take away your will for happiness at the time you begin to be happy, so too, a sinful will, should it ever be yours in the future, will not cease to be your will because God foreknew its future.

8. See, if you will, how anyone could make such a blind assertion as this: "If God has foreknowledge of my future will, then I am necessitated to will what He has foreknown, since nothing can happen differently than God has foreknown it. But if I am necessitated, we must admit that I no longer will freely, but of necessity." What sheer folly! Why could not something happen other than God foreknew, if what God foreknew as a future will is not a will? I pass over the equally astounding assertion, which I mentioned a moment ago, of the man who said he was necessitated to will the way he did. He is trying to destroy the will by presupposing

---

[1] A further passage alleged by Pelagius as supporting his doctrine of man's moral sufficiency.

necessity, for if he is necessitated to will, how can he will when there is no will?

If he says, instead, that the will itself is not within his power because he is necessitated to will, he will come up against the same answer you gave when I asked whether you would be happy in the future against your will. You replied that you would already be happy if it were within your power, for you said you had the will, but not yet the power, to become happy. At that point I interjected the remark that the voice of truth was making itself heard in you, for we cannot deny that we have the power unless we fail to make our own the very thing we are willing. But if the will itself is not at our disposal while we will, then, of course, we are not willing at all. But if it is impossible for us not to will while we are willing, then the will is present to us whenever we will. There is nothing in our power except that which is present while we are willing. Unless, then, it is within our power, our will is no will. Furthermore, it is because the will is in our power that it is free. What is not within our power, or cannot be, does not come under our freedom.

Accordingly, we do not deny God's foreknowledge of all things future, and yet we do will what we will. Since God has foreknowledge of our will, its future will be such as He foreknows it. It will be a will precisely because He foreknows it as a will, and it could not be a will if it were not in our power. Hence God also has foreknowledge of our power over it. The power, then, is not taken from me because of His foreknowledge, since this power will be mine all the more certainly because of the infallible foreknowledge of Him who foreknew that I would have it.[2]

---

[2] Consistent with the main purpose of defending man's freedom against the Manichaeans, Augustine insists that God's foreknowledge does not destroy but rather presupposes such freedom. Efforts to interpret his words in favor of the respective schools of Molina and Bañez have proved inconclusive. As S. Grabowski observes: "In this matter no support for either side can be gained from the writing of Saint Augustine" *(The All-Present God* [Saint Louis 1954] 154).

Ev. See, now I no longer deny that everything must happen as God foreknew that it would and that He foresees our sins in such a way that our will still remains free and subject to our power.

Chapter 4

9. *Aug.* What, then, is it that perplexes you? Unmindful, possibly, of our conclusion in the first discussion, are you going to deny that we are not forced to sin by anyone else, whether he is superior, or inferior, or equal to us, but that it is we who sin by our own will?

Ev. I dare not deny any of these points at all. But I still have to admit that I do not see how these two notions are not at variance, namely, God's foreknowledge of our sins and the freedom of the will in sinning. We must admit that God is just and has foreknowledge. But I would like to know what kind of justice it is that makes God punish sins which are committed of necessity, or how those things do not take place necessarily which He foreknew would happen, or how we can fail to ascribe to the Creator whatever occurs of necessity in His creatures.

10. *Aug.* What basis do you have for your opinion that our free will is at variance with God's foreknowledge? Is the reason foreknowledge, or God's foreknowledge?

Ev. Chiefly because it is God's foreknowledge.

Aug. Well, then, if *you* foreknew that someone was going to sin, would he have to sin?

Ev. Indeed he would. Unless I foreknew what is certain, I would not have foreknowledge.

Aug. Therefore, what God foreknows must come about, not because God foreknows it, but only because it is foreknown. If foreknowledge is not certain, there is no foreknowledge.

Ev. I agree. But what are you driving at?

Aug. If I am not mistaken, it is the fact that you would not necessarily be making a man sin because you foreknew he was going to sin. Your foreknowledge would not itself make him sin, though he is certainly going to sin; otherwise you would not foreknow that it would happen. Therefore, just as these two are not at variance, namely, your foreknowledge of what another will do and his freedom to do it, so, though God does not force anyone to sin, yet He foresees those who are going to sin by their own will.

11. Why, then, should a just God not punish sins which He has not forced anyone to commit because of His foreknowledge? Just as you do not compel past events to happen by your memory of them, so God does not compel events of the future to take place by His foreknowledge of them. Again, just as you recall certain things that you have done, though you do not do all the things you remember, so God foreknows all things whereof He is the Cause, though He is not Himself the Cause of all that He foreknows. He is not the cause of evil deeds, but only their avenger.

You must see from this what that justice is which makes God punish sins, since He does not perpetrate what He knows is going to happen. For if He ought not to punish sinners because He foreknows that they are going to sin, then neither ought He to reward the righteous, since He foresees equally well that they will do what is right. Let us rather acknowledge that God's foreknowledge requires that nothing future be hidden from His view, while His justice demands that sin, being a voluntary offense, should not go unpunished by His judgment, since it was not necessitated by His foreknowledge.

Chapter 5

12. Now your third question raised the problem of how we can fail to ascribe to the Creator whatever takes place of

necessity in His creation.[1] This problem should not readily cast uncertainty on that precept of religious conduct which obliges us to render thanks to the Creator. Even if He had assigned us a lower place in His creation, we should in all justice praise His bountiful goodness. Though weakened by sin, our soul is yet more noble and perfect than if it were to be changed into that light which we behold with our eyes. And you are certainly aware how greatly God is praised for the excelling quality of this light by souls, even when they have become enslaved to the bodily senses. Consequently, the fact itself that sinful souls incur blame should no longer perplex you and make you say to yourself that it would have been better had they never existed. They incur blame when we compare them with themselves and see what they would be if they had not willed to sin. Nevertheless, God their Maker deserves the highest praise that man can give Him, not only because He deals justly with them as sinners, but also because He has so fashioned their souls that, even when stained by sin, they are in no way surpassed in dignity by that physical light for which He is nonetheless justly praised.

13. Though you may not perhaps allege that it would have been better if these souls had never existed, I would also caution you against saying that they should have been created differently. Whatever right reason suggests to you as more perfect, you may be sure that God has already made it, for He is the Creator of all things good. Whenever you suppose that something better should have been made, because you are unwilling to have anything less perfect exist, this is not right reason but a want of understanding stemming from envy. It is as if you should wish that the earth had not been made, once you had gotten a view of the heavens. This attitude is

---

[1] The two previous questions raised by Evodius at the beginning of the former chapter inquired whether God can justly punish sins committed of necessity, and whether God's foreknowledge does not necessitate the course of future events.

entirely wrong. You might have reason to find fault if you saw that the earth had been created while the heavens had been passed over since you might allege that the earth should have been made according to your idea of what the heavens should be. But when you see that the heavens too have been made according to the idea you had in mind for the earth, though it is called the heavens rather than the earth, I do not think you should ever begrudge existence to a less perfect creature or to the earth since you have not been deprived of something more perfect.

Again, there is such variety with respect to the parts of the earth itself that no form of earthly beauty can occur to the mind which has not been made somewhere over the whole expanse of the earth by God, the Creator of all things. We can pass so gradually from the most fertile and fairest tracts of land to the most barren and unproductive through those in between, that you do not dare to find fault with any part except by comparing it with something better. In this way you mount all the levels of excellence until you reach the best kind of land, though you would not want this alone to exist. But what a difference there is between the earthly universe and the heavens! In between are found moisture and air, and from these four elements are formed all the many various natures and kinds of things whose number, though incalculable for us, is known to God. There may be something in nature which you do not conceive of in your mind, but it is impossible that something not exist which you truly conceive of in your mind. You cannot conceive of anything better in the creation which has escaped the knowledge of the Creator. It is really the nature of the soul to live in union with the Divine Ideas[2] and it depends upon them whenever it pronounces one thing to be better than another. If it sees

---

[2] Augustine's doctrine of illumination is intimately connected with his notion of the Divine Ideas. For an interesting presentation of this teaching in the light of its Platonic background, cf. *De diversis quaestionibus 83* q. 46.

the truth, and understands it, it does so in the light of those Ideas with which it is united. So the soul must believe that God has made what his right reason tells him should have been made, even though he fails to see it among the things created. Even though a man were unable to see the heavens with his eyes and yet could rightly conclude by his reason that such a thing should be made, he would have to believe it was made, though he could not see it with his eyes. Only in the light of those Ideas, after which all things have been made, could he see in his mind why something had to be made. One cannot form a true conception of anything not present in these Ideas anymore than he can find something there which is not true.

14. Most men go astray on this point when, having perceived more perfect realities with their mind, they try to find them with their eyes in the wrong places. It is as if a man with an intellectual grasp of perfect roundness should become indignant at not finding it in a nut, supposing that he had never seen anything round expect this fruit. So it is with men who see perfectly well that a creature is better if, while possessed of free will, it has nevertheless remained ever united to God and has never sinned. When they look at the sins of men, they are grieved, not simply because men do not give up sinning, but because they have been created at all. God, they tell us, should have created us so that we would always will to enjoy His changeless truth but never will to sin.

These men should put an end to their complaining and indignation. The fact that God has created men does not force them to sin just because He has given them the power to do so if they choose. Furthermore, there are angels who have never sinned and who never will sin. If you are elated by a creature that perseveres fully in its will not to sin, there can be no doubt that you are right to prefer it to one that sins. But just as you give this creature a preference in your thinking, so has God the Creator given it preference in the ordering of the universe. You must believe that a creature of this kind exists in the higher realms and has its abode on high in heaven. For if the Creator shows His goodness in making a creature who He foresees is going to sin, He cannot fail to show that same goodness in making one that He foreknew would not sin.

15. A creature so sublime as this finds its eternal happiness in the endless enjoyment of its Creator, which it merits by its unwavering will to hold fast to justice. The sinful creature, too, has its proper place in the order of things. Through sin it has lost its happiness, but not its power to recover happiness. It is certainly better than the creature that is held captive forever by its will to sin. It occupies a middle place between the latter and the other which is ever steadfast in its will for justice, because it can regain its high estate by humble repentance. For God has not withheld His bountiful goodness from making a creature which He foreknew would not only sin, but would persist in its will to sin. Just as a stray horse is better than a stone that does not go astray through a lack of self-movement and sense perception, so a creature which sins by its free will is more excellent than one that does not sin because it is without free will. And just as I might praise a wine as good in its own way and blame a man who became drunk from this wine, nevertheless, I would set a higher value on this man, whom I reproved and who is still drunk, than I would on the wine which I praised and which made him drunk. So too, the bodily creature should be duly praised according to its rank, while they are deserving of blame who, through the intemperant use of it, are turned away from the perception of truth. Here again, despite their perversity and a kind of intoxication, these men excel that bodily creature, however praiseworthy in its own way, which has brought them to ruin by intemperate desire; more excellent, not through the demerit of their sins, but because of the abiding dignity of their nature.

16. It follows then, that any soul is of greater excellence than any kind of body, and that the sinful soul is never changed into a body, however great has been its fall. The identity of the soul's nature is not lost completely so that it never loses its superiority over the body. In the world of bodies, light holds the first place. Hence the least soul must be ranked above the best body. It may happen that one body is better than another which has a soul, but it is never better than the soul itself.

Why then, should not God be praised, and why should His unspeakable praises not be proclaimed far and wide? For He has made souls destined to abide by the laws of justice, and also others that He foresaw would sin, or even persevere in their sins. Even souls like these are still more excellent than creatures that cannot sin because they do not enjoy the rational and free choice of the will. These, in turn, are still better than the most resplendent light shed by any kind of body, such as that which some men make the great mistake of worshiping in place of the nature of the most-high God Himself.[3]

In the arrangement of bodily creatures, all the way from the clusters of the stars down to the number of our hairs, the beauty of these good things is achieved so progressively that it would be utterly absurd to ask what this or that is doing there, for all things have been created in their proper order. How much more absurd it is to speak this way about any kind of soul at all which, no matter how far its beauty has diminished or deteriorated, will, without a doubt, always surpass in dignity any kind of bodily reality.

17. Reason and utility judge things in a different light. Reason judges them in the light of truth and is guided by sound judgment in subordinating lower things to those higher. Utility tends, generally, from a habit of convenience to value more highly things which reason shows to be of less

---
[3] An allusion to the Manichaean identification of the sun with God. Cf. *C. Secundinum Manichaeum* 1.20.

value. Though reason ranks the heavenly bodies far above those of earth, what worldly-minded man would not rather have many stars missing in the heavens than to have a single bush missing in his field, or a cow from his herd? Older people either disregard entirely, or at least patiently await for correction, judgments made by children who prefer the death of any man, except a few whose love brings them joy, to the death of a pet-sparrow; all the more so, when it is a man who frightens them, while the sparrow sings well and is attractive. Something the same is done by those whose intellectual growth has enabled them to advance in wisdom whenever they come upon men of poor judgment. Such praise God for His lesser creatures because they are better suited to their carnal senses while, in regard to His higher and nobler creatures, they either give Him little or no praise, or even censure Him or try to improve upon Him, or do not believe that He is their Maker. Those wiser men should accustom themselves either to disregard such judgments completely, if they cannot correct them, or to endure them patiently until they can correct them.

Chapter 6

18. In view of all this, that notion is far from true which would have us impute the sins of a creature to the Creator, even though those things have to take place which He foreknew would happen. You, for your part, assert that you do not see how we can avoid imputing to God whatever is bound to take place in His creature. I, on the contrary, see no way, and I would deny outright that there is, or can be, any way, to impute to God whatever must occur in His creature by reason of its sinful will.

If anyone says he would rather not exist than be unhappy, I will reply: "You are not telling the truth, for you are unhappy even now, yet you do not wish to die, for the simple reason that you wish to exist. Therefore, though you do not wish to be unhappy, you still wish to exist. Be thankful, then, for the fact that you will to exist so that you may be rescued from what you do not want to be. You willingly exist, and you are unwilling to exist unhappily. But if you are ungrateful for your will to exist, it is only right that you be compelled to be what you do not will to be. So I praise the goodness of the Creator because you have what you wish, even though you are ungrateful. I praise the justice of Him who orders all things, because you have to suffer unwillingly for your ingratitude."

19. If he should say, "I do not wish to die, not because I prefer an unhappy existence to no existence at all, but because I may be more unhappy after death," I will reply: "If this is unjust, you will not be more unhappy; but if just, let us praise Him whose laws have decreed that this shall be your state." If he says, "How am I to presume that I shall not be unhappy," I will reply: "If your future state is in your own power, either you will not be unhappy, or you will be justly unhappy because you have not ruled over your life justly. Or, again, if you have the will, but not the power, to rule over your life, then, not being in your own power, you are either in the power of no one or of someone else, unwillingly or willingly. If you are in no one's power, you either want it this way, or you do not. But you cannot be so unwillingly unless some other force has overpowered you; yet no force can overpower a man who is not in another's power; and if you are not in another's power through your own volition, we must conclude again that you are in your own power. Again, either you are justly unhappy for not having ruled over your life justly, or your future, whatever it is, will be of your own choosing, so that you will still have reason to thank the Creator for His goodness. But if you are not in your own power, then he who has you in his power is either stronger than you, or weaker. If he is weaker, you are

at fault and your unhappiness is just, because you can overcome someone weaker if you want to. If, being weaker, you are in the power of someone stronger, you simply have no right to think that so rightful an order of things is unjust." So I was perfectly right when I said, "If this is unjust, you will not be more unhappy after death; but if just, let us praise Him whose laws have decreed that this shall be your state."

Chapter 7

20. But suppose he says, "It is because I am already existing that I prefer to be unhappy rather than not to exist at all. But if I could have been consulted before I existed, I would have chosen not to exist rather than to be unhappy. The fact itself that I now fear not to exist though I am unhappy is part of that very unhappiness which makes me will what I ought not to will, for I ought rather to will not to exist than to be unhappy. But now I admit that I really do prefer unhappiness to nothingness. And the more unwise I am to make such a choice, the unhappier it is, and it is all the more unhappy, as I see more clearly that I should not have made this choice."

I will reply: "Be all the more cautious not to blunder at the very point where you fancy you are seeing the truth. Now if you were happy, you would surely prefer to exist rather than not to exist. Even now, unhappy as you are, you nevertheless prefer to be unhappy rather than not to exist at all, though you do not wish to be unhappy. Make every effort, then, to understand how great a good existence itself is, which is desired by the happy and unhappy alike. If you weigh this matter well, you will see that you are unhappy to the extent that you fail to draw near to the Being that exists supremely, and that your failure to perceive this

Supreme Existence is why you think it is better for someone not to exist than to be unhappy. You will further realize that you nevertheless wish to exist for the simple reason that you owe your existence to Him who exists supremely."

21. If, then, you would escape unhappiness, have a love for this will to exist which is within you. In fact, the more you will to exist, the closer you will come to Him who exists supremely. And now give thanks that you do exist. Though you are less perfect than those who are happy, you are yet superior to beings which lack even the will to be happy; yet many of these things are praised even by men who are unhappy. Nevertheless, all things are rightly deserving of praise by the very fact that they exist, since they are good inasmuch as they exist.

The greater your love to exist, the more strongly will you desire eternal life and you will long all the more to become so disposed as to have no attachment to things temporal; for our affections have been branded with the love of temporal things and bear the stamp of them. Before coming to be, temporal things do not exist; while existing, they are already passing away; once having passed away, they exist no longer. Hence, while belonging to the future, they do not yet exist, and once they have passed away, they no longer exist. How, then, shall we take lasting possession of them, since coming to exist is the same for them as to be going out of existence? But the man who loves existence, looks upon these things as good inasmuch as they exist, and loves that which exists forever. And if his love of the former left him inconstant, he will be made strong by his love of the latter. If he wasted himself on the love of transitory things, he will be made firm by the love of that which endures. He will stand firm and come into the possession of that same existence which he desired when he feared not to exist and was unable to stand firm, being ensnared by the love of things that pass away.

You should, therefore, experience no regret, but rather great elation, over the fact that you prefer even an unhappy existence to the termination of an unhappy existence, since you would not then be existing at all. If, to your initial will to exist, you expand your existence more and more, you will advance higher and become eminently fitted for that which exists supremely. You will thus preserve yourself from any kind of fall whereby the lowest thing in existence passes into non-existence, dragging along with it the impetuosity of its lovers. Hence he who would rather not exist for fear of being unhappy must be unhappy, because it is impossible for him not to exist. But the man who loves to exist more than he detests existing unhappily should exclude what he dislikes by enhancing that which he loves. When he begins to enjoy perfect existence in keeping with his nature, he will not be unhappy.

Chapter 8

22. See how absurd and inconsistent it is for anyone to say that he would rather not exist than be unhappy. A man who says he would rather have this than that is making a choice of something, whereas non-existence is not something, but nothing. It is logically impossible, therefore, for you to make a choice when the object of your choice does not exist. You assert that you really wish to exist, though you are unhappy, but say that you should not wish this. What should you will, then? I should will rather not to exist, you say. If this is what you should wish, it is better, but, since that cannot be better which does not exist, you should not, therefore, wish it at all. Furthermore, the natural insight that prompts you not to will non-existence is more trustworthy than the supposition which makes you think you should have willed it. Again, when a man has attained what he rightly chose as something to be desired, he necessarily becomes a better man. But he cannot become better if he is not going to exist. No one, therefore, can logically choose not to exist.

Nor should we be unsettled by the judgment of those men who have been driven by unhappiness to take their own lives. Either they have sought to find refuge where they imagined they would be better off, and this view, however they may have come to it, is not opposed to our line of reasoning; or if they thought they would no longer exist at all, we will be far less unsettled by the illogical choice of men who make "nothing" the object of their choice. If anyone chooses nonexistence, he is obviously choosing "nothing," even though he is unwilling to give this for an answer.

23. Allow me, however, to express my own view, if I can, about this whole question. In my opinion, no one who takes his life or in any way desires death, really feels certain that he will not exist after death, even though he holds it somewhat as an opinion. Opinion is found in a man who exercises his reason or belief in a matter that is either true or false, while feeling derives its force either from custom or nature. The possibility that opinion and feeling may be different is readily seen from the fact that we frequently think we should do one thing, while we find delight in doing something else. Sometimes, too, feeling is more trustworthy than opinion, when the latter arises from error and feeling springs from nature. A sick man, for instance, is often enticed by cold water which would be good for him to drink, though he believes it will hurt him if he drinks it. Sometimes opinion is more trustworthy than feeling, as when a man takes the word of medical science that cold water is bad for him, when in fact it is, and yet he is delighted to drink it. At other times, both are true, as when that which is beneficial is not only thought to be so, but also gives delight. At other times, both are wrong, as when something harmful is thought to be beneficial and gives us endless delight. Usually, however, a right opinion corrects the wrong custom, while a wrong opinion vitiates what is right by nature, for such is the power which reason exercises in its rule and supremacy.

Consequently, when anyone is driven by unbearable hardships to desire death wholeheartedly, in the belief that he will not exist after death, he decides upon death and grasps for it. Opinion leads him to entertain the false notion of a complete extinction, whereas feeling suggests a natural desire to be at rest. But the state of rest is not the same as nothing; on the contrary, a thing at rest exists more perfectly than that which is not at rest. In fact, restlessness makes us vacillate in our affections so that one of them destroys the other, while rest possesses a constancy which is uppermost in our mind when we say of anything that it exists. Accordingly, every desire on the part of a man's will for death is directed, not towards extinction after death, but towards rest. Though he has the mistaken belief that he will not exist, he still has a natural desire to be at rest, that is, to enjoy a more perfect existence. Hence, just as no one can possibly find delight in not existing, so it should never happen that anyone should be ungrateful towards the goodness of his Creator for his existence.

Chapter 9

24. Suppose someone should say that it was not difficult or laborious for an omnipotent God to see to it that everything He made should so maintain its proper place that no creature would come to the extremity of unhappiness; for, being omnipotent, He could have done so, and, being good, He could not be envious. I will say, in reply, that the orderly arrangement of creatures extends all the way from the highest to the lowest according to certain just gradations in such a way that only envy could prompt a man to say that a creature should not exist, or that it should be different. For if he wants it to be the same as something higher, then such a creature is already existing and possesses such excellence that nothing more should be added, since it is perfect in its kind. If he maintains that the lower creature should also have this excellence, he either wants to add to the higher, which is already perfect, and then he is wanting in moderation and justice; or he wants to destroy the lower creature, and then he becomes malicious and envious.

But if he asserts that it should not exist, he is still malicious and envious, because, while opposed to its existence, he is still compelled to praise it, even though it is of a lower rank. It is as if he were to say that the moon should not exist. For he must admit, or else be guilty of an absurd and obstinate denial, that even the light of a lamp, though much less luminous, has a beauty of its own, is a suitable ornament in the darkness, is well suited for use at night, and, in all these respects, is deserving of praise in its own small way. How, then, can he rightly presume to say that the moon should not exist when he realizes he would be open to ridicule if he were to say that the lamp should not exist?

Now if he does not deny that the moon should exist, but says that it should be like the sun, he fails to realize that he is merely saying that there should be two suns but no moon. Here he is doubly mistaken: he wants to add to the perfection of the universe by desiring another sun and to detract from its perfection by taking away the moon.

25. Here he may point out that he has no fault to find with the moon, since it is not made unhappy by reason of its inferior brightness, but that he is saddened over the plight of souls, not because of their darkened condition, but on account of their unhappiness. Let him note carefully that the moon's brightness has no more to do with unhappiness than does the brightness of the sun with happiness, for although they are heavenly bodies, they are bodies nevertheless with respect to the kind of light that can be seen by our bodily eyes. Bodies, as bodies, are capable neither of happiness nor of unhappiness, though they may be the bodies of men who are happy or unhappy.

But the analogy drawn from such luminous bodies can be instructive. As you examine the difference among these bodies and see that some are brighter, it is wrong for you to ask that darker bodies be removed or be made equal to those that are brighter. But if you make everything bear upon the perfection of the universe, the various grades of luminous bodies will enable you to see all the more clearly the fact that they all exist. You will further perceive that the perfection of the universe requires that the presence of things more perfect shall not entail the absence of those less perfect.

Consider in the same light the differences that also exist among souls. Here, too, you will discover how the unhappiness, which you deplore, contributes to the perfection of the universe, since some souls merit unhappiness because of their sinful will. And it is far from true to assert that God should not have made such souls, when we owe him praise for having also made other creatures far inferior to the condition of unhappy souls.

26. But my opponent, apparently, has another objection occasioned by his failure to grasp what has been said. Suppose, he says, that even our unhappiness fills out the perfection of the universe; then, in the event that we would always be happy, something would be wanting to the perfection of the universe. Thus, if the soul comes to an unhappy state only through sin, then our sins are necessary for the perfection of the universe, which God has made. How, then, is it just for God to punish sin when, unless there was sin, His creation could not be whole and entire?

Here is my answer. Neither sin nor unhappiness is necessary for the perfection of the universe, but souls, taken simply as souls, are necessary. They can sin if they will, and if they do, they become unhappy. If their unhappiness were to continue once their sins were taken away, or if it were present before they sinned, one might rightly contend that the order and government of the universe are defective. Again, if sins are committed and there is no unhappiness, the order of things is no less vitiated by injustice. When happiness is found in those who do not sin, the universe is in perfect order. Likewise, when unhappiness befalls those who sin, the universe remains no less perfect. The universe is always complete and perfect by every kind of nature for the reason that souls are not absent from it, whether it be those whose unhappiness results from sin, or those whose happiness comes from doing what is right. For sin and the punishment of sin are not any sort of nature, but are states found in nature, the former, voluntary, the latter, penal. The voluntary state is a shameful one when sin is committed. Consequently, a penal state is applied to the sinful state to assign the nature a place which is fitting for its condition, and to compel it to be in harmony with the beauty of the universe. In this way the penalty for sin makes amends for the shamefulness of the sin.

27. By sinning, therefore, the higher creature is punished by the lower creatures, because the latter are of such lowly condition that they can be embellished even by debased souls and so be brought into harmony with the beauty of the universe. What is so great in a house as a man, and what so mean and low as the sewer of the house? Yet, when a slave is apprehended in some misdeed for which he deserves to be made to clean the sewer, he enhances it by his own disgrace. Both of these things, the slave's disgrace and the cleaning of the sewer, now combined and reduced to a distinctive kind of unity, are blended and woven into the ordering of the household so that the beauty of their unity conforms to the harmony of the entire household. Yet, if the slave had not willed to do wrong, some other provision for cleaning the household necessities would have been available for the running of the house.

What is so low in all nature as an earthly body? Yet even the sinful soul so embellishes this corruptible flesh as to impart to it a beauty all its own and a life-giving movement. Through sin, such a soul is unsuited for a heavenly abode but is suited for an earthly habitation as a means of punishment. Hence, no matter what choice the soul makes, the universe, whose Creator and Ruler is God, remains ever beautiful through the harmonious arrangement of its parts. When the most excellent of souls dwell in the lowest of creatures, they do not enhance them by their unhappiness, which they have not, but by making the right use of them. But if sinful souls were permitted to dwell in the higher regions, this would be wrong, because they are not suited for things that they cannot use properly and to which they add nothing by way of embellishment.

28. Consequently, though this earthly orb is reckoned among things corruptible, it still keeps intact, as far as it can, the image of the higher realities of which it is continuously pointing out to us certain examples and signs. If we see some great and good man sacrificing his body to be burned from a sense of duty, we do not call this a punishment for sin, but a proof of courage and patience. And though this horrible corruption is destroying his bodily members, we love him more than if he were not undergoing such suffering, and we actually marvel that the soul's nature is not altered by the changes in the body. But when we see the body of a ruthless robber destroyed in a similar way as a punishment, we approve this orderly process of the law. Both men, then, enhance such torments, but the first does so on the merit of his virtue, the other, by the demerit of his sin. If, after his exposure to the flames, or even beforehand, we should see the good man transformed into a state suited for a heavenly abode and transported to the stars, we would certainly rejoice. But if, whether before or after his punishment, we should see the wicked thief raised to an everlasting place of honor, despite

the persistence of his evil will, who of us would not take umbrage at this? Hence, both can enhance the dignity of the lower creation, but only one can do so for the higher.

This reminds us to take note that the first man enhanced the mortal character of our flesh as a suitable punishment for sin, and that our Lord also enhanced it so that in His mercy He might free us from sin. The just man could have a mortal body and, if he persevered in justice, could attain the immortality of the saints, which is impossible for the wicked man so long as he remains wicked. I refer to the immortality proper to heaven and to the angels; not to those angels about whom the Apostle says: "Know you not that we will judge the angels,"[1] but to those of whom the Lord says: "For they will be equal to the angels of God."[2] Men, whose vainglory prompts them to desire equality with the angels, do not will to be equal to the angels but to have the angels equal to them.[3] If they persist in this will, their punishment will be equal to that of the angels who love their own power more than that of Almighty God. Since these have not sought God through the lowly entrance of humility, which the Lord Jesus Christ has shown us in His own life, and have been unforgiving and proud during life, they will be placed on His left side where He will say to them: "Depart into everlasting fire which was prepared for the devil and his angels."[4]

Chapter 10

29. Sins spring from two sources, our own thoughts and the persuasion of others, and I believe that the Prophet was referring to these when he said: "From my hidden sins

---

[1] 1 Cor. 6.3.
[2] Luke 20.36.
[3] Here I have adopted the Maurist reading . . . *non ideo volunt esse angelis, sed angelos sibi,* rather than that of Professor Green, which omits *angelos.*
[4] Matt. 25.41.

cleanse me, O Lord, and from the sins of others spare thy servant."[1] Both sources, of course, are voluntary. Just as a person who sins by thought does not do so against his will, so when he consents to another's evil persuasion, he does so only by his will. Yet, to sin not only through one's own thoughts without being persuaded to do so by another, but also to persuade someone else by envy or deceit to sin, is a more grievous offense than being induced to sin by the persuasion of another. Accordingly, the Lord's justice is vindicated by His punishing both kinds of sin.

This issue, too, was weighed on the scales of justice, namely, that the devil should not be denied his power over men whom his evil persuasion had made subject to him. It would have been unfair for the devil not to rule over one whom he had made his captive. It is unthinkable that the perfect justice of the supreme and true God, which encompasses all things, should fail to impose order even upon the ruin suffered by sinners.

But since man had sinned less grievously than the devil, he was enabled to recover salvation by the very fact that he was given in bondage, even in his mortal flesh, to the prince of this world, namely, the lowest and mortal region of the universe, in bondage, that is, to the prince of all sinners and the ruler of death. Conscious now of his mortal condition, living in dread of injury and destruction from the meanest and most contemptible beasts, even the smallest of them, insecure for his future, man grew accustomed to check sinful delights, and, most of all, to curb pride, which led to his fall and which is the one vice that rejects the healing remedy of mercy. What indeed stands so much in need of mercy as an unhappy man, and what is so undeserving of mercy as the unhappy man who is proud?

30. So it has come to pass that the Word of God, through whom all things have been made and who is the source of

---

[1] Ps. 18.13-14

happiness in the Angels, has reached out in His mercy even to our misery, and has become flesh and has dwelt among us. And though not yet equal to the Angels, man could thus eat the Bread of Angels if the Bread of Angels should Himself deign to become equal with men. Nor has His coming down to us made Him abandon the Angels, but He is wholly present at the same time to them and to us. He nourishes the Angels within by His divinity, and teaches us by outward signs through the human nature that is ours. By faith He prepares those whom He will nourish by the vision of His countenance, as He does for the Angels.

Rational creatures find their most perfect nourishment, so to speak, in this Word. And, though the human soul is rational, it was held captive by the bonds of death as a penalty for sin, debased to the point that it must toil to grasp things invisible by inferences drawn from things that are visible. This Food of rational creatures has been made visible to our eyes, not by any change in His nature, but by putting on our nature, that He may recall us from the pursuit of visible things to His divine nature which is invisible to our eyes. In this way the soul discovers the outward lowliness of Him whom it had inwardly abandoned in its pride, and by imitating the visible example of His humility, the soul will return to the heights of things invisible.

31. Having put on man's nature, God's Word and only Son has also brought under man's power the devil, whom He has ever held, and will ever hold, under the power of His law. He has wrested nothing from the devil by tyrannical force but has subdued him by the law of justice. After the woman had been deceived and man had fallen because of the woman, the devil laid claim to the entire offspring of the first man, as to sinners subject to the law of death. He did so from a malicious desire to harm them, though in accordance with strict justice. The devil's power prevailed until he put to death the Just One, in whom he could show nothing deserving of death, not only because, though guiltless, He was slain, but also because He was born free from the influence of lust. The devil had subjected his captives to lust that he might make his own whatever was born of it, as fruit from his own tree, motivated of course by covetousness, but not without a just title of ownership.

It is, then, a matter of strict justice that the devil should be forced to set free all those who believe in Him whom he put to death so unjustly. Thus, by suffering death for a time, these discharge their debt, and, by living for all eternity, they live in Him who paid a debt for them, which He Himself did not owe. But the devil could in justice keep as his companions in eternal damnation those whom he had persuaded to remain obstinate in their unbelief. Thus man, whom the devil had subdued, not forcibly but by persuasion, was not wrested forcibly from the devil. Besides, having justly suffered the further humiliation of having to serve the devil to whom he had consented in doing evil, man was justly set free by Him to whom he consented in doing good, because, in consenting to evil, man had sinned less grievously than the devil had done by his evil suggestion.

Chapter 11

32. God therefore made all creatures, not only those that would persevere in virtue and justice, but also those that would sin. He did not make them to sin, but to be an adornment of the universe, whether they willed to sin or not. If there were no souls to occupy the highest place in the order of the created universe, such that should they will to sin, the universe would be undermined and ruined, something of great importance would be lacking in the creation; for there would be lacking that very thing whose absence would disturb the stability and orderly arrangement of the universe.

Such are the excellent, holy, and sublime creatures comprising the Powers of heaven and beyond, over whom God alone rules, and to whom the whole world has been made subject. Without the exact and perfect discharge of their duties by such creatures, it would be impossible for the world to exist. Again, if there were no souls that would choose either to sin or not to sin, the order in the universe would not be impaired, though something of great importance would thus be lacking. Rational souls do in fact exist, unequal, of course, in function to higher souls, but equal to them in nature. And there are many classes of things made by the Most High God, which, though still lower than these, are yet worthy of praise.

33. The nature of those exercising a higher function is such that the order of the universe would suffer not only if this nature were non-existent but also if it were to sin. The nature of souls having lower functions is such that the universe would be less perfect only if they did not exist, but not if they were to sin. Upon the former nature there has been conferred the power to maintain all things in order as its own special function and one which cannot possibly be lacking in the created order. It is not because it has received this function that it perseveres in its good will; rather, it has received this function because God, who assigned it, foresaw that it would so persevere. It does not, however, maintain all things in order by its own authority, but by fidelity to His authority and the devout discharge of His commandments "from whom and through whom and in whom all things have been made."[1]

To the former there has also been granted the exalted power to maintain all things in order, provided, of course, it was sinless, though it does not possess this power exclusively but only in conjunction with the latter, since it was foreknown that it would sin. Spiritual natures can be joined together and separated without any increase or decrease in bulk. Con-

---

1 Cf. Rom. 11.36

sequently, the task of the higher would not be made easier by their union with the lower nor rendered more difficult if the lower should desert its function because of sin. Though spiritual creatures may possess their individual bodies, they cannot be joined or separated by reason of place or physical bulk but only by a sameness or difference in their inclinations.

34. When the soul has been assigned its rightful place, subsequent to its sinning, among the lower and mortal bodies, it does not rule over its own body with complete freedom but only according as the laws of the universe permit. Nevertheless, such a soul is not thereby made inferior to a heavenly body to which even earthly bodies have been made subordinate. Certainly, the tattered clothing of a condemned slave is inferior to that worn by a well-deserving slave who is highly esteemed by his master. But the slave himself, because he is a man, is better than any kind of costly attire. The higher spiritual nature, then, residing in a heavenly body, adheres to God, and, through its angelic power, is able to lend adornment even to earthly bodies and to rule them according to the command of Him whose will it beholds in some ineffable manner. The lesser spiritual nature, weighed down by a mortal body, can scarcely exercise inner control over the very body which oppresses it, and yet it lends it as much adornment as possible. Upon other bodies that surround it from without, it exercises an outward but weaker influence so far as is possible.

Chapter 12

35. We may thus infer that, even had the spiritual nature never willed to sin, nothing in the way of suitable adornment would have been lacking to the lowest level of corporeal creation. For what is capable of ruling the whole, can also rule over a part, though that which can do something less, cannot necessarily accomplish something greater. The fully competent physician can also heal a bodily sore effectively, but it does not necessarily follow that a man who is useful in treating a sore can cure every kind of human disorder. Indeed, if we consider the true force of our reasoning which makes it perfectly clear that there had to exist a creature that never sinned and never will sin, that same reasoning will show us that such a creature refrains from sin by its free will and is free from sin, not by compulsion, but of its own accord. However, if it were to sin—though it has not done so, just as God foreknew—nevertheless, if it were to sin, the indescribable force of God's power would suffice to rule this universe, so that by assigning all things their due and proper place, He permits nothing shameful or unbecoming to exist throughout His entire domain. Even without the agency of any powers created for this very purpose, and even if all the angelic natures had sinfully defected from His commands, God would rule over all things by His own power in the best and most suitable way possible. Nor would He on this account be harboring any ill-will towards the existence of spiritual creatures, since His bountiful goodness has also created bodily creatures which are far inferior to spiritual creatures, even when these latter sin. Hence, anyone who gazes thoughtfully upon the heavens and the earth and things visible, all arranged in classes according to their proper form and mode of being, will believe that God alone is their Maker and acknowledge that He deserves praise beyond the power of words to express. On the other hand, if there is no better plan for ordering the universe than that the power of angels should govern all things in virtue of their natural excellence and the good dispositions of their will, then, even if all the angels were to sin, they would not have left the Creator of angels without the resources to rule over His own domains. God's goodness would not fail through any kind of weariness nor would His Omnipotence be found wanting in the face of difficulty to create other angels and assign them to the positions which the others had deserted through sin. And if spiritual natures were to suffer just condemnation, they could not, however numerous they might be, obstruct the order of things which makes just and appropriate provision for those who deserve condemnation. Wherever, therefore, we direct our attention, we find that God deserves praise far beyond the power of language to express, for He is the perfect Creator and most just Ruler of all natures.

36. Finally, let us leave the contemplation of this beauty of the universe to those who can do so through God's gift, and let us not try to lead men by means of words to the contemplation of things ineffable. And yet, on account of certain loquacious men, who are either fickle or deceitful,[1] let us examine this important question as briefly as possible.

Chapter 13

Every nature capable of becoming less good is a good nature, and every nature becomes less good when it is corrupted. Now, either corruption does no harm to a nature and it is not corrupted, or, if the nature is corrupted, it suffers harm from such corruption. If it suffers harm, corruption destroys something of its goodness and makes it less good. If corruption deprives it entirely of all its good, then what remains will no longer be capable of corruption because there will be no good to be lost by further corruption; for that is not corrupted which can suffer no harm from corruption. Again, a nature which does not undergo corruption is incorruptible. Consequently, there will be a nature which corruption has made incorruptible, which is altogether absurd.

Therefore, it is perfectly true to assert that every nature, insofar as it is a nature, is good. For, if it is incorruptible, it is better than a corruptible nature, while, if it is corrupti-

---
[1] A reference to the Manichaeans.

ble, it is undoubtedly good, since it becomes less good when undergoing corruption. Now every nature is either corruptible or incorruptible, and therefore every nature is good. I use the term "nature" to indicate what is also commonly called "substance." Hence every substance is either God or from God, since every good is either God or from God.

37. Now that we have firmly settled upon these principles as a kind of point of departure for our reasoning, give your attention to what I am going to say. Every rational creature endowed with free choice of the will is undoubtedly worthy of praise, provided it perseveres in its enjoyment of the highest and changeless good; and every nature which endeavors so to persevere is also worthy of praise. On the other hand, every nature that fails to persevere in this good and is unwilling to exert itself to this end is blameworthy to the extent that it fails to abide in the good and makes no effort to do so.

If, therefore, a created rational nature receives praise, then no one can doubt that He who created it is worthy of praise; and if it is blameworthy, no one can doubt that its Maker receives praise even when it is an object of reproach. For when we blame it for not having the will to enjoy the highest and changeless good, namely, the Creator, we are surely rendering praise to God. How great a good, then, is God, the Creator of all things! How deserving He is of praise and honor beyond the power of our words or thoughts to express! For we can neither be praised nor blamed without giving Him praise. We cannot be blamed for not abiding in Him unless this is our greatest, highest, and principal good. And why is this so, if not because God's goodness is ineffable? What justification can we find in our sins for blaming God when it is impossible to blame our sins without giving praise to God?

38. Then again, when we blame these things themselves, is it not their vice alone that is blamed? Moreover, you cannot blame the vice in a thing without praising its nature. Either what you blame is natural to the thing and not a vice at all, and then it is you that should be corrected, rather than what you are wrongly blaming, so you will know how to blame the right things; or, if it is a vice that may be rightly blamed, it must also be against nature. All vice, precisely because it is vice, is against nature. If it does not harm a nature, it is not vice; if it is a vice because it harms nature, it is a vice because it is against nature. But if a nature is corrupted by another's vice, and not by its own, it is unjust to blame it, and we must ask whether that nature whose vice could corrupt another nature does not itself suffer corruption by its own vice. What does it mean for a thing to be vitiated, except that it is corrupted by vice?

Furthermore, a nature that is not vitiated is free from vice, whereas that which corrupts another nature by its vice is certainly possessed of vice. Hence, a nature that can corrupt another with its vice is itself first vitiated and already corrupted. We may thus conclude that all vice is against nature, even against the very nature of the thing that has it. Accordingly, since it is only the vice in a thing that is blamed, and, since something is a vice because it is against the nature that has it, we cannot properly blame the vice in a thing without praising its nature. You are rightly displeased with the vice only because it vitiates something in the nature that pleases you.

Chapter 14

39. We must see whether it is also true to say that a nature is corrupted by the vice of another when it has no vice of its own. If a nature possessed of vice approaches another nature in order to corrupt it and finds nothing in it capable of corruption, it does not corrupt it. But if it does find something corruptible, it joins forces with the vice of the other to bring about its corruption. If a stronger nature is unwilling, it cannot be corrupted by a weaker, but if it is willing to be corrupted, its corruption starts with its own vice rather than with the other's. In the same way, a nature cannot be corrupted by one its equal if it is unwilling. Any nature in a vicious condition that accosts one free from vice in order to corrupt it, comes to it, by that very fact, not as its equal, but as one already weaker by reason of its vice.

But if a stronger nature corrupts one that is weaker, this comes about either because there is vice in both, if it comes from the evil desires of both, or it results from the vice of the stronger when its nature is of such excellence that, even though vitiated, it ranks above the lower nature that it corrupts. How could anyone rightly blame the fruits of the earth simply because men do not put them to good use when such men are already corrupted by their own vice and, in turn, corrupt these fruits by misusing them for sinful pleasure? Yet, only a fool could doubt that, even in its vitiated state, human nature is more excellent and stronger than any kind of fruit, even when it is unspoiled.

40. It is possible for a stronger nature to corrupt a weaker one and to do so without any vice on either part, if by vice we mean that which is blameworthy. Who, for instance, would dare to blame a frugal man who looked for nothing more in these fruits than natural replenishment, or who would blame the fruits themselves because they are corrupted by his use of them for food? In ordinary usage this is not called corruption since, most of the time, the term usually denotes a vice.

We can easily observe this fact too, that when a stronger nature corrupts one weaker, it does not do this to satisfy its own needs, as, for example, when it punishes a fault according to the demands of justice. It is with such a rule in mind that the Apostle says: "If any man corrupt the temple of God, God will corrupt him."[1] Or, again, such corruption is seen in the arrangement of changeable things which give way to one another according to laws eminently designed for the government of the universe according to the natural capacity of each part. If the sun's brightness should injure someone whose eyes are too weak by nature to withstand its light, we should not imagine that the sun causes this alteration in the eyes to supply a deficiency in its own light or through any vice on its part. In any case, the eyes themselves should not be blamed because they obeyed their owner's command to look into the light or because they were injured by yielding to the light itself.

Consequently, of all the forms of corruption, only that can be rightly blamed which involves vice. The others should either not even be called corruption, or, in any case, they cannot possibly be blameworthy since they do not involve vice. Indeed, the word "blame" *(vituperatio)* is thought to be derived from *vitium* and *paratum,* meaning something prepared exclusively for vice, namely, that which is properly due to vice.

41. Now, as I started to say, a vice is evil simply because it is against the nature itself that has it. Hence it is clear that the very thing whose vice is being blamed is itself deserving of praise because of its nature, and that we must therefore acknowledge that, in blaming their vices, we are bestowing praise upon the natures, upon those natures, that is, whose vices are being blamed. Since vice is opposed to a thing's nature, its malice increases as the integrity of the nature decreases. Whenever, therefore, you blame the vice, you really praise the thing that you would want to see possessed of its integrity. And where is this integrity found, except in the nature? A nature that is perfect not only deserves no blame, but also merits praise according to the excellence of its nature. You call what is wanting to the natural perfection

---

[1] 1 Cor. 3.17.

of a thing a vice, thereby showing plainly enough that you are pleased with the nature and would like to see it perfect, which is why you blame its imperfection.

Chapter 15

42. If, then, the beauty and dignity of natures infected with vice are enhanced even when we blame their vices, how much more should God, the Creator of all natures, be praised for such natures, even in their vitiated condition! Though they owe their natures to Him, they become vitiated to the extent that they depart from the design by which God has made them. Moreover, they are blameworthy to the extent that, in recognizing the design wherein they were fashioned, we blame them because we do not find this in them. And if this very design, by which all things have been made, namely, the supreme and changeless Wisdom of God, is something which truly and supremely exists, as indeed it does, then you must see in what direction a thing is tending which departs from this design. But unless it were voluntary, this defect would not be blameworthy. Consider, if you will, whether it would be right for you to blame something which exists the way it should exist. I do not think so; rather you would blame that which is not what it should be. No one is indebted for something he has not received. And to whom is one indebted, except to him from whom he has received that which makes him a debtor? Even payments made in the form of a bequest are made for him who made the bequest. And payment made in favor of the rightful heirs of creditors is really paid to the creditors who have been succeeded by their rightful heirs. Otherwise, this should not be called a payment, but a transfer or donation, or whatever else such transactions are called.

Hence, it would be utterly absurd of us to assert that temporal things should not perish. Their status in the order of nature is such that, unless they pass out of existence, things future could not succeed those that are past, and the beauty of the ages could not reach its full and natural perfection. They act according to the efficacy they have received and, to this extent, make return to Him to whom they are indebted for whatever existence they have. Anyone who laments the passing of these things should reflect on his own words, at least on those which voice his complaint, to see if his complaint is just and based upon prudence. If he is enamored by some of his words because of their sound and is unwilling to have them pass away and give place to the rest so that his whole discourse can be framed by the succession of his words, we will judge that he is afflicted with a strange kind of insanity.

43. No one therefore can rightly blame those things for their failure to continue; they pass away because they received no further existence, so that all things may run their course according to their appointed times. And no one can say that something should have remained in existence when it could not exceed the limits assigned to it.

Whether they sin or not, it is in rational creatures that the beauty of the universe achieves its final and most fitting perfection. Now they either do not sin [when they complain about the transitory nature of things], which would be a perfectly absurd thing to say, since one at least commits sin by condemning what is no sin; or they deserve no blame for their sin, which is just as absurd, for then we shall actually begin to praise evil deeds and the whole direction of man's thinking will be thrown into confusion and cause an upheaval in life; or an action will be blamed which was done as it should have been done, and this will give rise to abominable folly, or, to put it more mildly, to a most unfortunate kind of error; or, if we are constrained, as we are, by the truth of our reasoning to blame sins, and to blame rightly whatever does not exist as it should, then ask what the sinful nature owes and you will find that it owes the debt of good deeds; ask to whom it owes this debt and you will find that it is God. It is from Him that the soul has received the power to act rightly when it so wills, and also from Him that it is made unhappy if it fails to act rightly, and made happy if it does act rightly.

44. Since no one prevails over the laws of the Almighty Creator, the soul may not fail to pay what it owes. It does so either by making good use of what it has received, or by forfeiting what it was unwilling to use rightly. Accordingly, if it does not pay with just acts, it will pay by suffering unhappiness, because the term "debt" holds for both cases. We might also express this by saying that if the soul does not pay by doing what it ought, it will pay by suffering what it ought. There is, however, no temporal interval between these two. It is not as though the soul fails in its duty at one time and suffers its due punishment at another. The beauty of the universe may not be disfigured even for an instant by having the ugliness of sin without the beauty of a just punishment. Whatever is punished now in utmost secrecy is reserved to the future judgment for its manifestation and painful experience of unhappiness. Just as one who is not awake is sleeping, so too, the man who fails to act as he ought experiences at once the suffering he deserves, because the happiness that comes from justice is so great that one cannot depart from it except to embark upon unhappiness. In all cases of defection, things suffering defection have either not received further existence, and there is no fault—just as even while they were existing, there was no fault since they did not receive further existence —or else they are unwilling to be what they were given the power to be, if they had so willed. And since what they received is something good, they are guilty if they fail to will it.

Chapter 16

45. God, however, is a debtor to no one since He confers everything gratuitously. And if anyone should say that something is due him from God because of his merits, his existence, at least, is something not owed him, for nothing was owed him when he did not exist. Besides, what merit is there in turning to Him from whom you have your existence, that you may enjoy a more perfect existence from Him who has given you your existence? What, then, have you given God in advance that you can demand as a debt? When you refuse to turn to Him, He is not the loser, but you yourself. Without Him you would be nothing, and He is so much the cause of your existence that, unless you make due acknowledgment to Him for your existence by turning to Him, you will not, it is true, be non-existent, but you will be unhappy all the same.

All things, therefore, owe to Him, first of all, such existence as they have by their natures; next whatever further perfection they can achieve, if they so will, according to the will they have received, and according to what it is their duty to become, and for all that they ought to be. No one is at fault for what he has not received, but he is justly at fault for not doing as he ought. Now he has an obligation to do so if he has received free will and all the power that is needed.

46. When anyone does not act as he ought, this, far from being a fault on the part of the Creator, even redounds to His praise, because such a one suffers due punishment. The very fact that one is blamed for not doing what he ought to do, is simply to give praise to God to whom he owes a debt. If you receive praise for seeing what you are obliged to do, though you can only see this in Him who is the changeless Truth, how much more should He be praised who has both laid a command upon your will and has given you the power to fulfill it, and has not allowed your refusal to go unpunished?

If everyone must render what he has received, and if man has been so made that he sins of necessity, then it is his duty to sin. Therefore, whenever he sins, he is doing what he ought to do. If it is wicked to make such an assertion, then no one is forced by his nature to sin.[1] Neither is he forced to sin by another's nature, for no one sins so long as what happens to him is against his will. If he suffers justly, his sin is not in suffering against his will, but in his having sinned by such willful action that he now suffers a just punishment against his will. If he suffers unjustly, how does he sin? For there is no sin in suffering something unjustly, but rather in perpetrating some unjust action. But if no one is forced to sin, either by his own nature or by someone else's, it follows that he sins by his own will.

If you wish to impute the sin to the Creator, you will exonerate the sinner who has done nothing that falls outside the designs of the Creator. But if it is just to defend the sinner, he has not sinned, and there is nothing to impute to the Creator. Let us, therefore, praise the Creator, whether the sinner can be defended or not. If he is justly defended, he is not a sinner; praise God, then. But if he cannot be defended, he is a sinner insofar as he turns away from the Creator. So give praise to the Creator. Accordingly, I do not see how we can impute our sins to God, our Creator, and I declare that there is no way possible, and that none in fact exists. I do find that He is deserving of praise even in these very sins, not merely because He punishes them, but also because they are committed at the very moment that one departs from His truth.

Ev. I am perfectly willing to accept these points and I give them my approval. And I agree it is perfectly true that it is altogether impossible to impute our sins rightly to our Creator.

Chapter 17

47. But I would still like to know, if this is possible, why

---
[1] Also appropriated by Pelagius against Augustine's teaching on grace.

one nature does not sin, which God foreknew would not sin, and why another does sin, which He foresaw was going to sin. I am no longer of the opinion that, because of God's foreknowledge, the one is forced to sin while the other is not forced to sin. But unless there were some cause for it, rational creatures would not be divided into some that never sin, others that continuously sin, and others, in between, as it were, that sometimes sin and at other times turn to doing what is right. What is the cause for the separation into these three groups? Now I do not want you to reply that it is the will, for I am looking for the cause of the will itself. Since they all have the same nature, there must be some cause why one never wills to sin, why another always wills to sin, and why another wills to sin at one time but not at another. This much alone seems clear to me, namely, that there has to be a cause for this threefold division of the human will, but what it is, I do not know.

48. *Aug.* Since the will is the cause of sin, and you are looking for the cause of the will itself, supposing I were to find this, will you not be looking for the cause of this cause which I have found? What limit will there be to our inquiry, and where will our investigation and discussion end, since there is no need to carry your inquiry beyond the root of the matter? Beware of supposing that anything could possibly be truer than the saying that "avarice is the root of all evil,"[1] namely, the desire for more than is sufficient. Sufficiency is measured by what each nature requires for its preservation according to its class. The word avarice, in Greek, *philarguria,* is not to be understood merely in terms of silver and coins, from which the Greek term is more properly derived, since, among the ancients, coins were made from silver or, as was more commonly the case, from a silver alloy, but must be understood in regard to everything that is desired immoderately whenever anyone simply wants more than is sufficient. Such

---

1 1 Tim. 6.10.

avarice is cupidity, and cupidity is a perverse will. A perverse will, therefore, is the cause of all evil. If this were natural, it would certainly preserve the nature and not be destructive of it, and consequently it would not be a perverse will. Hence the conclusion that the root of all evil is not in accord with nature, which is a sufficient rejoinder against those who want to reproach nature. But if you are looking for the cause of this root, how will it be the root of all evil? For there will be a cause of this cause and, as I said, when you find it, you will look for what caused it and there will be no end to our inquiry.

49. But what could possibly come before the will to be its cause? Either the will is itself the cause, and there will be no regress from this root of the will, or it is not the will, and the will is without sin. Consequently, either the will itself is ultimately the cause of sin, or the ultimate cause of sin is without sin. Sin can be justly imputed to no one but a sinner, and can therefore only be justly imputed to one who wills it.[2] But I fail to see why you wish to look for something else. Finally, whatever is the cause of the will is certainly either just or unjust. If just, whoever obeys it will not be sinning; if unjust, it must not be obeyed and one will not commit sin.

Chapter 18

50. Or is there perhaps some violent cause that compels one against his will? Now, must we go on repeating the same things over and over again? Recall the previous points which we mentioned at length concerning sin and free will. If it is difficult to commit them all to memory, keep this brief point in mind. Whatever the cause of the will, if a man is unable to resist, there is no sin in his yielding to it; if he can resist, he must not yield to it and there will be no sin. Or does it perhaps deceive a man caught off his guard? Then

---

[2] Another passage directed by Pelagius against Augustine.

let him take care not to be deceived. Or is the deception so powerful that it is simply impossible to be on one's guard against it? If this is the case, there is no sin, for how can anyone sin where he cannot possibly be on his guard? But sins are committed, and therefore it is possible to be on one's guard.

51. And yet there are things done even from ignorance which are condemned and judged as deserving of correction, as we read on the authority of the Sacred Writers. For example, the Apostle says: "I obtained mercy, because I acted in ignorance."[1] And the Prophet says: "Remember not the deeds of my youth and of my ignorance."[2] Actions performed of necessity are blameworthy when a man has the will to do right and cannot do so. Hence the words of the Apostle: "For the good which I will, I do not; but the evil which I will not, I do"; and, "To will is present with me, but to accomplish that which is good, I find not";[3] and, "The flesh lusteth against the spirit, and the spirit against the flesh. For these things are contrary one to another, so that you do not what things you will."[4] But these things are all the lot of men who spring from the time of man's condemnation to death; for if this is not a punishment for man, but is something natural, then there is no sin. If man does not depart from the natural condition in which he was made, which cannot be improved upon, then, in doing these things, he is only acting as he should. But if man were good, he would be in a different condition. But because he exists the way he does, he is not good now and does not have it in his power to become good, either because he does not see what kind of man he ought to be, or, though seeing this, he is unable to become what he sees he ought to be. Can there be any doubt that this is a punishment?

Now every punishment, if just, is a punishment for sin,

---
1 1 Tim. 1.13.
2 Ps. 24.7.
3 Rom. 7.19, 18.
4 Gal. 5.17.

and is called a penalty. But if the punishment is unjust, and there is no doubt that it is a punishment, then it has been inflicted on man by some ruler who is unjust. Besides, since only a fool would doubt the omnipotence and justice of God, this is a just penalty and is inflicted as punishment for some kind of sin. For no unjust ruler could ever steal man from God, unknown to Him, or wrest him from God against his will, as if God were too weak and were so subject to threats or violence that this ruler might afflict man with unjust punishment. It remains, then, that this is a just punishment springing from man's condemnation.

52. We must not be surprised that man in his ignorance does not enjoy the free choice of will to choose the right thing to do or, though aware of what is right and with a will to do it, that he is unable to accomplish it against the opposition of carnal habits which have somehow become ingrown in nature by the vehemence present in the act of human generation. It is a perfectly just penalty for sin that man should forfeit what he would not put to good use when he could easily do so, if he were willing. That is to say, a man who fails to do what he knows is right, and a man who was unwilling to do what was right when he could, forfeits the power to do so when he wants to have it.

These two punishments, ignorance and difficulty, are truly present in every soul that sins. Through ignorance, the soul is tainted with error; through difficulty, it suffers anguish. But to accept falsity for truth, so as to err unwillingly, and to be unable to refrain from lustful acts through the resistance of carnal habits, these are not of man's nature as he originally existed, but are a punishment of man inflicted after his condemnation. When we speak of the will's freedom to do what is right, we are speaking, of course, of that freedom with which man was created.[5]

---

[5] In the *Retractations* (1.9.5), Augustine reproduces section 51 entire and the second paragraph of section 52 to show how he had anticipated, as it were, certain Pelagian objections to his teaching on grace.

Chapter 19

53. Here there arises a question which is often mulled over by men who grumble and are ready to blame anything at all for sin, except themselves. They say, for example: "If Adam and Eve sinned, what have we poor creatures done that we should be born with the blindness of ignorance and with the anguish of difficulty? First, in ignorance of what we ought to do, we fall into error; then, when the precepts of justice begin to be made known to us, we have the will to fulfill them and cannot do so because some kind of compulsion from carnal concupiscence resists our efforts." In reply to such men, I will answer briefly that they should be quiet and should stop murmuring against God. They might have grounds to complain if no man had ever triumphed over error and lust. But there is everywhere present One who makes manifold use of creatures, at the service of Him their Lord, to recall the man who has turned away from Him, to teach him when he believes, to console him when he has hope, to encourage him when he loves, to assist his efforts, to hear him when he prays. You are not charged with a fault because you are in ignorance against your will, but because you fail to seek knowledge that you do not have. Nor are you at fault because you do not bind up your wounded members, but because you neglect Him who wants to heal them. These are personal sins of your own. No man has been denied a knowledge of the benefit of inquiring after something where ignorance is of no benefit, or of how he should make humble avowal of his weakness so that, while searching after knowledge and confessing his weakness, he may be assisted by Him who experiences neither error nor difficulty in coming to our aid.

54. Wrong actions done by anyone from ignorance and the inability to perform good acts that he wants to, are called sins for the very reason that they have their origin in the first sin, which was voluntary, and it is this previous sin which has merited these consequences. We use the term "tongue" not only for the bodily member which moves about in our mouth when we speak, but also for the effect produced by this movement of the tongue, namely, the arrangement and sequence of words. It is in this sense that we say that Greek is one tongue, and Latin another. Similarly, we use the term "sin" not only in the strict sense of a fault which one commits knowingly and willingly, but also to indicate the effects which follow necessarily as punishment for such sin.

So, too, we use the term "nature" in different senses. In the strict sense, we speak of man as having a specific nature in which he was originally created in the state of innocence as one of a class. We use it in another sense to indicate the nature into which we are now born as mortal creatures, ignorant and slaves to the flesh, following the sentence of condemnation which was passed upon the first man. It is in this sense that the Apostle says: "For we were also by nature children of wrath, just as the others."[1]

Chapter 20

55. As we are born from the first union, subject to ignorance and difficulty and death, because through sin our first parents were cast headlong into error, misery, and death, so too has it pleased the justice of the Supreme God and Ruler of the universe, first to reveal His justice by punishment at the time of man's origin, and then, as man advanced in time, to manifest His mercy as a Liberator. Though under a sentence of condemnation, the first man was not deprived of the happiness of having children. It was possible that even from his offspring, however carnal and mortal, something should appear and, in its own way, be a thing of beauty and an adornment for the earth. Yet, equity would not allow Adam

---
1 Eph. 2.3.

to beget offspring better than himself. But it was only right that, from the moment of turning to God, each one should not only be unhampered in his desire but should even be aided in overcoming the punishment which man had merited at the beginning by turning away from God. In this way, too, the Creator of the universe showed how easy it would have been for man, had he so willed, to preserve the condition in which he was created since even his offspring were able to overcome the condition that was theirs by birth.

56. Again, if only a single soul was created from which are derived the souls of all men that are born, who can say that he did not sin when the first man sinned? But if souls are created one by one in each man that is born, it is not incongruous, but rather altogether fitting and in accord with order, that the evil merits of a former soul should be the natural inheritance of one that follows, and that the good merits of the succeeding soul should be the natural possession of the former. How is it unworthy of the Creator that He should have chosen even this way to show how the soul's dignity so far excels bodily creatures that one soul can begin to rise up from that condition which another had come to by its fall? When the sinful soul has reached the condition of ignorance and difficulty, this is properly called a punishment because the soul was better before this punishment. If, not only before sinning, but before beginning upon life, one soul begins to exist in the same condition to which another had come after a sinful life, it still possesses no small good for which to give thanks to its Creator, since even at the time of its creation and beginning, it is more excellent than the best of bodies. That the soul should not only enjoy a natural superiority over all bodies, but should also have power, with its Creator's help, to perfect itself and be able to acquire and possess by its pious efforts all the virtues by which it is freed from the anguish of difficulty and the blindness of ignorance —all these are no ordinary blessings.

If this is so, ignorance and difficulty will not be a punishment for sin to souls at birth, but a stimulus to make progress and the first step on the way to perfection. It is no small advantage that the soul, previous to any merit for good works, should have received a natural power of discernment to enable it to rank wisdom above error, and rest above difficulty, so it can attain these, not through birth, but by its own effort. But if a soul is unwilling to do so, it will be justly held as guilty of sin for not having made good use of the power it received. Though born in a state of ignorance and difficulty, it is not compelled by any necessity to remain in that state in which it was born. No one but God Almighty could be the Creator of such souls, who creates them before they love Him and perfects them once they have loved Him. He gives them being when they do not exist, and confers happiness upon those that love Him as the Source of their existence.

57. But if there are any souls already existing in some secret habitation, which God has assigned them, and these are sent forth to animate and rule over the bodies of individual men at birth, they are sent for this particular task. They must govern well the body, born under the punishment of sin, namely, the sentence of death incurred by the first man, that is, they must curb it through the practice of virtue and bring it into a just and lawful subjection so as to win for the body, too, a state of heavenly immortality in due order and at the appropriate time. When these souls embark upon the present life and endure the burden of carrying about this mortal frame, they must also endure the forgetfulness of their former life and the travail of the present one. The result will be ignorance and difficulty, which, in the case of the first man, was the penalty of death in order to bring him to an awareness of the miserable state of the soul; whereas, for these souls, this furnishes them an opportunity to restore the state of incorruption to the body. Again, this is spoken of as sin only because the flesh, which springs from a sinful source, causes ignorance and difficulty in the souls that enter it. But the blame for this is not to be placed either upon these souls or upon their Creator.

The Creator has given them the power to discharge faithfully these burdensome tasks and has provided a way of faith for the blindness resulting from forgetfulness. Most of all, He has given them the power of discernment which makes every soul acknowledge that it should seek to know where ignorance is of no avail, that it should strive unremittingly to discharge its difficult tasks in order to overcome the difficulty of doing what is right, and should implore help from its Creator to assist it in its efforts. Outwardly, by His Law, and inwardly, by speaking to the depths of man's heart, He directs the soul to exert itself, while He prepares a state of glory in the Blessed City for those who triumph over him who led the first man to unhappiness and overcame him by his wicked persuasion. These men accept such unhappiness in order to overcome him by the excellence of their faith. It is no small glory to be engaged in a warfare in which we overcome the devil by accepting that very punishment which enables him to boast that he has made man his captive. But any man who is so captivated by the love of the present life that he neglects this duty will have no right whatever to charge this criminal desertion to the command of the Ruler. Rather, being subject to the Ruler of all things, he must take his place on the side of him in whose shameful service he found such delight as to desert his own ranks.

58. But if souls existing elsewhere are not dispatched by the Lord God, but come of their own accord to dwell in bodies, it is easy to see why the Creator should not be blamed at all for whatever ignorance and difficulty have resulted from their own free choice. Even if God had sent them Himself, He would be altogether blameless, since, despite their ignorance and difficulty, He has not withdrawn from them the freedom to ask and seek and strive, but is ready to

give to those who ask, to show the way to those who seek, and to open to those who knock. To souls that are zealous and well-disposed, He would bestow the power to overcome such ignorance and difficulty and gain the crown of glory. To those, however, that are neglectful and wish to allege weakness for their sins, He would not reproach their ignorance and difficulty as sinful. Yet, because they have chosen to remain in such a state rather than to arrive at the truth and a ready will, He will inflict a just punishment upon them because they lacked the zeal to seek and learn, to make humble confession of sin, and to pray.

Chapter 21

59. No one should rashly affirm any one of these four views about the soul: 1) souls come into existence by generation; 2) souls are newly created for each one who is born; 3) souls already existing elsewhere are sent by God into bodies; 4) souls descend into bodies of their own accord.[1] Either this question has not yet been explained and clarified by Catholic commentators of the Sacred Scripture, as the obscurity and perplexity of the matter warrant, or, if this has been done, such writings have not yet come into my hands. Only let our faith keep us from thinking anything false or unworthy of the Creator's nature, for we make our way to Him along the road of piety. If, therefore, we conceive of Him otherwise than as He is, we will be driven towards vanity, not towards happiness. But if we conceive of creatures otherwise than as they are, there is no danger, provided we do not regard our

---

1 Only the first two of these, namely, spiritual generationism and creationism, are seriously considered. From a letter to Jerome (*Ep.* 166), it would appear that Augustine inclined towards creationism but found himself unable to explain the transmission of original sin in such an hypothesis. Actually, the problem of the soul's origin remained unsolved for him even to the end of his life. Cf. *Retractations* 1.1.3; *Opus imperfectum contra Iulianum* 2.178.

knowledge as certain. In our pursuit of happiness, it is not the creature, but the Creator, that we are commanded to seek. If our convictions about the Creator are other than what they should be, we are victims of a most pernicious kind of error. For no one can reach the happy life by tending towards something that either does not exist, or if it does exist, cannot make him happy.

60. In order to contemplate eternal truth in a way that will enable us to enjoy it and cling to it, a path through temporal things, suited to our infirmity, has been marked out for us, namely, that we accept on faith past and future events so far as this suffices for men on their journey towards things eternal. These teachings of faith are so regulated by God's mercy as to give them the greatest authority. Things present, however, as far as creatures are concerned, are perceived as transitory through the inconstancy and changing nature of the body and soul. We cannot know things of this kind at all unless we experience them. We must accept, then, on divine authority whatever we are told about any creature at all, whether past or future. Some, however, passed away before we could perceive them, while others have not yet come into our sense experience. Nevertheless, we must readily believe them because they help us very much to strengthen our hope and to arouse our love. At the same time, they remind us of our deliverance which God has not failed to provide throughout the orderly course of the ages.

Now any error that masquerades as divine authority can be best refuted by this line of reasoning; namely, can we show that it believes, or asserts as true, that there exists any form of beauty, even though changeable, apart from God's creation, or that any changeable form of beauty exists in God's nature, or that it maintains that God's nature is something of greater or less perfection than the Trinity? The Christian exercises all possible vigilance towards a pious and careful understanding of the Trinity and directs all his progress towards this end. But this is not the place for a discussion on the unity of the Trinity and on the equality and properties of each Person in the Trinity. To recount certain truths concerning the Lord God, Author of all things and the Source of their ordered perfection, the Ruler of the universe, truths that pertain to salutary faith and provide gentle nourishment and a useful support for the soul's first efforts to rise from the things of earth to those of heaven—this is easy to do, and many have already done it. But to give a thorough treatment of this whole question, and present it so that every man's intelligence can be sufficiently won over to the clear light of reason, so far as is possible in this life, and to express it in words, or even in our thoughts, can hardly seem an easy task for any man, or, at any rate, for us.

Now, then, let us proceed with what we have undertaken so far as we are given help and leave to do so. As for things created, we must promptly believe whatever is related to us about the past or is prophesied about the future, if this helps to promote sound religion by awakening in us a sincere love of God and our neighbor. Against unbelievers, however, we must defend it to the point of either crushing their unbelief by the weight of authority, or by showing them as best we can, first, that it is not foolish to believe such things; secondly, that it is foolish not to believe them. Nevertheless, we ought to refute false teaching about the present, particularly, about things unchangeable, rather than what concerns the past and the future, and should disprove such teaching by means of clear arguments.

61. Within the order of temporal events, our expectation of the things to come should certainly occupy our attention more than an inquiry into things of the past since, even in the Sacred Books, the events narrated as past are represented either as a type, or promise, or a witness of things to come. Actually, even where things of the present life are concerned, whether favorable or unfavorable, little concern is shown for one's past condition, but the weight of anxiety rests wholly upon one's hopes for the future. By a kind of natural instinct within us, things that have happened to us, once they are over, are regarded as though they had never taken place as far as having any influence upon our happiness or unhappiness is concerned. What harm can come to me if I do not know when I began to exist since I know that I now exist and do not despair of existing in the future? I do not turn my thoughts to things of the past, as if I lived in fear over a disastrous error for having thought of them otherwise than they were, but I direct my course towards what the future holds for me, under the merciful guidance of my Creator. Consequently, if I entertain any false belief or view about my future existence, or about God with whom I shall be existing in the future, I must strenuously avoid any such error. Otherwise, I shall either fail to make the necessary preparation, or I shall be unable to reach the goal I have in mind because I have mistaken one thing for something else.

Thus, if I were to buy a coat, it would not be a handicap were I to forget about last winter, but it would be, if I thought there were no threat of cold for the future. Similarly, my soul will not be handicapped if it chances to forget something it endured in the past, provided it is careful now to fasten its attention upon the goal for which it is admonished to prepare itself from now on. Again, for example, no harm would come to a man sailing for Rome if he were to forget from what shore he had set sail, so long as he knew how to steer his course from the position where he happened to be. But it would do him no good to remember the shore from which he embarked on his journey if he miscalculated about the port of Rome and should suffer shipwreck upon the shoals. So, too, if I do not remember the time my life began, this will be no hindrance to me so long as I know what the end is wherein I am to find rest. Any recollection or conjecture about the beginning of my life would be no help to me if I should run upon the reefs of error by holding views unworthy of that same God who alone is the end of the soul's labors.

62. These remarks should not be construed as meaning that we would prohibit men who are capable from inquiring according to the divinely inspired Scriptures as to whether souls are generated from souls, or are separately created for each body they animate, or are sent from elsewhere by God's command to govern and animate the body, or make their own way into bodies of their own volition. We do not forbid such inquiry if reason demands that we examine and discuss these things in order to solve some important question, or if we are granted leisure from more important matters for an inquiry and examination of these matters. Rather, my remarks were intended to prevent a person from showing unreasonable displeasure in a question of this kind towards one who does not accept his view because of a doubt that may be all too human. Besides, even if someone should acquire a certain and clear grasp of this matter, he must not suppose that someone else has lost all hope of the things to come just because he does not remember his origins in the past.

Chapter 22

63. Whatever the status of the problem, namely, whether we should omit it altogether or defer it for consideration at another time, this will not prevent us from seeing clearly the truth of the matter at hand, that souls suffer punishment for their sins and do so without detriment to the majesty of God's nature, which remains inviolate, all-just, steadfast, and unchanging. As we have already explained at some length, these sins must be imputed to the will alone and we need look no further for the cause of sin.

64. But if ignorance and difficulty are man's natural state, then it is from this condition that the soul begins to progress and advance towards knowledge and a state of rest until the happy life is fully realized in it. If, of its own accord, the soul neglects to make such progress in a knowledge of higher things and in the practice of piety, though it has not been denied the power to do so, then it deserves to be plunged into a worse state of ignorance and difficulty, which is already penal in character, and it takes its place among lower creatures according to a universal governance that is perfectly fitting and proper. The soul is charged with guilt, not because of its natural condition of ignorance and weakness, but because it made no effort to acquire knowledge and did not apply itself sufficiently to obtain the power to do what is right. Ignorance of language and inability to speak are natural to the infant. Such ignorance and difficulty in speaking are not only blameless under the rules of grammar, but are even a source of pleasure and delight for our human sensibilities. It was no fault of the child that it failed to acquire this ability, nor has it through its own fault lost the ability after having once acquired it.

Consequently, if our happiness consisted of eloquence, and if it were accounted a crime to make a mistake in speaking, as it is when we perform sinful acts in life, certainly no one would be blamed for being an infant, because it is from this state that a beginning is made towards attaining eloquence. If, however, because of a perverse will, one should remain in such a state, or should fall back into it, he would clearly be deserving of condemnation.

So even now, if ignorance of the truth and difficulty in doing right are natural to man and are the point of departure whence man begins his ascent to the happy state of wisdom and rest, no one is justified in reproaching happiness for its natural origin. But if a man is unwilling to advance or is willing to be a backslider, he rightly deserves to suffer the penalty.

65. But the soul's Creator is to be praised in every respect, either because He endowed the soul from the very beginning with a capacity for the highest good, or because He helps it to advance, or because He implements its progress and brings it to perfection, or because He subjects it to order by condemning it according to its just deserts whenever it sins, that is, when it either refuses to raise itself from its initial state to perfection, or when it falls back after it has made some progress. He did not therefore create it evil just because it was not so perfect then as when it received the power to become so later on. For all perfections found in bodies are far inferior to the soul in its original state, and yet any person of sound discernment would judge that even these deserved to be praised for what they are. The soul's ignorance of what it ought to do stems from the fact that it has not yet received this knowledge. But it will receive this too if it makes good use of what has already been given it, for it has received the power to seek it with diligence and devotion, if only it chooses to do so. Again, the soul finds itself unable to do at once what it sees ought to be done because it has likewise not yet received this power. One part of it, the higher, has gone ahead to perceive the good of a righteous act, but another part, the more sluggish and carnal element, is not brought into conformity with this view. Hence the soul is prompted by this very difficulty to beg Him for help in making progress, from whom it sees it owes its start.

This is why it loves God all the more, since it is elevated to its happy state, not by its own resources, but by the mercy of Him to whose goodness it owes its existence. The more it loves God, the Source of its existence, the more securely does it find repose in Him and the more fully does it experience the joys of His eternity.

We would be wrong to call the young and tender sapling barren, even though it goes through several summer seasons without bearing fruit until the proper time arrives to show its fruit. Why, then, should the soul's Creator not be praised with all due reverence if He has given the soul a kind of beginning that enables it to mature with the fruits of wisdom and justice by its efforts and growth, and when He has so dignified it that it is within its power to reach out for happiness, if it wills to do so?

Chapter 23

66. An insidious objection is often levelled against this line of reasoning by ignorant men concerning the death of young children and the bodily sufferings with which we often see them afflicted. What need, they ask, was there for a child to be born when it departed this life before it could set out to merit in life? Or, what will be its destiny in the future judgment, seeing that it has no place either among the just, since it performed no good deeds, or among the wicked, since it did nothing sinful?

Here is my answer to their objection. Viewing the universe as a whole and the perfect order prevailing throughout the entire creation spread over time and place, it is impossible that the creation of any man would be superfluous in a universe where not even the creation of a single leaf of a tree is superfluous. What is really superfluous is any inquiry about the merits of one who has acquired no merits. We need have no fear that there may be a life in between virtue and vice, or that the Judge may pass a sentence halfway between reward and punishment.

67. Here, too, men are in the habit of asking what benefit comes to young children from the sacrament of Christ's baptism, since they often die after receiving it and before they could know anything about it. On this point, it is piously believed, and quite rightly so, that the child benefits from the faith of those who present it for baptism. Such a belief finds support in the salutary authority of the Church, so that each one may realize how beneficial his own faith is for himself when it can also be turned to the benefit of others who do not yet have faith of their own. What benefit did the widow's son derive from his own faith, which he certainly did not possess once he was dead, whereas his mother's faith was instrumental in his being raised from the dead?[1] How much more, then, can the faith of another provide for the child whose lack of faith cannot be imputed to it?

68. A more serious complaint, almost compassionate in tone, is frequently voiced concerning the bodily suffering which afflicts young children. Because of their age, they are without sin, provided the souls animating them did not exist before they became human beings. What evil have these done, they ask, that they should undergo such sufferings? You might think there could be a reward for innocence before a person is able to cause harm! But God accomplishes some good in reforming the lives of older people when these are chastised by the suffering and death of their little ones so dear to them. Why should this not happen since, once it is over, it will be as if it never happened for those who suffered it? On the other hand, those for whose sake this has happened, will either become better if, after having profited from these temporal trials to reform their lives, they will choose to live more righteously; or they will have no excuse when they are punished at the future judgment if they failed to make use of the suffering of this present life to turn their desires towards life eternal. Besides, who can tell what good recompense God, in His hidden designs, has in store for these children when, as a result of their suffering, the harshness of parents is softened, their faith is strengthened, and their compassion is made evident to all? Though they have performed no good acts, they have nevertheless endured these sufferings without having committed any sins. It is not without reason that the Church proposes for our veneration as martyrs,

---
1 Cf. Luke 7.12-15.

even the infants who were slain when the Lord Jesus Christ was being sought out for destruction by Herod.

69. These carping critics, who neglect to study such questions carefully but go about airing their opinions garrulously, usually try to shake the faith of those less instructed on the problem of pain and hardships also suffered by animals. What evil have even these deserved, they ask, or what can they hope for in the way of good that they should suffer such distress? They speak or think this way because they take a very unfair view of things and, incapable as they are of understanding the nature and excellence of the highest good, they would have everything conform to their own idea of what it is. They cannot conceive of a supreme good beyond the highest bodies which have a heavenly nature and are not so subject to corruption. Hence, without any regard for order, they make the unreasonable demand that animals should suffer neither death nor corruption in their bodies, as if they were not mortal, though they are on the lowest plane, or as if they were evil, just because the heavenly bodies are better.

Besides, the pain experienced by beasts reveals clearly a power of the animal soul which is wonderful and admirable in its own way. The very fact of their suffering makes it quite clear how much these souls strive for unity in ruling over their bodies and imparting life to them. For what is pain, if not a conscious struggle against disintegration and dissolution? Hence it is as plain as day how eager and tenacious the soul is to preserve unity throughout. It directs its attention to suffering within the body and is troubled by the deterioration of its unity and integrity, not in a voluntary or indifferent way, but with resistance and by putting up a struggle. Except for pain in the animal, we would have no evidence of the intense desire for unity in the lower living things. Without such evidence, we would not be made sufficiently aware that all these have been constituted by the supreme, sublime, and unspeakable unity of their Creator.

70. Indeed, if you reflect upon this matter reverently and carefully, you will see that all the beauty and movement of those creatures which come to man's attention speak words of instruction for us. Through the variety of their movements and tendencies, as by so many different tongues, they everywhere proclaim and cry out that we should recognize their Creator. Of those creatures that experience neither pain nor pleasure, there is not one that is not impelled by its unity to realize its distinctive beauty, or, in a general way, to achieve a degree of permanence within its nature. So too, among creatures that experience the anguish of pain or the delight of pleasure, there is none whose aversion to pain and desire for pleasure does not thereby attest to the fact that it shuns disintegration and seeks unity. In their very desire to know, wherein rational souls find a natural delight, they reduce all the objects of their perception to a unity, while, in the avoidance of error, they simply shun the confusion caused by meaningless equivocation. Why is all equivocation troublesome, if not for the fact that it has no fixed unity? Accordingly, it is now evident that whether they cause or suffer harm, whether they give or receive pleasure, they all suggest and proclaim the unity of the Creator.

But if ignorance and difficulty with which this present life must take its beginning are not the natural condition of souls, then we must conclude that these have either been assumed as a debt or have been imposed as a punishment. Now I think we have had enough discussion on these points.

Chapter 24

71. We should ask what the first man himself was like when he was created, rather than how his descendants have been propagated. Some think they are displaying great acumen when they propose the question as follows. If the first man was created wise, why, they ask, was he misled, and if he was created foolish, how can God not be the cause of vice, since folly is the greatest of the vices? They speak as if it were impossible for human nature to be endowed with some intermediate state, besides folly and wisdom, which could be called neither folly nor wisdom. Actually, a man begins to be either foolish or wise, and must be called one or the other, only from the time he is able to possess wisdom and when, by neglecting to do so, his will is guilty of the vice of folly. No one is foolish enough to call an infant foolish, though it would be more absurd of him to want to call it wise. Though already a human being, the infant cannot be called either wise or foolish.

Hence it is clear that human nature is endowed with an intermediate state which you may not properly call either folly or wisdom. Consequently, if anyone were born with a soul in the same state as those who lack wisdom through negligence, no one could properly call him foolish, since he could tell that his conditions arose, not from vice, but from nature.

Folly is not any kind of ignorance at all about what we should seek and avoid, but an ignorance born of vice. This is why we do not say that irrational animals are foolish, since they have not been endowed with the power to become wise. But we often use terms in a way that is similar, but not the same. Though blindness is the most serious of all defects in the eye, it is not a defect in newborn puppies, and cannot, properly speaking, be termed blindness.

72. Accordingly, if a man was created in a state where, though yet unwise, he could receive a command that he ought certainly to obey, it is neither surprising that he could be seduced, nor an injustice that he should suffer punishment for failing to obey. Neither is the Creator the cause of his vice, since it was not yet a vice for man to be without wisdom when he had not yet received the power to have it. Yet he did have something that would enable him to advance towards what he did not yet have, provided he was willing to make good use of it. It is one thing for a man to be rational, it is something else to be wise. Through reason, man became a fit subject for commands, and he must show himself faithful to these and so fulfill all that is commanded of him. Just as it is natural for reason to grasp a command, so too, it is the observance of such a command that gains for us the possession of wisdom. What nature does in the way of grasping the command is accomplished by the will in carrying it out. And as rational nature merits, in a way, to receive a command, so too, it is the observance of it that merits the bestowal of wisdom.

Now, from the time a man begins to be capable of receiving a command, from that moment he begins to have the power to sin. Before a man becomes wise, he can sin in two ways, either by failing to make himself fit to receive the command, or by not observing the command once he has received it. But if a man already wise turns from wisdom, then he sins. Just as the command does not issue from the person commanded, so too, wisdom does not come from the person who is enlightened but from Him who is the Source of enlightenment.

Is there any reason then why man's Creator should not be praised? Man is something good, and because he is capable of receiving a command, he is something better than the beast. He is better yet when he has already received a command, better yet when he has obeyed it, and still better when he is made happy by the eternal light of wisdom.

The malice of sin consists in a man's failure either to accept the command, or to observe it, or to be steadfast in the contemplation of wisdom. This enables us to see how the first man could be seduced by sin, even though he was created wise. Since this sin was within his free choice, it entailed a just penalty by reason of God's law. It is in this sense too that the Apostle says: "Professing themselves to be wise, they became foolish."¹ For pride turns a man from wisdom and folly follows in its wake. Surely, folly is a kind of blindness, as the same Apostle indicates, where he says: ". . . and their foolish heart was darkened."² Now what is the cause of this darkness, but the turning away from the light of wisdom? And what causes this turning away, if not the fact that man, whose good is God, wills to be his own good, just as God is His own good? Whence the words of Scripture: "My soul is troubled in my own regard,"³ and, "Taste, and you shall be as gods."⁴

73. In examining this matter, some are disturbed by the question as to whether the first man fell from God through folly, or whether he became foolish by falling from God. If you answer that he fell from wisdom through folly, it will appear that he was foolish before he fell from wisdom, so that folly was the cause of it. Likewise, if you reply that he became foolish by falling, they will ask whether, in doing so, he acted foolishly or wisely. If he acted wisely, he did what was right and committed no sin; if he acted foolishly, then, they say, it was the folly already found in him that made him fall since, without folly, he could not do anything foolish. This makes it clear that there is some middle state through which a man passes from wisdom to folly. We cannot say that this state resulted either from folly or wisdom, and it is one that men in this life can only understand in terms of its contraries. Thus, no mortal can become wise unless he passes from folly to wisdom. If the transition itself is made foolishly, it is certainly not done well, which would be a very foolish thing to say; if the transition is made wisely, then wisdom was already present in man before he passed over to wisdom, which is something equally absurd. This makes it clear that there is a middle state which cannot

---
1 Rom. 1.22.
2 Rom. 1.21.
3 Ps. 41.7.
4 Gen. 2.5.

go by either name. So, too, when the first man passed from the heights of wisdom to folly, the transition was neither foolish nor wise. It is something like sleep and wakefulness, where falling asleep is not the same as sleeping and where awakening is not the same as being awake, but where there is a passing from one state to another. There is, however, this difference, that the latter generally happen involuntarily, while the former are always voluntary, which is why the punishments that follow are perfectly just.

Chapter 25

74. But the will is not drawn to any action unless something is perceived. It is within anyone's power to accept or reject something, but it is not in his power to be unaffected by what he sees. We must acknowledge that the soul is affected by the things it perceives, both of a higher and lower order, so that a rational being may take what it chooses from each, and, on the merit of what it takes, there follows unhappiness or happiness. In the garden of paradise, for example, God's command belonged to the perception of higher things, the suggestion of the devil, to things below. Neither the command enjoined upon him by God nor the suggestion made by the devil was in the power of man. Just how free man was from having to yield to the lower attraction of what he perceived, when he was free from the constraints of difficulty and living a sound life of wisdom, can be seen from the fact that even foolish men overcome this attraction as they approach wisdom, even though they find it hard to forego the deadly delights of their pernicious habits.

75. A question may arise at this point. If man was confronted by both classes of objects that he perceived, God's precept on the one hand, and the serpent's suggestion on the other, how was it suggested to the devil himself to pursue

wickedness and so fall from his place on high? If he had not been affected by something he perceived, he would not have chosen to do what he did, for, unless something had entered his mind, he would not have turned his thoughts at all to wickedness. How, then, did it enter his mind to embark upon something which would make a devil out of a good angel?

One who wills, certainly has to will something, and unless this something is either suggested externally by the bodily senses, or arises in the mind in some hidden way, he cannot will it. We must distinguish, then, two classes of things that are perceived. The first comes from the will of one who makes use of persuasion, as the devil did, when man sinned by yielding to him. The second class comprises things which come to the attention of the mind or to the bodily senses. Apart from the Changeless Trinity, which does not fall under the soul's comprehension but rather transcends it, the things that it perceives are these: first, the soul itself, by which we perceive that we are alive; secondly, the body, which is governed by the soul, enabling the soul to move whatever member is needed to perform an act at the time. Bodily things, on the other hand, are all subject to the perception of the bodily senses.

76. In contemplating supreme wisdom—which, being unchangeable, is not the soul—the mutable soul also gets a view of itself and somehow comes into its own mind. This is only possible because of the difference that separates the soul from God, though even the soul is something which, after God, can be a source of delight. But it is better for the soul when it forgets itself in its love of the unchangeable God, or utterly despises itself by comparison with Him. If, on the other hand, it gets in its own way, so to speak, and takes delight in itself, by a perverse imitation of God in its desire to enjoy its own power, then the more it wants to be greater, so much does it become less. Thus, "pride is the beginning of all sin, and the beginning of pride is man's apostasy from God."[1]

---
[1] Ecclus. [Sirach] 10.15, 14.

In addition to his pride, there was the devil's insidious ill-will to urge upon man that very pride which he realized had brought damnation upon himself. Hence the provision that man should receive a corrective punishment rather than one which would entail his destruction. Thus, while the devil made himself an example of pride for man, the Lord, through whom we have the promise of life eternal, offered himself to man as an example of humility. Consequently, since Christ has purchased us by His blood, after having endured indescribable trials and suffering, let us cling steadfastly to our Liberator with such great love and be so transported by the light of His countenance that the sight of things below may not turn us from the higher vision. And even though some suggestion inspired by a desire for things below should enter our mind, the thought of eternal punishment and the torments suffered by the devil should bring us back to our senses.

77. Such is the beauty of justice and the delight of that eternal light, namely, changeless truth and wisdom, that, even were one permitted to abide in it only for the space of a single day, yet, for this alone, he would rightly and justly regard as nought the countless years of the present life, though they were filled with delights and an affluence of temporal goods. These words of the Psalmist: "For better is one day in thy courts over thousands,"[2] were expressed with no small degree of genuine fervor. They can also be understood, however, in another sense, where a thousand days may stand for the changing character of time, while one day stands for the changelessness of eternity.

I do not know that I have passed over any point needed to answer your questions, so far as the Lord has seen fit to allow me. And even if some question does come to your mind, the limits of this book compel me to bring it to an end and to rest at last from our discussion.

---

2 Ps. 83.11.

RETRACTATIONS, Book 1, Ch. 9

THE FREE CHOICE OF THE WILL

1. While still sojourning in Rome, we decided to inquire into the origin of evil by way of a discussion. Our discussion was so directed as to lead us to a possible understanding, through rational reflection and inquiry, of what we already believed about the matter, so far as God might assist our inquiry and, since we were agreed, once the arguments had been carefully examined, that evil came about only by the free choice of the will, the three books which resulted from this discussion were entitled "The Free Choice of the Will." I completed the second and third of these, as best I could at the time, after my ordination to the priesthood at Hippo Regius.

2. So many subjects were discussed in these books that some questions which came up were deferred, either because I could not solve them or because they would have required a lengthy discussion just at that time. But whatever solutions were proposed in either case, even when it was not clear which of those proposed for these same questions was closer to the truth, our reasoning led us nevertheless to this conclusion, that wherever the truth lay, we should believe, and even make it clear, that God is to be praised. This discussion was undertaken because of those who deny that evil has its origin in the free choice of the will and contend that if this were the case, God is at fault, since He is the Creator of all natures. In line with their wicked error—they are the Manichees—they would thus introduce a kind of changeless evil nature, coeternal with God. Since this was the problem under consideration, there is no discussion in these books concerning the grace of God by which He so predestines His elect that He Himself even makes ready the wills of those among them who are already making use of their free choice. But when-

ever there was occasion to mention this grace, this was done in passing, and not as a defense of grace by means of painstaking arguments, as if this were the subject under discussion. To inquire into the origin of evil is one thing; to inquire how we can return to our original good, or to one that is better, is another matter.

3. Accordingly, the recent Pelagian heretics, who would assert the free choice of the will so as to leave no place for God's grace, since they maintain that it is given in accordance with our merits, must not be elated, as though I had defended their course; for I said many things in these books in favor of free will as the circumstances of the discussion demanded. In the first book I did, in fact, state that "evil deeds are punished by God's justice," and added, "unless they were committed voluntarily, their punishment would not be just" (1.1.1). Again, when I said that the will is so great a good that it is deservedly preferred to all bodies and external goods, I said: "I believe you see then that it lies within our will either to enjoy or to lack so great and true a good as this. For what is more within the power of the will than the will itself?" (1.12.26) And, in another place: "How are we justified then in regarding as doubtful the fact that it is by the will that we merit and live a good and praiseworthy life, and, by the same will, a life that is shameful and unhappy, even though formerly we were never wise?" (1.13.28) Again, in another place: "Accordingly, any man with the will to lead a good and upright life, provided he prefers this will to all fleeting goods, will acquire so great a possession with such great ease that to have what he wills is the same thing as to will it" (1.13.29). Similarly, I said elsewhere: "Certainly, the eternal law, which it is now time to consider again, has unalterably decreed that merit is in the will, whereas reward and punishment are identified with happiness and unhappiness" (1.14.30). And, in another place: "We also agreed that what each man chooses to pursue and embrace is within the power of the will to determine" (1.16.34). And in the second book: "For man himself, insofar as he is man, is something good because he can live an upright life whenever he so wishes" (2.1.2). And I said in another place: ". . . moral conduct is only possible by free will" (2.18.47). And in the third book: "What need, then, is there to look for a cause of that movement by which the soul turns from the unchangeable to a changeable good? We agree that it belongs to the soul alone and is voluntary, and, consequently, culpable. Furthermore, all practical instruction in this matter has this for its aim, that, renouncing and restraining this kind of movement, we turn our will from the instability of temporal things to the enjoyment of the everlasting good" (3.1.2). And, in another place: "The voice of truth is making itself heard very well in you. If our act of willing is not in our power, then you could not be conscious of anything else that is. Hence nothing is so much in our power as the will itself, for it is there at hand the very instant that we will something" (3.3.7). Again, in another place: "If you receive praise for seeing what you are obliged to do, though you can only see this in Him who is the changeless truth, how much more should He be praised who has both laid a command upon your will and has given you the power to fulfill it, and has not allowed your refusal to go unpunished?" Then I went on to add: "If everyone must render what he has received, and if man has been so made that he sins of necessity, then it is his duty to sin. Therefore, whenever he sins, he is doing what he ought to do. If it is wicked to make such an assertion, then no one is forced by his nature to sin" (3.16.46). And again: "But what could possibly come before the will to be its cause? Either the will is itself the cause, and there will be no regress from this root of the will, or it is not the will, and the will is without sin. Consequently, either the will itself is ultimately the cause of sin, or the ultimate cause of sin is without sin. Sin can be justly imputed to no one but a sinner, and can therefore only be justly imputed to one who wills it" (3.17.49). And, a little later: ". . . for how can anyone sin where he cannot possibly be on his guard? But sins are committed, and therefore it is possible to be on one's guard" (3.18.50). Pelagius used these statements of mine as evidence in a book of his. When I answered this book, I decided to entitle the book *Nature and Grace*.

4. Because no mention of grace was made in these and similar statements of mine, since we were not dealing with this question at the time, the Pelagians think or might think, that I held their views. But they are mistaken to think so. To be sure, it is the will that enables us to sin and to live a good life, and this was the problem under consideration in those statements of mine. Unless, therefore, the will is freed from the servitude which makes it "the servant of sin," and unless it is helped to overcome its vices, it is impossible for mortal men to lead righteous and godly lives. And unless this gift of God, which makes the will free, came before the act of the will, it would not be given because of the will's merits, and would not be grace, which, of course, is given freely. I have treated this subject sufficiently in other works of mine, where I refute these enemies of God's grace, the most recent of the heretics. Yet, even in this book, *The Free Choice of the Will*, which was not written against them, since they were not yet in existence, but against the Manichees on the subject of free will, I did not altogether pass over in silence this grace of God which they attempt to destroy by their base blasphemies. As a matter of fact, I stated in the second book: ". . . not only the great but even the least goods exist through Him alone from whom all good things come, namely, from God." And I added shortly afterwards: ". . . these virtues which enable us to live rightly are great goods whereas all forms of bodily beauty are the least goods, since we can live rightly without them. But the powers of the soul, without which there can be no right living, are intermediate goods. No one

puts virtues to bad use, since the function of virtue is the good use of those things which we can also put to bad use. No one makes bad use of what he puts to good use. Accordingly, the vast liberality of God's goodness has brought into existence not only the great, but also the intermediate and least goods. His goodness is more to be praised for the great than for the intermediate goods, and more for the intermediate than for the least goods, but still to be praised more for all of them than if He had not given them existence at all" (2.19.50). And in another place: "Only make sure to hold firm to your religious conviction that you know of no good, either by the senses, or by the intellect, or in any other way, that does not come from God" (2.20.54). Again, in another place, I stated: "But, since man cannot rise of his own will as he fell of his own will, the right hand of God, namely, our Lord Jesus Christ, is outstretched to us from above. Let us embrace Him with a strong faith, await Him with a sure hope, and love Him with an ardent charity" (*ibid.*).

5. Again, in the third book, following the words which, as I mentioned, Pelagius took for his own use from my works— ". . . for how can anyone sin where he cannot possibly be on his guard? But sins are committed, and therefore it is possible for one to be on his guard" (3.18.50)—I went on to say: "And yet there are things done even from ignorance which are condemned and judged as deserving of correction, as we read on the authority of the Sacred Writers. For example, the Apostle says: 'I obtained mercy, because I acted in ignorance.' And the Prophet says: 'Remember not the deeds of my youth and of my ignorance.' Actions performed of necessity are blameworthy when a man has the will to do right and cannot do so. Hence the words of the Apostle: 'For the good which I will, I do not; but the evil which I will not, I do'; and, 'To will is present with me, but to accomplish that which is good, I find not'; and, 'The flesh

lusteth against the spirit, and the spirit against the flesh. For these things are contrary one to another, so that you do not what things you will.' But all these things are the lot of men who come to exist from the time of man's condemnation to death; for if this is not a punishment for man, but is something natural, then there is no sin. If man does not depart from the natural condition in which he was made, which cannot be improved upon, then, in doing these things, he is only acting as he should. But if man were good, he would be in a different condition. But because he exists the way he does, he is not good now and does not have it in his power to become good, either because he does not see what kind of man he ought to be, or, though seeing this, he is unable to become what he sees he ought to be. Can there be any doubt that this is a punishment? Now every punishment, if just, is a punishment for sin, and is called a penalty. But if the punishment is unjust, and there is no doubt that it is a punishment, then it has been inflicted on man by some ruler who is unjust. Besides, since only a fool would doubt the omnipotence and justice of God, this is a just penalty and is inflicted as punishment for some kind of sin. For no unjust ruler could ever steal man from God, unknown to Him, or wrest him from God against His will, as if God were too weak and were so subject to threats of violence that this ruler might afflict man with unjust punishment. It remains, then, that this is a just punishment arising from man's condemnation" (3.18.51). And, in another place: "But to accept falsity for truth, so as to err unwillingly, and to be unable to refrain from lustful acts through the resistance of carnal habits, these are not of man's nature as he originally existed, but are a punishment of man inflicted after his condemnation. When we speak of the will's freedom to do what is right, we are speaking, of course, of that freedom with which man was created" (3.18.52).

6. See! Long before the Pelagian heresy arose, we carried on this discussion as if we were already engaged in debate

against the Pelagians. For we stated that while all things good—great, intermediate, and least—are from God, free will is found among the intermediate goods, because we can also make bad use of it; yet, it is a kind of good without which we cannot live a good life. The good use of the will is already virtue, and virtue is found among the great goods which no one can put to a bad use. And, since we said that all goods, great, intermediate, and least, are from God, it follows that the good use of the will, which is virtue, is also from God and is numbered among the great goods. Mention was then made of the misery, inflicted in all justice upon sinners, from which they are freed by God's grace, for man could fall of himself, that is, by his free will, but could not rise again. Ignorance and difficulty, which all men suffer from the moment of birth, belong to that misery arising from man's just condemnation, and no one is freed from this evil except by the grace of God. Through their denial of original sin, the Pelagians refuse to admit that this misery derives from a just condemnation. Nevertheless, even though ignorance and difficulty were the original and natural condition of man, God should not be blamed but praised, as I argued in that same third book. This discussion must be regarded as directed against the Manichees, who do not accept the Sacred Scriptures of the Old Testament, where original sin is recounted. And these have the wicked effrontery to contend that whatever we read about original sin in the Letters of the Apostles has been inserted by corrupters of the Scriptures, as if it were something the Apostles never said. But against the Pelagians we must defend what is set forth in both parts of the Scripture, which they profess to accept.

This work opens with the words: "Tell me, please, whether God is not the cause of evil."

GRACE AND FREE WILL

(De gratia et libero arbitrio)

INTRODUCTION

THE TREATISE *Grace and Free Will* marks the beginning of a new and final phase in Saint Augustine's long and tireless polemic on the subject of divine grace. Between the years of 412 and 420, he had devoted no fewer than nine works,[1] exclusive of pertinent sermons and letters, to a refutation of the Pelagian errors[2] and to a defense of the Church's traditional teaching on the necessity and absolute gratuity of grace in the work of man's salvation. In fact, it was largely through his personal efforts and intervention that these errors were condemned by more than two hundred and forty bishops at the Council of Carthage in 418. Later that same year the Council's action was confirmed by Pope Zosimus in his celebrated *Epistola Tractoria*,[3] which was endorsed by nearly the entire episcopate. Although Augustine emerged victorious from the controversy, further difficulties arose later from a new and unexpected source.

In the same year that witnessed the condemnation of Pelagianism, Augustine had addressed a letter to the Roman priest Sixtus,[4] later Pope Sixtus III, in which he outlined the errors of Pelagius and defended the doctrine that no merit

---

[1] These include the following works: *De peccatorum meritis et remissione et de baptismo parvulorum, De spiritu et littera, De natura et gratia, De natura et origine animae, Contra duas epistolas Pelagianorum, De perfectione iustitiae hominis, De gestis Pelagii, De gratia Christi et de peccato originali, De nuptiis et concupiscentia.*
[2] The best modern and comprehensive study of Pelagius is that of G. de Plinval, *Pélage: ses écrits, sa vie, et sa réforme* (Lausanne 1943). Cf. also J. Ferguson, *Pelagius: A Historical and Theological Study* (Cambridge 1956).
[3] Only fragments of the *Epistola* survive, including that found in Augustine's letter to Optatus (190.23).
[4] *Ep.* 194.

245

whatever is possible without grace, even to the point of asserting that "in crowning our merits, God does nothing more than crown His own gifts." Several years later, probably in 426, a copy of this letter fell into the hands of Florus, a monk of the community at Hadrumetum,[5] during a visit to the monastery in his native city of Uzala, presided over by Bishop Evodius.[6] A copy of the letter was dictated to Florus who had it brought back to Hadrumetum, while Florus himself went on to Carthage.[7] Unknown to the superior, Valentine, the letter was read to uninstructed members of the community. Some denied its authenticity; others opposed its contents as altogether incompatible with their personal efforts in the voluntary practice of virtue. Upon his return to Hadrumetum Florus informed Valentine of the dissension occasioned by Augustine's letter. While the dissenters numbered only five or more, Valentine resolved to restore peace and unity by seeking clarification of the letter. He turned first to Evodius, but when the latter's reply failed to satisfy the monks,[8] he addressed himself to a highly respected priest, Sabinus, whose efforts were apparently also unavailing. As a last resort, Valentine permitted two of the monks opposed to Augustine's teaching, Felix and Cresconius, to journey to Hippo with the controversial letter. While providing them with the necessary funds, he gave them no introductory letters so as not to appear sympathetic to their views. Actually,

---

5 The present-day city of Sousse in Tunisia.
6 A native of Tagaste, Evodius was present at the death of Monica at Ostia and later became a member of Augustine's first community at Tagaste. After Augustine's ordination to the priesthood at Hippo in 391, he joined the community established there on property donated for the purpose by Bishop Valerius. In two of Augustine's Dialogues, *The Greatness of the Soul* and *The Free Choice of the Will*, he serves as interlocutor.
7 The main events of this episode are described in two letters of Augustine to Valentine (*Epp.* 214, 215) and in Valentine's reply (*Ep.* 216).
8 The complete text of Evodius' letter, first published by Dom Morin in 1896, was re-edited by him in 1901 (*Revue bénédictine* 18.241-256); this second edition is reprinted in A. Hamman (ed.), Migne, *Patrologia Latina: Supplementum* 2 (Paris 1960) 332-334.

Valentine, as well as the community at large, acknowledged both the authenticity of the letter and the orthodoxy of its contents. The monks were joined sometime later at Hippo by the same Felix who had dictated the copy of Augustine's letter to Sixtus at Uzala and brought it to Hadrumetum.

Because of the monks' desire to return to their own monastery for Easter, Augustine supplemented his oral explanations with a more detailed account in a letter to Valentine, which he read to them. Finally, when the monks agreed to remain for Easter, he reviewed with them various documents which had exposed and condemned the Pelagian heresy. These included, in addition to a second and shorter letter to Valentine, letters sent to Pope Innocent concerning the Councils of Carthage and Numidia, as well as the lengthier account submitted by five of the bishops, including the Pope's reply; also, the report of the Council of Africa sent to Pope Zosimus, together with his reply in the *Epistola Tractoria*, and a report of the anti-Pelagian measures adopted by the recent plenary Council of Africa. He also read them his latest treatise, *Grace and Free Will*, addressed to Valentine, and composed during the monks' sojourn at Hippo. In reply to Augustine's two letters, Valentine assures him that the treatise has happily achieved the desired result of restoring peace and harmony in the community.

As Augustine points out at the beginning of this work, and again in a brief account of it in the *Retractations*,[9] the treatise is specifically directed against those who regard any defense of grace as a denial of free will, which they boldly defend at the expense of grace, asserting that this is given according to our merits. Because of the Saint's insistence and emphasis upon the radical insufficiency of man's will to merit the first grace and to persevere until death without the gratuitous assistance of God's grace, the work may properly be regarded as the first to be occasioned by the rising tide

---

9 2.66.

of Semi-Pelagianism,[10] which was to occupy the rest of his declining years.

No exact date can be assigned for the composition of *Grace and Free Will*. Since, however, it occupies the second last place in the chronological ordering of the *Retractations,* completed in 427, it was most probably composed during the Easter period of 426 or 427.

The present translation has been made from the text of the Maurist (Benedictine) Edition, as reproduced in J. P. Migne's *Patrologia Latina* 44.

---

10 Until the late sixteenth century the doctrinal errors attributed to Cassian, the monks of Marseilles, and Faustus of Riez, were designated collectively as *Massilienses* and *Pelagianorum reliquiae*. The term "Semi-Pelagianism," employed for the first time during the celebrated controversy, *De auxiliis,* came into general usage only after the first years of the seventeenth century.

SELECT BIBLIOGRAPHY

Text and Translations:

Maurist Edition: *Sancti Augustini Hipponensis episcopi Opera* 10 (Paris 1696) 717-744. Reproduced, with few variants, by:
Migne, J. P. *Patrologia Latina* 44 (Paris 1861) 881-912.
Chéné, J.—Pintard, J. *Sur la grâce et libre arbitre* (Bibliothèque Augustinienne: Oeuvres de saint Augustin 24 [Paris 1962] 90-207; 769-783).
Galati, L. *La grazia e il libero arbitrio* (Rome 1959).
Holmes, P.–Wallis, R. "On Grace and Free Will," in Dods, M. (ed.), *The Works of Aurelius Augustine* 15 (The Anti-Pelagian Works of St. Augustine 3; Edinburgh 1876) 13-67.
Kopp, S. *Aurelius Augustinus, Schriften gegen die Semipelagianer, lateinisch-deutsch: Gnaden und freier Wille, Zurechtweisung und Gnade* (Würzburg 1955).
Vega, G. de, *De la Gracia y del libre albedrío* (Biblioteca de Autores Cristianos 50: Obras de San Agustín 6 [2 ed. Madrid 1956] 225-301).

Secondary Works:

Bovy, L. *Grâce et liberté chez saint Augustin* (Montreal 1938).
Chéné, J. *La théologie de saint Augustin: Grâce et prédestination* (Le Puy-Lyon 1961).
La Bonnardière, A. M. "Quelques remarques sur les citations scripturaires du *'De gratia et libero arbitrio,'*" *Revue des études augustiniennes* 9 (1963) 77-85.
Léon-Dufour, X. "Grâce et libre arbitre chez saint Augustin," *Recherches de science religieuse* 30 (1940) 129-163.
Rondet, H. "La théologie de la grâce dans la correspondance de saint Augustin," *Recherches Augustiniennes* 1 (1958) 303-315.
Sage, A. "'Preparatur voluntas a Domino,'" *Revue des études augustiniennes* 10 (1964) 1-20.

GRACE AND FREE WILL

Chapter 1

1. So far as the Lord has deigned to assist me, I have already examined and set down a number of things in writing[1] on account of men who so extol and defend man's free will that they dare to deny and attempt to do away with the grace of God whereby we are called to Him and are delivered from our evil merits, and through which we acquire good merits enabling us to reach eternal life. But seeing that there are some who so defend God's grace that they deny man's free will, or who think that free will is being denied when grace is defended, I have taken care, impelled by our charity for one another, to address something on this matter to your Charity, brother Valentine, and to the rest of you, who serve God together.

Reports about you have reached me, brethren, by some in your community who have come to us and by whom we have forwarded this writing, that there are dissensions among you on this subject.[2] Accordingly, dearly beloved, I would first of all admonish you to give thanks to God for what you understand so you will not be confused by the abstruse nature of the question at hand; but as for whatever is still beyond reach of your mind, pray for understanding from the Lord, while preserving at the same time peace and charity one with another. And until He Himself leads you to grasp what you do not yet understand, walk along that way which has enabled you to reach this goal. This is the admonition given by the

---
1 Cf. Introduction, p. 245, n. 1.
2 Cf. Introduction, p. 246f.

Apostle Paul who, after having said he was not yet perfect,[3] went on to add a little later: "Let us then, as many as are perfect, be of this mind."[4] That is to say, we are perfect only to the extent that we have not yet come to that perfection which is in store for us. The Apostle goes on to add at once: "And if in any point you are minded otherwise, this also God will reveal to you."[5] Nevertheless, let us follow that path which has brought us to our present goal. As a matter of fact, by walking according to what we have attained, we shall, with God's revelation to us, be able to reach what we have not yet attained if we are otherwise minded, provided we do not forsake all that He has already revealed.

Chapter 2

2. Now He has revealed through His Sacred Scriptures that there exists in man the free choice of the will. I will show how He has revealed this, not in the language of men, but in that of God. First of all, the commandments of God themselves would be of no avail to man unless he had the free choice of the will whereby by fulfilling them he could attain the promised reward. For they were given so that man might have no excuse on the score of ignorance, as the Lord says in the Gospel with reference to the Jews: "If I had not come and spoken to them, they would have no sin. But now they have no excuse for their sin."[1] To what sin does He refer but to that heinous sin which He foreknew would be theirs even as He was so speaking, namely, that by which they would put Him to death? For until Christ had come to them in the flesh, they had no sin. The Apostle likewise says: "The wrath of God is revealed from heaven against all ungodliness

---
3 Cf. Phil. 3.12.
4 Phil. 3.15.
5 Phil. 3.16.

---
1 John 15.22.

and wickedness of those men who in wickedness hold back the truth; seeing that what may be known about God is manifest to them. For God has manifested it to them. For since the creation of the world his invisible attributes are clearly seen—His everlasting power also and divinity—being understood through the things that are made. And so they are without excuse."[2] How does he mean that they are "without excuse," except by reference to a kind of excuse that usually prompts human pride to voice such protestations as: "If I had only known, I would have done it, and consequently I did not do so because I did not know better"; or, "If I only knew how, I would do it, and therefore I do not do so because I do not know how"? This kind of excuse is taken away from them when a precept is given or when the knowledge of how to avoid sin is made clear to them.

3. But there are men who even try to use God himself to excuse themselves. It is to such that the Apostle says: "Let no one say when he is tempted, that he is tempted by God; for God is no tempter to evil, and he himself tempts no one. But everyone is tempted by being drawn away and enticed by his own passion. Thus when passion has conceived, it brings forth sin; but when sin has matured, it begets death."[3] In a similar vein Solomon's Book of Proverbs has the answer for those who would use God Himself to excuse themselves: "The folly of a man supplants his steps, and he frets in his mind against God."[4] And the Book of Ecclesiasticus has this to say: "Say not: It is through God that I fell away; for you ought not to do the things that he hates. And do not say: He has caused me to err, for he has no need of the sinful man. The Lord hates all abomination, and they that fear God shall not love it. God made man from the beginning and left him in the hand of his counsel . . . If you are willing, you will keep the commandments and fulfill faithfully his good

---

2 Rom. 1.18-20.
3 James 1.13, 15.
4 19.3.

pleasure. He has set water and fire before you: stretch forth your hand to whatever you will. Before man is life and death . . . whatever he shall choose shall be given him."[5] There we have a perfectly clear statement of the free choice of the human will.

4. What of this fact, that God in so many passages commands that all His precepts be kept and carried out? How can He command if there is no free choice? And what of that "blessed man" about whom the Psalmist says that "his will has been according to the law of the Lord"?[6] Does he not make it perfectly clear that it is by the will that a man takes his stand on the side of God's law? Finally, there are many commandments that in one way or another refer by name to the will. For example: "Be not overcome by evil, but overcome evil with good."[7] And there are similar passages, such as: "Do not become like the horse and the mule, who have no understanding";[8] and, "Do not cast off the counsels of thy mother";[9] and, "Be not wise in your own conceit";[10] and, "Do not fall away from the correction of the Lord";[11] and, "Neglect not the law";[12] and, "Do not refrain from helping the needy";[13] and, "Plan no evil against thy friends";[14] and, "Mind not the deceit of a woman";[15] and, "He would not understand that he might do well";[16] and, "They were unwilling to take correction."[17] What do such numerous passages from the Books of the Old Testament show, except that man's will is possessed of free choice?

---
5 15.11-17.
6 Ps. 1.2.
7 Rom. 12.1.
8 Ps. 31.9.
9 Prov. 1.8.
10 Prov. 3.7.
11 Prov. 3.11.
12 Prov. 3.1.
13 Prov. 3.27.
14 Prov. 3.29.
15 Prov. 5.2.
16 Prov. 36.3.
17 Prov. 1.30.

The Books of the New Testament also, composed by the Evangelists and Apostles, what other lesson do they teach us where they say: "Do not lay up for yourself treasures on earth";[18] and, "Do not be afraid of those who kill the body";[19] and, "If anyone wishes to come after me, let him deny himself";[20] and, "Peace on earth among men of good will"?[21] And the Apostle Paul says: "Let him do what he will, he does not sin if he should marry. But he who stands firm in his heart, being under no constraint, but is free to carry out his own will, and has decided to keep his virgin—he does well."[22] The Apostle likewise declares: "If I do this willingly, I have a reward";[23] and in another passage: "Be sober as just men, and do not sin."[24] And again, ". . . so that your readiness to begin may be equalled by your desire to carry it through."[25] And writing to Timothy, he says: ". . . for when they [young widows] have wantonly turned away from Christ, they wish to marry";[26] and, in another place: "And all who wish to live piously in Christ Jesus will suffer persecution."[27] And, addressing Timothy himself, he says: "Do not neglect the grace that is in you."[28] And addressing himself to Philemon, he says: ". . . that your kindness may not be as it were of necessity, but voluntary."[29] He even admonished slaves themselves to give service to their masters "from the heart, with a good will."[30] In a similar vein, Saint James says: "Therefore, my brethren, do not err . . . and do not join faith in our Lord Jesus Christ to partiality towards persons,"[31]

---
18 Matt. 6.19.
19 Matt. 10.28.
20 Matt. 16.24.
21 Luke 2.14.
22 1 Cor. 7.36-37.
23 1 Cor. 9.17.
24 1 Cor. 15-34.
25 1 Cor. 8.11.
26 1 Tim. 5.11.
27 2 Tim. 3.12.
28 1 Tim. 4.14.
29 Philem. 14.
30 Eph. 6.6-7.
31 James 2.1.

and, "Do not speak against one another."[32] And Saint John writes in his Epistle: "Do not love the world,"[33] as well as other testimonies of a like nature.

Now wherever there is the express statement not to do this or that, and whenever the performance of the will is required to do or refrain from some action, in keeping with God's commandments, that is sufficient proof of the free choice of the will. Let no man, therefore, blame God in his heart whenever he sins, but let him impute the sin to himself. Nor does the fact that something is done in accordance with God's will transfer such an act from one's own will. Indeed, when one does it of his own free will, then it deserves to be called a good work and one for which we are to expect a reward from Him of whom it is said that "He will render to everyone according to his deeds."[34]

Chapter 3

5. Any excuse that men are wont to allege on grounds of ignorance is taken away from those who know the commandments of God. But neither will they be without punishment who are ignorant of God's law. "For whoever have sinned without the law, will perish without the law; and whoever have sinned under the law, will be judged by the law."[1] I do not think that the Apostle meant to say that those who sin in ignorance will suffer worse punishment than those who know the law. It would seem that it is worse to perish than to be judged. But as the Apostle was speaking here of the Gentiles and of the Jews, since the former are without the law while the latter have received it, how can anyone dare say that those Jews who sin under the law will not perish?

---
32 James 4.11.
33 1 John 2.15.
34 Matt. 16.27.

---
1 Rom. 2.12.

For they have not believed in Christ, and it has been said of them that "they shall be judged by the law." For without faith in Christ no man can be set free, and consequently they will perish by the judgment.

Now if those ignorant of the law are in a worse condition than those who know the law, how can this saying of our Lord in the Gospel be true: "That servant who knows not his master's will and did things deserving of stripes, will be beaten with few. But that servant who knows his master's will and did things deserving of stripes, will be beaten with many stripes"?[2] As you see, this passage shows clearly that a man who knows sins more gravely than one who does not know. But we must not on this account take refuge in the darkness of ignorance so as to find there an excuse for our conduct. Not to know is one thing, unwillingness to know is another. The will is surely at fault in the kind of man of whom it is said that "He would not understand that he might do well."[3] But even the ignorance that is found, not in those unwilling to learn, but in those who, so to speak, simply do not know, is not such as to excuse anyone from the punishment of everlasting fire, even if his unbelief resulted from his never having heard what he should believe; but his suffering may perhaps be somewhat mitigated. For there was reason for the Psalmist to say: "Pour out your wrath upon the nations that know you not."[4] And the Apostle says that ". . . he will come in flaming fire to inflict punishment on those who do not know God."[5] Nevertheless so that no one of us may say, "I did not know," "I did not hear," "I did not understand," the human will is cited to show that we can have this very knowledge of God where it says: "Do not become like the horse and the mule which have no understanding."[6] But worse is the state of that man of whom it is

---

2 Luke 12.48, 47
3 Ps. 35.4.
4 Ps. 78.6.
5 1 Thess. 1.7-8.
6 Ps. 31.9.

said: "The stubborn slave will not be corrected by words; for even if he understands, he will not obey."[7] But when a man says: "I cannot do what is commanded because I am overcome by my concupiscence," he no longer has ignorance for an excuse; neither does he blame God in his heart, but he acknowledges his inner evil state and grieves over it. Yet, it is to such a one that the Apostle says: "Be not overcome by evil, but overcome evil with good."[8] And it is certainly the freedom of the will that is being cited whenever someone is told: "Be not overcome by evil." For, to be willing or unwilling has to do with each man's will.

Chapter 4

6. But one should be wary lest all such scriptural testimonies in defense of free will (and there are doubtless many others) be so construed as to leave no place for God's help and grace in leading a good and upright life deserving of an eternal reward. There is the added danger that when a man, miserable as he is, is leading a good life and doing good, or rather, when he imagines he is doing so, he will dare to glory in himself and not in the Lord and put his hope for a good life in himself, thus incurring the curse of the Prophet Jeremia where he says: "Cursed be the man that trusts in man, and makes strong the flesh of his arm, and whose heart departs from the Lord."[1]

You must understand, brethren, these words of the Prophet. Because he did not say: "Cursed be the man that trusts in himself," some one might suppose that the words, "Cursed be the man that trusts in man," meant that no one should place his hope in any other man, but in himself. It was, then, to

---
7 Prov. 29.19.
8 Rom. 12.21.

1 Jer. 17.5.

clarify his admonition that man should not put his trust even in himself that, following his statement that man should not put his trust even in himself, the Prophet immediately added the words: "And make strong the flesh of his arm." By "arm" he meant the "power to act," while the term "flesh" must be understood as "human frailty." Hence a man "makes strong the flesh of his arm" when he judges that a poor weak power, namely, a human power, is sufficient of itself to do good and does not place his hope in help from the Lord. This was why the Prophet added the words: "and whose heart departs from the Lord." This is the teaching of the Pelagians, which is not an old heresy but one that sprang up not so long ago. After a rather lengthy polemic against this heresy, the matter came before the councils of the bishops as a last resort. I have forwarded you the Proceedings of some of these, but not of all, for your perusal.[2] Let us, then, not put our hope in man in the performance of good so as to make strong the flesh of our arm, and let our heart not depart from the Lord, but rather turn to Him and say: "Be thou my helper, forsake me not; do not despise me, O God, my Savior."[3]

7. So, dearly beloved, let us also see what testimonies there are from revelation having to do with grace, without which we are incapable of doing good, just as we have shown from the scriptural testimonies above that there is the power of free choice in man for living a good life and for doing good. And I shall first of all say something about the life itself which you profess; for unless you felt a contempt for the pleasures of marriage, you would not even be gathered together in the kind of community where you lead a life of continence. Now it was while the Lord was speaking in this vein and when the disciples remarked to Him: "If the case of a man with his wife is so, it is not expedient to marry," that He replied: "Not all accept this teaching, but those

---

2 Cf. *Ep.* 215.
3 Ps. 26.9.

to whom it has been given."⁴ And when the Apostle said to Timothy: "Keep yourself chaste,"⁵ was it not to his free will that he appealed? In this same connection, he also pointed to the power of the will where he says: "Being under no constraint, but free to carry out his own will to keep his virgin."⁶ And yet, "not all accept this teaching, but those to whom it has been given." As for those to whom it is not given, they either do not will it or they fail to carry out what they will; whereas those to whom it is given are of such a will they carry out what they will. That this teaching, therefore, which all do not accept, be accepted by some, is a matter both of God's gift and of man's free choice.

8. In a further reference to conjugal chastity itself, the Apostle says expressly: "Let him do what he will; he does not sin if he should marry."⁷ But this too is God's gift, as the Scriptures say: "It is by the Lord that the woman is joined to her husband."⁸ So it is that the Teacher of the Gentiles commends by his words both conjugal chastity, which excludes adultery, and a more perfect kind of chastity which rules out the desire for intercourse, while showing that the former and the latter are both the gift of God. Writing to the Corinthians, he also admonishes married couples not to deprive one another of the marriage debt, though, following this warning, he went on to say: "Yet I would that you all were as I am myself"; for he himself refrained indeed from all intercourse. He then proceeded to say: "But each one has his own gift from God, one in this way, and another in that."⁹

What else but free will is indicated by these many precepts in God's law which forbid the commission of fornication and adultery? For these precepts would not be given unless man possessed a will of his own whereby to obey God's command-

---
4 Matt. 19.10-11.
5 1 Tim. 5.22.
6 1 Cor. 7.37.
7 1 Cor. 7.36.
8 Prov. 9.14.
9 1 Cor. 7.7.

ments. And yet, without this gift of God it is impossible to obey the precepts of chastity. That is why the Writer declares in the Book of Wisdom: "And as I knew that I could not otherwise be continent, except God gave it, this also was a matter of wisdom, to know whose gift it was."[10] On the other hand, "everyone is tempted by being drawn away and enticed by his own passion"[11] so that he fails to observe the holy precepts of chastity. If someone should say of these commandments: "I will to observe them but I am overcome by my concupiscence," the Scripture will address to his will the very reply I mentioned above: "Be not overcome by evil, but overcome evil with good."[12] But it is grace that helps to achieve this, and, unless we are assisted by grace, the law will only be a power of sin. Unless we have the spirit of grace to assist us, concupiscence is increased and strengthened by the law and its prohibitions. This is the very thing which the Teacher of the Gentiles says Himself: "Now the sting of death is sin, and the power of sin is the law."[13] Now you see why a man will say: "I will to observe the commandment, but I am overcome by the power of my concupiscence." Even when his will is called into play and he is told: "Be not overcome by evil," what good is this to him unless the command can be carried out with the help of grace?

The Apostle himself added this as a sequel when, having said that "the power of sin is the law," he immediately added these words: "But thanks be to God who has given us the victory through our Lord Jesus Christ."[14] Consequently, even the victory by which we are able to overcome sin is nothing other than the gift of God who assists our free will in such a struggle.

9. This is why our heavenly Master also says: "Watch and

---

10 8.21.
11 James 1.14.
12 Rom. 12.21.
13 1 Cor. 15.56.
14 1 Cor. 15.57.

pray that you enter not into temptation."[15] In the struggle then against his concupiscence, let each one pray that he enter not into temptation, that is to say, let him pray not to be drawn away and enticed by this concupiscence. Now if a person overcomes concupiscence by a good will, he does not enter into temptation. But man's free will is not enough unless he is given the victory by the Lord in answer to his prayer that he be not led into temptation. In fact, what clearer evidence is there for pointing to God's grace than in the case where we receive what we ask for in prayer? For if our Lord had said: "Watch that you enter not into temptation," He would appear to have merely given an admonition to man's will, whereas when He added the words "and pray," He made it clear that it is God who helps us so that we do not fall into temptation. It is to man's free will that these words have been directed: "Son, do not fall away from the correction of the Lord."[16] And the Lord says: "I have prayed for thee, Peter, that thy faith may not fail."[17] Man, then, is aided by grace so that commands are not imposed upon his will to no purpose.

Chapter 5

10. When God says: "Turn to me . . . and I will turn to you,"[1] the one part, namely, that we turn to Him, apparently pertains to the will, while the other, namely, that He Himself will also turn to us, refers to His grace. The Pelagians may think they find support in this passage for their view that God's grace is given according to our merits. Indeed, Pelagius himself did not dare make such an assertion when his cause was being heard by the bishops in the East, namely,

---

15 Matt. 26.41.
16 Prov. 3.11.
17 Luke 22.32.

---

1 Zach. 1.3.

in Palestine where Jerusalem is located.² This charge too, among others, was made against him, that he declared that God's grace is given according to our merits. Such a view is so foreign to Catholic teaching and so destructive of Christ's grace that unless Pelagius had anathematized the view charged to him, he would himself have gone out from the Council under anathema. That Pelagius pronounced this anathema in bad faith is plainly shown in his later works in which he absolutely defends this view, that God's grace is given according to our merits. The Pelagians cull passages from the Scriptures such as the one I mentioned awhile ago—"Turn to me . . . and I will turn to you"—to show that it is according to our merits for turning to God that He gives us that grace by which He Himself also turns to us. Those who hold this view fail to observe that unless this turning of ours to God were itself also a gift, we could not say to Him: "O God of hosts, convert us";³ and, "Thou wilt turn, O God, and bring us to life"; and, "Convert us, O God, our Saviour."⁴ And there are other similar passages too numerous to mention. For certainly, this coming of ours to Christ simply means that we turn to Him through belief. And yet He tells us that "No one can come to me unless it be given him by my Father."⁵

11. There is this similar passage in the Second Book of Paralipomenon that certainly gives evidence of the freedom of the will: "The Lord is with you because you are with Him. If you seek Him, you shall find; but if you forsake Him, He will forsake you."⁶ But those who assert that grace is given according to our merits take these testimonies to mean that

---

2 A reference to the Council of some thirteen bishops at Diospolis summoned at the end of 415 by the Primate of Palestine, Eulogius, at which Pelagius was obliged to answer charges brought against his teaching on grace by two exiled Gallican bishops, Heros of Arles and Lazarus of Aix. In the absence of his accusers and by skillful evasions, Pelagius succeeded in avoiding condemnation.
3 That is, "turn us."
4 Ps. 84.7, 5.
5 John 6.66.
6 2 Par. 15.2.

our merit consists in our being present with God, while the grace conferred according to our merit results in this, that God Himself also becomes present with us. Likewise, that our merit consists in seeking God and that the grace to find Him is given us according to such merit. And in the First Book of Paralipomenon there is this passage which clearly indicates the freedom of the will: "And thou my son Solomon, know thy God and serve Him with a perfect heart and a willing mind; for the Lord searches all hearts and understands all the thoughts of minds. If you shall seek Him, you shall find Him; but if you forsake Him, He will cast you off forever."[7] But the Pelagians base their opinion of man's merit on this expression: "If you seek Him," and find support for their view that grace is given according to such merit from the expression: "Thou shalt find Him." And they do their utmost to show that grace is given according to our merits, namely, that grace is not grace. For, as the Apostle so clearly expresses it, where a return is made according to merit, "the reward is not credited as a favor, but as something due."[8]

12. Certainly, merit was found in the Apostle Paul, but while he was persecuting the Church, it was evil. Hence his own avowal: "I am not worthy to be called an Apostle because I persecuted the Church of God."[9] So it was while he possessed this evil merit that good merit was given him in return for his evil merit. That is why he went on to say: "But by the grace of God I am what I am." And, in order to show that there is also free will, he at once added: "And His grace in me has not been fruitless, but I have labored more abundantly than all of them."[10] He does, in fact, exhort man's freedom also in others where he says to them: "We entreat you not to receive the grace of God in vain."[11] How, indeed, could he make this plea if their reception of grace were to result in

---
7 28.9.
8 Rom. 4.4.
9 1 Cor. 15.9.
10 1 Cor. 15.10.
11 2 Cor. 6.1.

the loss of their own will? Nevertheless, so that it might not be supposed that the will is itself capable of anything good without the grace of God just because he had said: "His grace in me has not been fruitless, but I have labored more abundantly than all of them," he at once added: "yet not I, but the grace of God with me";[12] that is to say, it is not I, but the grace of God that is with me. Accordingly, it was neither grace alone nor he himself alone, but the grace of God and himself together. It was by God's grace alone, however, that he was called by a voice from heaven and was converted by so great and efficacious a call, seeing that his merits, though great, were evil. Elsewhere, too, he says to Timothy: "Enter into my sufferings for the Gospel through the power of God. He has redeemed us and called us with a holy calling, not according to our works, but according to his own purpose and the grace which was granted us in Christ Jesus."[13] Similarly, recalling those merits which were his own, but evil, he declares: "For we ourselves also were once unwise, unbelieving, going astray, slaves to various lusts and pleasures, living in malice and envy, hateful and hating one another."[14] What recompense, indeed, was there for such evil merits, but punishment? But as God renders good for evil through grace, which is not given according to our merits, that was accomplished which he then went on to describe in these words: "But when the goodness and kindness of God our Saviour appeared, not by reason of good works that we did ourselves, but according to his mercy, he saved us by the bath of regeneration and renewal by the Holy Spirit, whom he has abundantly poured out upon us through Jesus Christ our Saviour, in order that, justified by his grace, we may be heirs in the hope of life everlasting."[15]

---

12 1 Cor. 15.10.
13 2 Tim. 1.8-9.
14 Titus 3.3.
15 Titus 3.4-7.

Chapter 6

13. We prove by these and similar testimonies of Sacred Scripture that God's grace is not given according to our merits. We see, in fact, that it is given, and continues to be given daily, not only where there are no good merits, but also where there are many previous merits that are evil. But it is when grace is unmistakably given that even our own merits begin to be good, though only because of grace. For if it is withdrawn, man falls, and he is not raised up by his free will, but rather cast down. So even when a man begins to possess good merits, he ought not to ascribe them to himself but to God, to whom the Psalmist says: "Be thou my helper, forsake me not."[1] When he says "forsake me not," he makes it plain that if he were forsaken, he would be incapable of any good by himself. This is why he also declared: "And in my abundance I said: I shall never be moved,"[2] for he had judged that to be his own whereby he so abounded that he would never be moved. But in order to show him whose good it was whereof he was beginning to boast, as if it were his own, he was reminded by the gradual withdrawal of grace to avow: "O Lord, in thy favor thou gavest strength to my beauty. Thou turnest away thy face from me, and I became troubled."[3] Consequently, man has need of God's grace not only to be made just when he is wicked, when he is changed, that is, from a wicked to a just man, and when he is given good in return for evil, but grace must accompany him, and he must lean on it in order not to fall. This is why it is written of the Church in the Canticle of Canticles: "Who is this that cometh up clad in white, leaning upon her kinsman?"[4] For she who could not do this of herself has been made white. And who has made her white but Him who says by the prophet: "If your sins be

---

1 Ps. 26.9.
2 Ps. 29.7.
3 Ps. 29.8.
4 8.5 [LXX].

as scarlet, they shall be made white as snow"?⁵ She was not gaining any good merit then at the time she was made white. But now that she has been made white, she walks aright, provided only that she continues to lean upon Him who made her white. Accordingly, Jesus Himself, upon whom the Church leans, now that she has been made white, said to His disciples: "Without me you can do nothing."⁶

14. Let us then return to the Apostle Paul who, as we have certainly seen, obtained the grace of God, who gives good in return for evil merit. Let us see what he has to say as he nears death when, writing to Timothy, he declares: "As for me, I am already being poured out in sacrifice, and the time of my deliverance is at hand. I have fought the good fight, I have finished the course, I have kept the faith."⁷ He recounts these good merits as indeed his own and, just as after his evil merits he had obtained grace, so now, after his good merits, he may obtain the crown. And take note finally of what follows: "For the rest, there is laid up for me a crown of justice which the Lord, the just Judge, will give to me in that day."⁸ To whom could he give a crown, if the merciful Father had not given his grace? And how could this be a "crown of justice" unless grace, which makes the wicked just, had gone before? And how could the crown be given as due recompense unless grace had first been given freely?

15. But when the Pelagians contend that the only grace not given according to our merits is that which remits man's sins,⁹ whereas final grace, namely, eternal life, is awarded in return for previous merits, they must not go unanswered. If, in fact, their understanding of our merits is such that they know that even these are God's gifts, there would be nothing

---

5 Isa. 1.18.
6 John 15.5.
7 2 Tim. 4.6-7.
8 2 Tim. 4.8.
9 At the Council of Diospolis, Pelagius had formally repudiated the view attributed to his companion, Celestius, that pardon is granted to penitent sinners through their merits rather than by the grace and mercy of God. Cf. *De gestis Pelagii* 35.65.

reprehensible in such a view. But inasmuch as they so extol man's merits as to maintain that man has these of himself, the Apostle is absolutely right in replying to them: "For what singles thee out? What hast thou that thou hast not received? And if thou hast received it, why dost thou boast as if thou hadst not received it?"[10] To a person so-minded, one may say in all truth that it is His own gifts that God is crowning, and not your merits, if these merits come from yourself and not from Him. If they are merits such as these, they are evil and God does not crown them; and if they are good merits, they are God's gifts since, according to the Apostle James: "Every good gift and every perfect gift is from above, coming down from the Father of Lights."[11] This is also why John, Precursor of the Lord, says: "No man can receive anything unless it is given to him from heaven,"[12] and, indeed, from that heaven from which the Holy Spirit came when, "having ascended on high," Jesus led away "captivity captive and gave gifts to men."[13] Consequently, if your good merits are God's gifts, then He does not crown them as merits of yours, but as gifts of His own.

Chapter 7

16. Let us next consider those very merits of the Apostle Paul which he said the just Judge would repay with a "crown of justice," and see whether his merits are to be reckoned as his, namely, acquired by and for himself, or whether they are gifts of God. "I have fought the good fight," he says, "I have finished the course, I have kept the faith."[1] First of all, those good works would be nothing at all if they had not been preceded by good thoughts. Observe then what he says con-

---
10 1 Cor. 4.7.
11 James 1.7.
12 John 3.27.
13 Ps. 67.19; Eph. 4.8.
---
1 2 Tim. 4.7.

cerning these very thoughts when, writing to the Corinthians, he says: "Not that we are sufficient of ourselves to think anything, as from ourselves, but our sufficiency is from God."[2] Next, let us look at his merits one by one. "I have," he says, "fought the good fight." I want to know whether this power to fight came from himself or was given him from above. But it is inconceivable that such a great teacher as Paul would not have known the law of God who says to us in the Book of Deuteronomy: "Say not in thy heart: My own might and the strength of my own hand have given me all this power. But remember the Lord thy God that he hath given thee the strength to achieve such power."[3] And what is to be gained by a "good fight," unless it is followed by a victory? And who is it that gives the victory but Him of whom the Apostle says: "Thanks be to God who has given us the victory through our Lord Jesus Christ"?[4] And in another passage, right after he had quoted the words of the Psalm: "Because for thy sake we are put to death all the day long, and we are counted as sheep for the slaughter,"[5] he went on to say: "Because in all these things we overcome because of him who has loved us."[6] We overcome, therefore, not by ourselves, but through Him who has loved us.

The next merit he mentioned was this: "I have finished the course." But this was said by the very man who elsewhere asserts: "So then there is question not of him who wills nor of him who runs, but of God showing mercy."[7] There is no way to turn this sentence around and make it say: "It is a question not of God showing mercy, but of man's willing and running"; for anyone who would dare speak this way shows plainly that he is contradicting the Apostle.

17. The last merit mentioned by the Apostle was this:

---

2 2 Cor. 3.5.
3 8.17-18.
4 1 Cor. 15.57.
5 Ps. 43.22.
6 Rom. 8.36-37.
7 Rom. 9.16.

"I have kept the faith." But these words were spoken by the very man who says elsewhere: "I have obtained mercy from the Lord that I might be faithful."[8] For he did not say: "I have obtained mercy because I was faithful," but rather, "that I might be faithful," thereby making it plain that to have faith itself is only possible through God's mercy and that it is a gift of God. He teaches the same thing where he says: "For by grace you have been saved through faith; and that not of yourselves, for it is the gift of God."[9] The Pelagians might possibly allege that we have received grace because we have believed, so as to ascribe faith to themselves, and grace to God. This is why, having said "through faith," he added, "and that, not from yourselves, for it is the gift of God." Again, so that they might not assert that they had merited such a gift by their works, the Apostle at once added: "Not as the outcome of works, lest anyone may boast."[10] It was not that he denied good works, or stripped them of all value, for he states that God renders to each one according to his works, but rather, that works come from faith, and not faith from works. Accordingly, our works of justice come from Him who is also the source of our faith, about which it is said: "The just man lives by faith."[11]

18. Because they fail to grasp what the Apostle means where he says: "We reckon that a man is justified by faith independently of the works of the law,"[12] some men have understood him to say that faith is sufficient for man, even though he lives a bad life and is without good works.[13] It is unthinkable that the "vessel of election" should hold this

---

[8] 1 Cor. 7.25 ("faithful," i.e. believing).
[9] Eph. 2.8.
[10] Eph. 2.9.
[11] Rom. 1.17.
[12] Rom. 3.28.
[13] Some years earlier, probably in 413, Augustine composed a short treatise against this error, *De fide et operibus.* As he points out in the *Retractations,* it was directed against certain members of the laity "who so divorce Christian faith from good works that they are convinced that one is able to attain eternal salvation, not, of course, without faith, but without good works" (2.64).

view. It was he who, upon having stated in a certain passage: "For in Christ Jesus neither circumcision is of any avail, nor uncircumcision," added at once, "but faith which works through charity."[14] It is this same kind of faith which separates the faithful ones of God from the unclean devils, since even these, as the Apostle James says, "believe and tremble,"[15] though they do not perform good works. Theirs, then, is not that faith by which the just man lives, namely, a faith which so works through charity that God requites it with eternal life in accordance with its works. But as these same good works also come from God, who bestows faith and charity upon us, this same Teacher of the Gentiles has accordingly spoken of "eternal life" itself as a grace.

Chapter 8

19. A serious problem arises here which demands a solution, if only the Lord will provide us with it. For if eternal life is given in return for good works, as the Scripture clearly indicates where it says that "God will render to everyone according to his works,"[1] then how is it possible for eternal life to be a grace? For grace is not given in return for works, but freely, as the Apostle himself testifies: "Now to him who works, the reward is not credited as a favor but as something due."[2] Again, he says: "There is a remnant left, selected out of grace," and then adds: "And if out of grace, then not in virtue of works; otherwise grace is no longer grace."[3] How, then, is eternal life "grace," if it is obtained in virtue of works? May it be that the Apostle did not call eternal life a grace? On the contrary, he has said this so plainly that it is

---
14 Gal. 5.6.
15 James 2.19.

---
1 Rom. 2.6.
2 Rom. 4.4.
3 Rom. 11.5-6.

absolutely impossible to deny it. His words do not need a man of acute understanding, but one who merely pays attention. For, having said that "the wages of sin is death," he added at once: "But the grace of God is life everlasting in Christ Jesus our Lord."[4]

20. In my opinion, no solution for the problem is possible unless we see that our good works themselves, which enable us to receive eternal life, are referred to God's grace by reason of our Lord's words: "Without me you can do nothing."[5] In saying that "by grace you have been saved through faith, and that, not from yourselves, for it is the gift of God; not as the outcome of works, lest anyone may boast,"[6] the Apostle himself certainly saw that men might construe his words to mean that good works are not necessary for believers, but that faith alone is sufficient for them. Again, he also saw that men might possibly boast of their good works as if they were sufficient of themselves to perform them, and that is why he immediately added these words: "For we are his workmanship, created in Christ Jesus in good works, which God has made ready beforehand that we may walk in them."[7]

Why is it that in commending God's grace the Apostle should say: "Not as the outcome of works, lest anyone may boast," and then give as a reason: "For we are his workmanship, created in Christ Jesus in good works"? How, then, are we to understand the expression, "not as the outcome of works, lest anyone may boast"? Pay attention now and try to grasp the import of the expression, "not as the outcome of works." These refer to works that come from yourself, as your own, and not to those in which God has molded you, namely, works in which God has formed and created you. It is of these latter that the Apostle says: "We are his workmanship, created in Christ Jesus in good works." He was not speaking

---

4 Rom. 6.23.
5 John 15.5.
6 Eph. 4.8-9.
7 Eph. 4.10.

of that creation whereby we were made men, but of a creation whereof the Psalmist, who was fully a man, spoke when he said: "Create a clean heart in me, O God,"[8] and of which the Apostle says: "If then any man is in Christ, he is a new creature: the former things have passed away; behold they are made new! But all things are from God."[9] It follows then that we are molded, that is, formed and created, in good works which we ourselves have not prepared but "which God has made beforehand that we may walk in them." It follows, my dearly beloved, that if our good life is nothing more than the grace of God, then eternal life, the recompense for a good life is, without any doubt, also a grace of God; for it is freely given in recompense for that which has also been freely given. Now a good life that is so rewarded is itself simply a grace, whereas eternal life, which is given in return as a recompense, is a grace given for a grace, a kind of remuneration, as it were, in accordance with justice. Hence the truth, as it is indeed a truth, that God "will render to everyone according to his works."[10]

Chapter 9

21. But perhaps you will ask whether we have ever read the expression "grace for grace" in the Scriptures. Now you have the Gospel according to John, outstanding for its great clarity, where speaking of Christ the Lord, John the Baptist says: "And of his fullness we have all received, grace for grace."[1] It is, then, from His fullness that we have, each according to his capacity, received our several portions, so to speak, that enable us to lead a good life, "according as God

---
8 Ps. 5.12.
9 2 Cor. 5.17-18.
10 Matt. 16.27; Rom. 2.6.

---
1 1.16.

has apportioned to each one the measure of faith";[2] for "each one has his own gift from God, one in this way, and another in that."[3] And this is grace. But, over and above this, we shall also receive "grace for grace" when we will be given eternal life, of which the Apostle has said: "But the grace of God is life everlasting in Christ Jesus our Lord."[4] He had previously declared, and rightly so, that the wages of sin is death, seeing that everlasting death is a kind of payment given in return for service to the devil. Though he could have said, and rightly so, that the wages of a just life is life everlasting, he nevertheless chose to say: "The grace of God is life everlasting," so we might thus understand that God brings us to life everlasting, not for any merits of ours, but in accordance with His mercy. And it is to God that the Psalmist refers where, addressing his soul, he says: "Who crowns thee with mercy and compassion."[5]

But is not this crown given in return for good works? Yes, but inasmuch as good works in the just are performed by Him of whom it is said: "For it is God who of his good pleasure works in you both the will and the performance,"[6] this is why the Psalmist said: "Who crowns you with mercy and compassion." For it is through His mercy that we perform the good works for which a crown is given us in return. And we must not suppose that when he said: "For it is God who of his good pleasure works in you both the will and the performance," he was doing away with free will. If such were the case, he would not have declared previously: "Work out your salvation with fear and trembling."[7] For when they are given the command "to work," an appeal is made to free will, whereas the command to do this "with fear and trembling" is given so they will not take credit to themselves

---

2 Rom. 12.3.
3 1 Cor. 7.7.
4 Rom. 6.23.
5 Ps. 102.4.
6 Phil. 2.13.
7 Phil. 2.12.

for their good works and become elated over them as if they were their own. It is almost as if the Apostle, upon being asked why he had said "with fear and trembling," had explained this expression by saying: "For it is God who works in you." Indeed, if you are "in fear and trembling," you will not be elated as if these were your own good works since it is God who works in you.

Chapter 10

22. Accordingly, brethren, you should not do evil with your free will, but good, for this is what the law of God prescribes in the Sacred Scriptures, both in the Old and New Testaments. Yes, let us read and try with the Lord's help to understand what the Apostle means when he says: "For by the works of the Law no human being shall be justified before him, for through law comes the recognition of sin."[1] He did not say the "destruction" of sin, but its "recognition." Now when a man comes to a knowledge of sin, the law undoubtedly works wrath unless man is aided by grace to avoid what he knows is sinful. This is what the Apostle says in another place, and these are his own words: "The Law works wrath."[2] He said this because God's wrath is more severe towards a transgressor who knows sin by the law, and yet commits it. Such a man is indeed a transgressor of the law, as the Apostle also remarks in the same passage where he says: "For where there is no law, neither is there transgression."[3] This is why he also says in another place: "That we may serve in newness of spirit and not in oldness of letter."[4] By "oldness of letter," he would have us to understand the law, whereas by "newness of spirit," nothing else but grace. Furthermore, so that

---
1 Rom. 3.20. The Vulgate reads *ex operibus legis;* Aug. *ex lege.*
2 Rom. 4.15.
3 Rom. 4.15.
4 Rom. 7.6.

no one might think he was blaming the law, or finding fault with it, he immediately faced the problem by asking: "What shall we say then? Is the Law sin? By no means!" He then went on to say: "Yet I did not know sin save through the Law." This is what he stated where he had said: "Through Law comes the recognition of sin." "For I had not known lust," he says, "unless the Law had said: 'Thou shalt not lust.' But sin, having thus found an occasion, worked in me by means of the commandment all manner of lust, for without the Law sin was dead. Once upon a time I was living without law, but when the commandment came, sin revived, and I died, and the commandment that was unto life was discovered in my own case to be unto death. For sin, having taken occasion from the commandment, deceived me, and through it killed me. So that the Law indeed is holy and the commandment holy and just and good. Did then that which was good become death to me? By no means! But sin, that it might be manifest as sin, worked death for me through that which is good, in order that sin by reason of the commandment might become immeasurably sinful."[5] And writing to the Galatians, he says: "But we know that man is not justified by the works of the Law, but by the faith of Jesus Christ. Hence we also believe in Christ Jesus, that we may be justified by the faith of Christ, and not by the works of the Law; because by the works of the Law no man will be justified."[6]

Chapter 11

23. Why, then, do men so utterly vain and perverse as the Pelagians say that the Law itself is the grace of God which helps us not to sin? In making this assertion, do they not unhappily find themselves in contradiction with so great an

---
[5] Rom. 7.7-13.
[6] Gal. 2.16.

Apostle, and this beyond the shadow of a doubt? It is he who says that sin obtained its power against man by the Law and that it is by the commandment, though this is holy and just and good, that the Law does nevertheless kill man, bringing about his death by what is good; also, that man is not delivered from this death unless the spirit gives life to him whom the letter had killed, as he indicates in another passage where he says: "The letter kills, but the spirit gives life."[1] Nevertheless, blind as they are to God's light and deaf to His voice, the Pelagians stubbornly maintain that the letter, which kills, is what gives life and thus go counter to the spirit that gives life. "Therefore, brethren," if I may admonish you in the Apostle's own words, "we are debtors, not to the flesh, that we should live according to the flesh, for if you live according to the flesh, you will die; but if by the spirit you put to death the deeds of the flesh, you will live."[2] I have quoted this passage so that I might make use of the Apostle's words to deter your free will from evil and to exhort it to what is good. Nor should you on this account glory in man, that is to say, in yourselves, and not in the Lord, when you are not living according to the flesh, but are putting to death by the spirit the deeds of the flesh. So that those to whom he thus spoke might not be elated by thinking they could perform these good works by their own spirit rather than by God's, because he had said, "but if by the spirit you put to death the deeds of the flesh," he hastened to add: "For whoever are led by the spirit of God, they are the sons of God."[3] So whenever you put to death by the spirit the deeds of the flesh that you may live, give glory and praise and thanksgiving to Him by whose spirit you are so led that you can perform such works as make it manifest that you are sons of God, "for whoever are led by the spirit of God, they are the sons of God."

---

1 2 Cor. 3.6.
2 Rom. 8.12-13.
3 Rom. 8.14.

Chapter 12

24. As many, therefore, as are led by their own spirit, trusting in their own strength, and assisted only by the law, without grace, are not the sons of God. The same Apostle says of such men that ". . . being ignorant of the justice of God and seeking to establish their own, they have not submitted to the justice of God."[1] He said this about the Jews who, because of their self-confidence, rejected grace and as a result did not believe in Christ. The Jews, he says, seek to establish a justice of their own that comes from the Law; not that the Law was established by them, but rather that they had placed their justice in the Law which comes from God, by supposing that they were able of themselves to fulfill this Law. For they were ignorant of the justice of God, not that justice whereby God is just, but one that comes to man from God. And that you may understand why the Apostle asserted that theirs was a justice coming from the Law, whereas God's justice comes to man from God, hear what he has to say in another passage where, referring to Christ, he declares: "For his sake I have not only counted all things as loss but I also count them as dung that I may gain Christ and be found in Him, not having a justice of my own, which is from the Law, but that which is from faith in Christ, which is of God."[2]

Since the Law is not his but God's, what does he mean by saying, "not having a justice of my own, which is from the Law," except that, though it comes from the Law, he spoke of this justice as his own precisely because he supposed he could fulfill the Law by his own volition without the help of that grace which comes through faith in Christ? This is why, having said, "not having a justice of my own, which is from the Law," he followed with the words, "but that which is from faith in Christ, which is of God." Such justice was

---

[1] Rom. 10.3.
[2] Phil. 3.8-9.

unknown to those men who, as the Apostle remarks, "are ignorant of the justice of God," ignorant, that is, of that justice which comes from God (not the justice conferred by the letter that killeth, but by the life-giving spirit); to men who "seek to establish their own justice" which the Apostle declared to be of the Law when he said "not having a justice of my own which is from the Law." Such men have not "submitted to the justice of God," namely, to the grace of God. For they were living under the Law, not under grace, and were therefore under the dominion of sin from which man is freed, not by the Law, but by grace. This is why he says in another place: "For sin shall not have dominion over you, since you are not under the Law but under grace."[3] It is not that the Law is evil, but that it makes those under it guilty by giving commands without providing help to fulfill them. As a matter of fact, grace helps a person to become a doer of the Law, and, without such grace, a man living under the Law will be merely a hearer of the Law. Accordingly, addressing himself to men of this kind, the Apostle says: "You who would be justified in the Law . . . have fallen away from grace."[4]

Chapter 13

25. Who could be so deaf to the words of the Apostle, who so utterly foolish, and indeed, so insanely ignorant of what he is saying, as to dare affirm that the Law is grace when the Apostle, who did know what he was saying, declares openly: "You who would be the justified in the Law . . . have fallen away from grace"? But if the Law is not grace, seeing that it is not the Law which helps us to observe the Law itself, but grace, could it be that nature itself is grace? For this is what the Pelagians have also dared to assert. They

---
3 Rom. 6.14.
4 Gal. 5.4.

affirm that grace is the kind of nature wherein we have been so created that we possess a rational mind, enabling us to understand, and, being made after God's image, to rule over the fish and the birds of the air and over every animal that creeps on land. But this is not the grace which the Apostle commends to us through faith in Jesus Christ. For we certainly share this nature in common even with men who are wicked and unbelievers, whereas grace through faith in Jesus Christ is found only in those who have faith itself. "For not all men have the faith."[1] In short, just as the Apostle says in all truth to those who have fallen from grace in their desire to be justified by the Law: "For if justice is by the Law, then Christ died in vain,"[2] so too it could be said in all truth to those who think that the grace he commends and receives through faith in Christ is nature, and if justice comes from nature, then Christ died in vain. For the Law was then in existence, and yet it did not justify; and nature was then existing, and yet it did not justify. It was not in vain then that Christ died in order that the Law might be fulfilled through Him who declared: "I have not come to destroy the Law but to fulfill it";[3] and that our nature, lost by Adam, might be restored through Him who said He had come "to seek and to save what was lost."[4] It was in His future coming too, that the Fathers of old had put their faith.

26. The Pelagians likewise assert that God's grace, given through faith in Christ, and which is neither the Law nor nature, has power only to remit past sins and does not help us avoid future sins or to overcome temptations. But if this were true, then in our recitation of the Lord's prayer we would not add the words, "and lead us not into temptation" right after saying, "forgive us our debts as we also forgive our debtors."[5] We recite the former part of the prayer that our

---

1 2 Thess. 3.2.
2 Gal. 2.21.
3 Matt. 5.17.
4 Luke 19.10; Matt. 18.11.
5 Matt. 6.12-13.

sins may be forgiven, and the latter, that we may avoid sin, or overcome it. There would be no reason to make these petitions to our Father in heaven if we were able to do these things by human will-power. Now I would advise you and strongly urge you to read attentively the work of Saint Cyprian which he composed *On the Lord's Prayer* and, so far as God helps you, to understand and commit it to memory. You will note in this book how he addresses himself to the free will of those whom he is instructing in this treatise so as to make it clear that they are to ask in prayer for help to fulfill all that the Law commands. But this would certainly be meaningless if man's will were sufficient to do so without the help of God.

Chapter 14

27. But we have shown these men to be no defenders of free will, but rather its boastful destroyers. For the grace bestowed upon us through Jesus our Lord is neither the knowledge of God's law nor nature nor the mere remission of sin, but that grace which makes it possible to fulfill the Law so that our nature is set free from the dominion of sin. Since, as I say, the Pelagians have already been proven wrong on these points, they now resort to this device in their endeavor to show that God's grace is given according to our merits. They say this, for example: "Though grace is not given in view of good works, inasmuch as it is by grace that we do good, it is given nevertheless in view of the merits of a good will," since, as they maintain, "the good will of a man at prayer precedes his prayer, this will is, in turn, preceded by the will to believe, so that, consequent upon such merits, there follows the bestowal of grace by God who hears our prayers."

28. I have already discussed above the subject of faith,[1]

---
1 Cf. 7.16-17.

namely, the will to believe, so as to show that faith pertains to grace. The Apostle, for example, did not say, "I have obtained mercy because I was faithful," but rather, "I have obtained mercy to be faithful."[2] There are also other testimonies, including the passage: "Be wise unto sobriety, according as God has divided to everyone the measure of faith,"[3] and the passage I already quoted: "By grace you have been saved through faith; and that not from yourselves, but it is the gift of God."[4] Besides, there are his words to the Ephesians: "Peace be to the brethren, and love with faith, from God the Father and the Lord Jesus Christ."[5] And another passage where he says: "For you have been given the favor on Christ's behalf—not only to believe in him but also to suffer for him."[6] Both of these, therefore, namely, the will to believe and the patience to suffer, pertain to grace since, as he stated, both have been given. And there is the very important passage where he says: "Since we have the same spirit of faith . . ."[7] He does not say "knowledge of faith," but "spirit of faith." He put it this way that we might understand how faith is given even without our asking for it, so that other graces may be granted in answer to the prayer of faith. "How," he asks, "are they to call upon him in whom they have not believed?"[8] Accordingly, it is the spirit of grace that enables us to have faith so that we may, through faith, ask in prayer for the strength to do what is commanded of us. This is why the Apostle constantly puts faith before the Law, seeing that we are incapable of doing what the Law commands unless, through faith, we ask in prayer for the strength to do so.

29. For if faith pertains to the will alone and is not a gift

---

2 1 Cor. 7.25.
3 Rom. 12.3.
4 Eph. 2.8.
5 Eph. 6.23.
6 Phil. 1.29.
7 2 Cor. 4.15.
8 Rom. 10.14.

of God, then why do we pray that those who refuse to believe should come to believe? It would be absolutely useless for us to do this unless we were entirely correct in our belief that Almighty God can bring about a conversion of the will to believe even in those whose wills are perverse and hostile to the faith. The Psalmist does in fact put his finger on man's free will where he says: "Today if you shall hear His voice, harden not your hearts."[9] But if God were not able to take away even that hardness of heart, He could not declare through his Prophet: "I will take away the stony heart out of their flesh, and will give them a heart of flesh."[10] The fact that this prophecy was made with reference to the New Testament is clearly shown by the Apostle where he says: "You are our letter . . . written not with ink but with the spirit of the living God, not on tablets of stone but on fleshy tablets of the heart."[11] We are not to think that this was meant to imply that those who should live spiritual lives might live according to the flesh. What is meant is this: as a stone, with which a hardened heart is compared, is without any feeling, what was left for God but to compare a heart with understanding with flesh and its capacity for feeling? The Prophet Ezechiel expresses it this way: "I will give them another heart and give them a new spirit; and I will take away the stony heart out of their flesh, and I will give them a heart of flesh that they may walk in my commandments and keep my judgments and do them: and that they may be my people, and I may be their God."[12] Would it not be the height of absurdity for us to maintain that there was some antecedent good merit in any man's good will to bring about the removal of his stony heart when, in fact, this stony heart simply signifies a will that is obstinate and absolutely unbending in its opposition to God? For where a good will precedes, there is, to be sure, no longer a heart of stone.

---
9 Ps. 94.8.
10 Ezech. 11.19.
11 2 Cor. 3.2-3.
12 Ezech. 11.19-20.

30. In another passage, too, God makes it very plain through the same Prophet that it is He who brings about such changes, not by reason of any good merits found in men, but for His own name's sake, where He says: "It is not for your sake that I will do this, O house of Israel, but for my holy name's sake, which you have profaned among the nations whither you went. And I will sanctify my great name which was profaned among the Gentiles, which you have profaned in the midst of them: that the Gentiles may know that I am the Lord, saith the Lord God, when I shall be sanctified in you before their eyes. For I will take you from among the Gentiles and will gather you together out of all the countries and will bring you into your own land. And I will pour upon you clean water and you shall be cleansed from all your filthiness and I will cleanse you from all your idols. And I will give you a new heart and put a new spirit within you. And I will take away the stony heart out of your flesh and I will give you a heart of flesh. And I will put my spirit in the midst of you, and I will cause you to walk in my commandments and to keep my judgments, and do them."[13]

Who is so blind as not to see, who so stone-like as not to perceive, that this grace is not given according to the merit of a good will, when the Lord so testifies where He says: "I will do this, O house of Israel, for my holy name's sake"? Why, in fact, did He say, "I will do this, but for my holy name's sake," if not to keep them from supposing that this was done in view of their good merits, as the Pelagians are not unashamed to maintain? The Lord makes it clear that they not only had no previous good merits but even had evil merits when He says: ". . . but for my holy name's sake which you have profaned among the Gentiles." How can anyone fail to see that the profanation of the Lord's name is a dreadful evil? But yet "for my name's sake," He says, "which you have profaned," I will make you good, but not for your own sake

---
13 Ezech. 36.22-27.

"And I will sanctify my great name," He says, "which was profaned among the Gentiles, which you have profaned in the midst of them." He says He is going to sanctify His name which He had said before was holy. Now this is the very thing we pray for in the Lord's prayer when we say: "Hallowed be thy name," namely, that His name, which of itself is certainly ever holy, may be sanctified among men. There then follow the words: "That the Gentiles may know that I am the Lord, says the Lord God, when I shall be sanctified in you before their eyes." Accordingly, though He is Himself forever holy, yet is He sanctified among those on whom He bestows His grace when He removes from them the stony heart with which they had profaned the name of the Lord.

Chapter 15

31. But lest anyone should suppose that men do nothing themselves in this matter by their free will, it is accordingly said in the Psalm: "Harden not your hearts";[1] and in Ezechiel himself: "Cast away from you all your transgressions which you have wickedly committed against me and make to yourselves a new heart and a new spirit, and keep all my commandments. And why will you die, O house of Israel? For I desire not the death of him who dies, says the Lord God; be converted and live."[2] We should keep in mind that the God who tells us, "Be converted and live," is He to whom we pray, "Convert us, O God."[3] We should keep in mind that He says: "Cast away from you all your transgressions," even though it is He Himself "who justifies the impious."[4] We should keep in mind that He who says, "Make to yourselves a new heart and a new spirit," is the very one who declares: "I will give you

---
1 Ps. 94.8.
2 Ezech. 18.31-32.
3 Ps. 79.4; 84.5-7.
4 Rom. 4.5.

a new heart and put a new spirit within you."⁵ How then can He say, "Make to yourselves," when He says, "I will give you"? Why does God command something of us if He is going to give it Himself? Why does He give, if it is man who must act? Only because He gives what He commands, whenever He helps man to do what He commands.⁶ Free will is always present in us, but it is not always good. For it is either free of justice, while serving sin, and then it is evil; or it is free of sin, while serving justice, and then it is good. But the grace of God is always good and brings about a good will in a man who before was possessed of an evil will. It is by this grace, too, that this same good will, once it begins to exist, is expanded and made so strong that it is able to fulfill whatever of God's commandments it wishes, whenever it does so with a strong and perfect will. This is the force of those words of the Scripture: "If thou wilt keep my commandments . . . ."⁷ So let the man who has the will, but not the power, realize that he does not yet have a perfect will, and let him pray for a will strong enough to fulfill the commandments. This is certainly the way a man receives help to do as he is commanded. The will is of use only when we have the power, while the power is of use only when we have the will. What good is it to us if we will what we cannot do, or are unwilling to do what we are able to do?

Chapter 16

32. The Pelagians imagine they know something important when they assert "God would not command something that He knew man was unable to do." How could anyone be

---
5 Ezech. 36.26.
6 The same thought is expressed in the famous formula of the *Confessions: Da quod iubes et iube quod vis* (10.29.40; 10.37.60). In the *De dono perseverantiae* (20.53), composed in 429, Augustine reports how the Pelagian controversy was occasioned by Pelagius' reading of these passages.
7 Ecclus. [Sirach] 15.16.

ignorant of that? But God does give commands beyond our power precisely in order that we may know what it is we ought to ask of Him. For it is faith itself which accomplishes through prayer that which the Law commands. Now He who said: "If thou wilt, thou shalt keep the commandments," goes on to say a little later in the same Book of Ecclesiasticus: "Who shall set a guard before my mouth and a seal of wisdom upon my lips, that I fall not by them and that my tongue destroy me not?"[1] To be sure, he had already received these commands: "Keep thy tongue from evil and thy lips from speaking guile."[2] Inasmuch, then, as he spoke the truth in saying: "If thou wilt, thou shalt keep the commandments," why does he ask that a guard be set before his mouth as the Psalmist does where he asks: "Set a watch, O Lord, before my mouth"?[3] Why are God's commandments and his own free will not enough for him when in fact he will keep the commandments if he so wills? How many are the commandments of God directed against pride! He is familiar with them already, and he will keep them if he will have the will to do so. Why, then, does he say a little later: "O Lord, Father and God of my life . . . give me not haughtiness of my eyes."[4] Already the Law had commanded him: "Thow shalt not covet."[5] Let him therefore only do what is commanded since, if he so wills, he will keep the commandments. Why then does he go on to say: "Turn away from me all coveting"?[6] How many are the commandments of God directed against impurity! Let him only observe them because he will keep them if he so wills. Why is it then that he crys out to God: "Let not the greediness of the belly and the lusts of the flesh take hold of me"?[7] Were we to address these questions to him in person, he

---

1 22.23.
2 Ps. 33.14.
3 Ps. 140.3.
4 Ecclus. [Sirach] 23.4-5.
5 Exod. 20.17.
6 Ecclus. [Sirach] 23.5.
7 Ecclus. [Sirach] 33.6.

would reply altogether correctly and say: "From that prayer of mine wherein I beg these favors of God, you may see what was meant when I said, 'If thou wilt, thou shalt keep the commandments.'" Certainly, we do keep the commandments if only we have the will to do so. But inasmuch as "the will is prepared by the Lord,"[8] we must ask of Him that strength of will which is sufficient to bring our will to act. Certainly, in willing anything, it is we who will, but it is He who enables us to will what is good. And the words I quoted a short while ago refer to Him, namely: "The will is prepared by the Lord." It is further said of Him: "The steps of a man are directed by the Lord and He it is who wills his way";[9] and, "It is God who works in you even to will."[10]

In doing anything, it is certainly we who act, but it is God's act that enables us to act by His bestowal of efficacious power upon our will, as He says Himself: "And I will cause you to walk in my commandments and to keep my judgments, and to do them."[11] In saying, "I will cause you . . . to do them," what else is He saying but that, "I will take away the stony heart out of your flesh," which caused you not to do them, and, "I will give you a heart of flesh, which will cause you to do them"? And what else is meant here except that, "I will take away the obstinate heart which caused you not to do them and I will give you an obedient heart which will cause you to do them"? He who causes us to act is He to whom the Psalmist says: "Set a watch, O Lord, before my mouth,"[12] which is the same as to say: "Cause me to set a watch before my mouth." It was only after he had obtained this favor from God that he declared: "I have set a guard to my mouth."[13]

---

8 Prov. 8.35. Cf. A. Sage, " 'Preparatur voluntas a Domino,'" *Revue des études augustiniennes* 10 (1964) 1-20.
9 Ps. 26.33.
10 Phil. 2.13.
11 Ezech. 36.27.
12 Ps. 140.3.
13 Ps. 38.2.

Chapter 17

33. Whoever, therefore, has the will to keep God's commandment, but lacks the power, already possesses a good will, but one that is still small and feeble. But once he comes to have a great and robust will, he will have this power. When the martyrs, for example, carried out those great commandments, they did so with a great will, namely, with that great love whereof the Lord Himself says: "Greater love than this no one has, that one lay down his life for his friends."[1] This is also the reason why the Apostle says: "For he who loves his neighbor has fulfilled the law. For 'Thou shalt not commit adultery; Thou shalt not kill; Thou shalt not steal; Thou shalt not covet'; and if there is any other commandment, it is summed up in the saying, 'Thou shalt love thy neighbor as thyself.' Love does no evil to a neighbor. Love therefore is the fulfillment of the Law."[2]

When the Apostle Peter thrice denied the Lord out of fear, he did not yet have this love, for, as John the Evangelist says in his Epistle: "There is no fear in love, but perfect love casts out fear."[3] Yet, though it was not great or perfect, love was not wanting in Peter when he declared: "I will lay down my life for thee,"[4] inasmuch as he fancied he could do what he had the will to do. And who was it that had begun to impart to him this love, however small, but God who prepares our will and brings to perfection through His cooperation the work which His operation begins in us? For He who first works in us the power to will is the same who cooperates in bringing this work to perfection in those who will it. Accordingly, the Apostle says: "I am convinced of this, that he who has begun a good work in you will bring it to perfection

---

1 John 15.13.
2 Rom. 13.8-10.
3 1 John 4.18.
4 John 14.37.

until the day of Christ Jesus."[5] God, then, works in us, without our cooperation, the power to will, but once we begin to will, and do so in a way that brings us to act, then it is that He cooperates with us. But if He does not work in us the power to will or does not cooperate in our act of willing, we are powerless to perform good works of a salutary nature. With reference to His working in us the power to will, it is said: "For it is God who works also in you to will,"[6] whereas, concerning His cooperation in us, once we begin to will so that our volition brings us to act, the Apostle says: "Now we know that for those who love God all things work together unto good."[7] What does he mean by "all things," if not the terrible and cruel sufferings we now endure? To be sure, this yoke of Christ, so burdensome for our infirmity, is made light where there is love. For the Lord has said that His burden is light[8] for men such as Peter was at the time he suffered for Christ, not as he was when he denied Christ.

34. It is such a charity as this, namely, a will on fire with God's love, which is commended to us by the Apostle where he says: "Who shall separate us from the love of God? Shall tribulation, or distress, or persecution, or hunger, or nakedness, or danger, or the sword? Even as it is written: 'For thy sake we are put to death all the day long. We are regarded as sheep for the slaughter.' But in all things we overcome be-

---

5 Phil. 1.6.
6 Phil. 2.13.
7 Rom. 8.28. Here, as well as in the subsequent companion treatise *De correptione et gratia* (7.14), Augustine adopts the reading *cooperatur* instead of the Vulgate reading *cooperantur*, employed in his previous works. Taken in conjunction with the previous text from the Philippians, "For it is God who works *(operatur)* in you also to will," the reading *cooperatur* enables Augustine to draw the distinction between *gratia operans* and *gratia cooperans,* which corresponds with the distinction made above between "imperfect" and "perfect" love, as exemplified in the conduct of the apostle Peter. Theologians of the later Augustinian school will base their distinction of *gratia versatilis* (inefficacious grace) and *gratia efficax* (efficacious grace) on this passage of *Grace and Free Will.* The former, they contend, was sufficient for man in the state of innocence, whereas the latter is necessary for man after the Fall.
8 Cf. Matt. 11.30.

cause of him who has loved us. For I am sure that neither death, nor life, nor angels, nor principalities, nor things present, nor things to come, nor height, nor depth, nor any other creature will be able to separate us from the love of God, which is in Christ Jesus our Lord."[9] And in another passage: "And I point out to you a yet more excellent way. If I should speak with the tongues of men and angels, but do not have charity, I have become as sounding brass and a tinkling cymbal. And if I have prophecy and know all mysteries and all knowledge, and if I have all faith so as to remove mountains, yet do not have charity, I am nothing. And if I distribute all my goods to feed the poor, and if I deliver my body to be burned, yet do not have charity, it profits me nothing. Charity is patient, is kind; charity does not envy, is not pretentious, is not puffed up, is not ambitious, is not self-seeking, is not provoked; thinks no evil, does not rejoice over wickedness, but rejoices with truth; bears with all things, believes all things, hopes all things, endures all things. Charity never fails."[10] And a little later in the same passage: "There abide faith, hope, and charity, these three: but the greatest of these is charity. Aim at charity."[11] Likewise, writing to the Galatians, he says: "For you have been called to liberty, brethren; only do not use liberty as an occasion for sensuality, but by charity serve one another. For the whole Law is fulfilled in one word: 'Thou shalt love thy neighbor as thyself.' "[12] This is the very thing he says to the Romans: "For he who loves his neighbor has fulfilled the Law."[13] And in a similar vein to the Colossians: "But about all these things have charity, which is the bond of perfection."[14] Writing to Timothy, he says: "Now the end of the commandment is charity," a kind of charity, as he goes on to add, which is

---

9 Rom. 8.35-39.
10 1 Cor. 12.31; 13.1-8.
11 1 Cor. 13.13-14.1.
12 5.13-14.
13 13.8.
14 3.14.

"from a pure heart, and a good conscience, and an unfeigned faith."[15] Moreover, when he tells the Corinthians: "Let all that you do be done in charity,"[16] he makes it clear enough that even corrections are to be administered with charity, though they are felt to be sharp and bitter by those who are undergoing correction. Accordingly, once he had given this direction in another passage: "Reprove the irregular, comfort the fainthearted, support the weak, be patient towards all men," he at once added: "See that no one renders evil for evil to any man."[17] Even in correcting the irregular, therefore, we are not rendering evil for evil, but rather good for evil. And what else but love can do all this?

35. And there is the Apostle Peter who says: "But above all things have a constant mutual charity among yourselves; for charity covers a multitude of sins."[18] And the Apostle James likewise says: "If, however, you fulfill the royal law, according to the Scriptures, 'Thou shalt love thy neighbor as thyself,' you do well."[19] Similarly, the Apostle John declares: "He who loves his brother abides in the light";[20] and in another place: "Whoever is not just is not of God, nor is He just who does not love his brother. For this is the message that you have heard from the beginning, that we should love one another."[21] And again: "And this is his commandment, that we should believe in the name of his Son Jesus Christ, and love one another";[22] also: "And this commandment we have from him, that he who loves God should love his brother also."[23] And then a little later: "In this we know that we love the children of God, when we love God and do his commandments. For this is the love of God, that we keep his com-

---
15 1 Tim. 1.5.
16 1 Cor. 16.14.
17 1 Thess. 5.14-15.
18 1 Peter 4.8.
19 James 2.8.
20 1 John 2.10.
21 1 John 3.10.
22 1 John 3.23.
23 1 John 4.21.

mandments, and his commandments are not burdensome."[24] And in his Second Epistle we find it written: ". . . not as writing to thee a new commandment, but that which we have had from the beginning, that we love one another."[25]

36. The Lord Jesus Himself also declares that the whole Law and the Prophets depend upon the two precepts to love God and our neighbor.[26] In the Gospel of Mark we find this written concerning these two precepts. "And one of the Scribes came forward who had heard them disputing together; and seeing that He had answered them well, he asked him which was the first commandment of all. But Jesus answered him, 'The first commandment of all is: "Hear O Israel! The Lord our God is one God; and thou shalt love the Lord thy God with thy whole heart, and with thy whole soul, and with thy whole mind [and with all thy strength]." This is the first commandment. And the second is like to it: "Thou shalt love thy neighbor as thyself."[27] There is no other commandment greater than these.' "[28] He likewise declares in the Gospel of John: "A new commandment I give you, that you love one another: that as I have loved you, you also love one another. By this will all men know that you are my disciples, if you have love for one another."[29]

Chapter 18

37. All these precepts concerning love, or charity, would have been given men to no purpose if they did not have free choice of the will; for such is their nature and importance that whatever a man supposes he is doing well is not done well at all if it is done without charity. Now these precepts

---
24 1 John 5.2-3.
25 2 John 5.
26 Cf. Matt. 22.40.
27 Deut. 6.4-5; Lev. 19.18.
28 Mark 12.28-31.
29 13.34-35.

are given in both the Old and New Law, though the grace promised in the Old Law comes only with the New Law. Without grace, the Law is the letter that killeth, whereas, with grace, it is the life-giving spirit. Whence comes this love of God and neighbor in man, if not from God Himself? For if it does not come from God, but from man, then it is the Pelagians who have prevailed; but if it comes from God, then we have prevailed over the Pelagians. Let the Apostle John, therefore, sit in judgment between us and issue the command: "Dearly beloved, love one another."[1] When the Pelagians begin to feel elated at these words of the Apostle and to ask why this command is given us at all unless we are able of ourselves to love one another, the same John proceeds to confound them by saying: "For love is from God."[2] Charity, therefore, is not of ourselves, but of God.

Why then has the command been given, "Let us love one another, for love is of God," except that this precept should prompt our free will to ask for God's gift? And this would certainly be of no avail at all unless the will at first received some measure of love enabling it to ask for more, so as to fulfill what was commanded. When it says, "Love one another" —that is the Law; when it says, "love is of God"—that is grace. Certainly, God's "Wisdom carries law and mercy upon her tongue."[3] Whence it is written in the Psalm: "For the lawgiver shall give a blessing."[4]

38. Let no one then deceive you, my brethren, for we could not love God unless He first loved us. The same John makes this very clear when he says: "Let us therefore love, because God first loved us."[5] Grace makes us lovers of the Law, whereas the same Law, without grace, makes of us only prevaricators. And the Lord teaches us the same thing where He says to His Apostles: "You have not chosen me but I have

---
1 1 John 4.7.
2 1 John 4.7.
3 Prov. 3.16 [LXX].
4 Ps. 83.8.
5 1 John 4.19.

chosen you."[6] For if we first loved Him so as to merit His love in return, then we first chose Him so as to merit our being chosen by Him. But He who is Truth Itself says otherwise and openly contradicts such human vanity by declaring: "You have not chosen me." Consequently, if it is not you who have chosen, then it is certainly not you who have loved; for how could they choose Him whom they did not love? "But it is I," He says, "who have chosen you." And how could they possibly fail to choose Him afterwards, or fail to prefer Him to all the goods of this world? It was because they were chosen that they chose Him; they were not chosen because they had chosen Him. There would be no merit in men's choosing Him unless the action of God's grace in choosing them had gone before. This is why in imparting his blessing to the Thessalonians the Apostle Paul declares: "And may the Lord make you to increase and abound in charity towards one another, and towards all men."[7] He who gave this blessing to love one another is the same who gave us the love to love one another. Again, because some of them were sure to possess already the good dispositions he wished to be theirs, he went on to say in another passage, directed to the same Thessalonians: "We are bound to give thanks to God always for you, brethren, as is fitting, because your faith grows exceedingly and your charity each for the other increases."[8] This he said so that they might not be elated over this great blessing which they enjoyed from God, as if it were something they possessed of themselves. Seeing, therefore, that your faith grows exceedingly and your charity for each other increases, as the Apostle says, we ought to thank God in your regard, and not praise you as if you possessed all this of yourselves.

39. And writing to Timothy, he says: "For God has not given us the spirit of fear, but of power and of love and of

---

6 John 15.16.
7 1 Thess. 3.12.
8 2 Thess. 1.3.

prudence."[9] We are certainly not to understand from these words of the Apostle that the spirit of the fear of God is something that we have not received. It is unquestionably a great gift of God and one concerning which the Prophet Isaia says: "And the spirit of the Lord shall rest upon him: the spirit of wisdom and of understanding, the spirit of counsel and of fortitude, the spirit of knowledge and godliness, the spirit of the fear of the Lord."[10] The spirit of fear which we have received is not that which led Peter to deny Christ, but that fear whereof Christ Himself says: "Be afraid of him who has power to destroy both body and soul in hell. Yes, I say to you, be afraid of him."[11] Now He said this so that we might not deny Him by the kind of fear that had shaken Peter. It was because he wished to remove such fear from us that He had said earlier: "Do not be afraid of those who kill the body, and after that have nothing more that they can do."[12] It is not the spirit of such fear as this that we have received, but the spirit of power and of love and of prudence. Referring to this kind of fear, the same Apostle declares to the Romans: "We exult in tribulations, knowing that tribulation works out endurance, and endurance tried virtue, and tried virtue hope. And hope does not disappoint, because the charity of God is poured forth in our hearts by the Holy Spirit who is given to us."[13] It is not by ourselves, therefore, but by the Holy Spirit who is given to us, that this charity shown by the Apostle to be God's gift, is the reason why tribulation does not destroy patience but rather gives rise to it. Again, writing to the Ephesians, he says: "Peace to the brethren, and love with faith." Great blessings, indeed, but now let him tell us whence they come. "From God the

---

9 2 Tim. 1.7.
10 Isa. 11.23.
11 Luke 12.5.
12 Luke 12.4.
13 Rom. 5.3-5.

Father," he replies, "and the Lord Jesus Christ."[14] These great blessings then are none other than God's gifts to us.

Chapter 19

40. But it is not surprising that "the light shines in the darkness and the darkness grasps it not."[1] It is this Light that says to us in John's Epistle: "Behold what manner of love the Father has bestowed upon us that we should be called and should be the sons of God,"[2] while the Darkness tells us in the Pelagian writings: "Love comes to us of ourselves." If these men had true love, that is, Christian love, they would also know whence they come to have it, as the Apostle knew when he said: "Now we have received not the spirit of the world, but the spirit that is from God, that we may know the things that have been given us by God."[3] And John says: "God is love."[4] The Pelagians further maintain that they possess God and that this does not come from God but from themselves. And while they acknowledge that the knowledge of the Law comes to us from God, they would have it that charity comes from ourselves, being deaf to the words of the Apostle that "knowledge puffs up, but charity edifies."[5] What could be more inept, what could really be more absurd or more alien to the essential holiness of charity than to maintain that knowledge, which puffs up without charity, comes from God, while that which makes it impossible for knowledge to puff up, namely, charity, comes from ourselves? Again, when the Apostle speaks of "Christ's love which surpasses knowledge,"[6] what greater absurdity than to

---
14 Eph. 6.23.

---
1 John 1.5.
2 1 John 3.1.
3 1 Cor. 2.12.
4 1 John 4.16.
5 1 Cor. 8.1.
6 Eph. 3.19.

suppose that knowledge, which ought to be subject to charity, comes to us from God, while charity which surpasses knowledge, comes from ourselves? But true faith and sound teaching tell us that knowledge and love are both from God, since, as the Scripture says: "From his face came knowledge and understanding";[7] and, "love is of God."[8] We likewise read of the "spirit of knowledge and piety,"[9] and of the "spirit of power and of love and of prudence."[10] But charity is a greater gift than knowledge; for whenever knowledge is present in man, charity is necessary to keep him from being puffed up, whereas charity "does not envy, is not pretentious, is not puffed up."[11]

Chapter 20

41. I think I have argued at sufficient length against those who inveigh so violently against the grace of God. The will is not destroyed by grace, but is changed from a bad to a good will, and is aided by grace once it becomes good. I also believe that I have done so in such a way that it has been the Sacred Scriptures, rather than I, that have spoken to you by their very clear testimonies of the truth. If the Scripture is examined carefully, it will not merely show that God has power over the good wills of men which He has changed from being evil and which He directs toward the performance of good acts and life eternal once He has made them good. It will also reveal that those wills of men which remain creatures of this world are so subject to God's power that He can bend them wherever and whenever He pleases, whether by bestowing benefits upon some or by inflicting punishment upon others, according as He Himself ordains by His decrees, hidden of course from us, but perfectly just beyond all doubt.

[7] Prov. 2.6.
[8] 1 John 4.7.
[9] Isa. 11.2.
[10] 2 Tim. 1.7.
[11] 1 Cor. 13.4.

For we find that some sins are also a punishment for other sins, as instanced in those "vessels of wrath" which the Apostle speaks of as "ready for destruction";[1] or as in the hardening of Pharao's heart in order, as it is said, to manifest God's power in him;[2] and as in the flight of the Israelites from the face of the enemy out of the city of Hai because fear was instilled into their hearts so that they fled. And this was done to punish their sin, and to punish it as it deserved to be punished, which is why the Lord said to Josue, the son of Nun: "The children of Israel shall not be able to stand before his enemies."[3] What is the meaning of "shall not be able to stand"? Why did they not use their free will to stand rather than take flight because their wills were thrown into confusion by fear? Was it not for the simple reason that God, as Master of men's wills, can in His anger instill fear into the hearts of whomsoever He pleases? Was it not of their own free choice that the enemies of the Israelites fought against God's own people when they had Josue, son of Nun, as their leader? And yet the Scripture tells us that "it was by the will of the Lord that their hearts should be strengthened that they should fight against Israel . . . and should be destroyed."[4] Was it not of his own free will that the wicked man Semei, son of Gera, cursed King David? And yet what does David say, filled as he was with a true and deep and heavenly wisdom? What, I ask, does he say to the man who wanted to strike down his reviler? "What have I to do with you," he says, "ye sons of Sarvia? Let him alone and let him curse: for the Lord hath bid him curse David. And who is he that shall dare say, 'Why hath he done this?' "[5] Then, as if to give full

---

[1] Rom. 9.22. The Vulgate reads "ready for destruction." In the examples which follow Augustine illustrates his point that "some sins are even a punishment for other sins." In a letter to Sixtus, which occasioned the present treatise, he states that the heart is hardened, not by God's imparting malice to it, but by not imparting His mercy to it (*Ep.* 194.3.14).
[2] Cf. Exod. 9.16.
[3] Jos. 7.12.
[4] Jos. 11.20.
[5] 2 Kings 16.10.

approval to King David's judgment, the Sacred Scripture repeats the episode from a different starting point, saying: "And King David said to Abisai and to all his servants: Behold my son who came forth from my bowels seeketh my life: how much more now a son of Jemini? Let him alone that he may curse as the Lord hath bidden him. Perhaps the Lord may look upon my affliction, and the Lord may render me good for the cursing of this day."[6] How is it possible even for a wise man to understand how God could tell this man to curse David? Actually, He did not tell him this by way of a command, for then the man would have been praised for his obedience. Rather, God inclined his will, which was already perverted by its own wickedness, to a sin of this kind, in accordance with His own just and hidden judgment. It was in this sense that the Lord spoke to him. For if he had obeyed God's order, he would have deserved praise rather than blame, as we know he was punished afterwards because of this sin. Nor does the Scripture conceal the reason why God told him in this way to curse David, namely, why He caused his heart to fall into this sin or allowed it to do so. "Perhaps the Lord will look upon my affliction," he says, "and the Lord will render me good for the cursing of this day." Here you have a proof of how God uses even the hearts of wicked men to commend and help those who are good. It was thus that He made use of Judas in his betrayal of Christ and of the Jews who crucified Him. And, as a result of this, how great have been the blessings which He has bestowed upon the people who were to believe in Him? He even makes use of the devil himself, the worst of all, but does so in the best way possible to exercise and put to the test the faith and piety of good men; not for His own sake, since He knows everything before it happens, but for our benefit, since it was necessary that He should deal with us in this fashion.

---

6 2 Kings 16.11-12.

Was it not by Absalom's own will that he chose to follow advice that proved detrimental to him, though he only did so because the Lord had heard his father's prayer to this effect?[7] Accordingly, as the Scripture says: "And by the command of the Lord the good counsel of Achitophel was defeated, that the Lord might bring evil upon Absalom."[8] The counsel of Achitophel was called "good" because it served his purpose for the time, since it favored Absalom over his father whom he had risen up against in rebellion. And it might well have destroyed him if the Lord had not frustrated Achitophel's counsel by influencing the heart of Absalom to reject this counsel and to choose another which was not to his advantage.

Chapter 21

42. Who can help but tremble at the thought of these judgments of God whereby He accomplishes whatever He pleases even in the hearts of wicked men, while yet rendering to each according to his merits? Solomon's son, Roboam, rejected the salutary counsel of the elders, not to deal harshly with the people, and yielded to the words of men of his own age by replying with threats to those who should have been given a gentle reply. And how did this come about, except by his own will? But as a result of it, the ten tribes of Israel withdrew from him and set up for themselves another king, Jeroboam, that the will of God, who had been angered, might be accomplished, as He had also foretold that it would come to pass. For what does the Scripture say? "And the king condescended not to the people: for the Lord was turned away from him to make good his word, which he had spoken through Ahias, the Silonite, to Jeroboam the son of Nabat."[1]

---
[7] Cf. 2 Kings 15.31.
[8] 2 Kings 17.14.

---
[1] 3 Kings 12.15.

All this was certainly done by man's will, but in such a way that the "turning way" came from the Lord.

Just read the Books of Paralipomenon and this is what you will find written in the Second Book: "And the Lord stirred up against Jarom the spirit of the Philistines and of the Arabians who border on the Ethiopians. And they came up to the land of Juda and wasted it, and they carried away all substance that was found in the king's house."[2] Here we have a clear indication of how God stirs up enemies to lay waste those countries which He judges to be deserving of such punishment. And yet, was it not of their own will that the Philistines and Arabs came to lay waste the country of Juda? Or did they so come of their own will that the Scripture lies where it tells us that the Lord stirred up their spirit to do so? On the contrary. Both statements are true because they did come of their own will and God did stir up their spirit. The same thing could also be expressed by saying that God both stirred up their spirit and that they came nevertheless of their own will. For the Almighty, who cannot possibly will anything unjust, is able to set in motion even the inclinations of their will in men's hearts in order to accomplish through these men whatever He wishes to achieve through their agency. What meaning can these words have which the man of God addressed to King Amasias: "Let not the army of Israel go out with thee, for the Lord is not with Israel and all the children of Ephraim. And if thou think to prevail over them, God will put thee to flight before thy enemies; for it belongeth to God both to help and to put to flight"?[3] How does the power of God help some in war by giving them confidence, and turn others to flight by instilling them with fear, except for this reason, that He who has made all things as He willed in heaven and on earth, also works in the hearts of men? We also read of what Joas, King of Israel, said when he dispatched a messenger to King Amasias, who had a mind

---
2 2 Par. 21.16-17.
3 2 Par. 25.7-8.

to go to war with him. Having mentioned certain things, he went on to say: "Sit at home. Why provokest thou evil that thou shouldst fall and Juda with thee?"[4] The Scripture then went on to add: "And Amasias would not hearken to him because it was the Lord's will that he should be delivered into the hands of enemies because they sought after the gods of Edom."[5] There you see how God, wishing to punish the sin of idolatry, influenced the heart of this man with whom he was indeed justly angry, that he would not heed salutary advice but, in his contempt for it, would engage in battle, there to perish together with his army. Speaking through His prophet Ezechiel, God said: "And when the prophet shall err and speak, I the Lord have deceived that prophet: and I will stretch forth my hand upon him and I will cut him off from the midst of my people Israel."[6] We read in the Book of Esther how this woman from the people of Israel became the wife of a foreign king, Assuerus, in the land of captivity. It is recorded in this Book that when Esther was faced with the necessity of intervening for her people, whom the king had ordered to be slain wherever they might be found in his kingdom, she prayed to the Lord. The urgency of the situation made her venture into the king's presence contrary to the king's orders and to her own accustomed way of acting. Observe now what the Scripture says: "He looked upon her with the violent indignation of a bull; the queen was frightened and her color changed through faintness; she leaned upon the head of her maid-companion who went before her. And God changed the King and turned his indignation into gentleness."[7] It is also written in the Proverbs of Solomon: "Even as the rush of water, so the heart of the king is in the hands of the Lord; whithersoever he will he shall turn it."[8] And in Psalm 104, concerning the Egyptians, we read what

---

4 4 Kings 14.10.
5 2 Par. 25.20.
6 Ezech. 14.9.
7 Esth. 15.10-11 [LXX].
8 Prov. 21.1.

God did to them: "He turned their hearts to hurt his people and to deal deceitfully with his servants."[9] Observe also what is written in the Epistles of the Apostles. We read in the Epistle of the Apostle Paul to the Romans: "Therefore God gave them up in the lustful desires of their hearts to uncleanness"; and a little later: "For this cause God has given them up to shameful lusts"; and a few verses later: "And as they have resolved against possessing the knowledge of God, God has given them up to a reprobate sense, so that they do what is not fitting."[10] And in the Second Epistle to the Thessalonians, he has this to say of certain men: "For they have not received the love of truth that they might be saved. Therefore God sends them a misleading influence that they may believe falsehood, that all may be judged who have not believed the truth, but have preferred wickedness."[11]

43. From these and other similar testimonies of the inspired Books, which cannot all be mentioned for want of time, I think it is quite clear that God works in men's hearts to incline their wills to whatsoever way He wills: either to good in accordance with His mercy, or to evil in accordance with their evil merits, and this, indeed, by His own judgments, sometimes manifest, sometimes hidden, but always just.[12] You must keep this conviction firm and unshaken in your heart that in God there is no injustice. Accordingly, when you read the truth of the Scriptures and find that men are led astray by God, or that their hearts are dulled and hardened by Him, have no doubt that it was their previous evil merits that made them suffer their just penalties. You will thus not clash with that proverb of Solomon: "The folly of man perverts his ways, while he blames God in his heart."[13]

But grace is not given according to men's merits; otherwise grace is no longer grace, seeing that it is called grace precisely

---
9 Ps. 104.25.
10 Rom. 1.24, 26, 28.
11 2 Thess. 2.10-11.
12 Cf. Rom. 9.14.
13 Prov. 19.3.

because it is freely given. Now if God is able, either through good or bad angels, or in some other way, to work in the hearts of even wicked men according to their merits—though He is not the cause of their wickedness, which they have either contracted through original sin or have increased through their own will—what wonder is it that He should work good in the hearts of His elect through the Holy Spirit, when He has already brought about a change in these same hearts from evil to good?

Chapter 22

44. But suppose men do imagine that there are merits of some kind which they think come first in order that they may be justified by God's grace, though they fail to see that by making such an assertion they are simply denying grace. But, as I said, let them imagine anything they want to with regard to adults. In the case of infants, at least, the Pelagians do not know what to answer, since there is nothing voluntary in their receiving grace which they can allege as a cause of any previous merit. Moreover, while they are being baptized and made recipients of God's sacraments, we see how they even cry and put up a struggle, which should be imputed to them as a grave sin of irreverence if they already enjoyed the use of free will. And though they put up a struggle, grace nevertheless remains in them, obviously without any previous good merits; otherwise grace would no longer be grace. There are times too when this grace is conferred upon the children of unbelievers as when, in God's hidden Providence, they fall somehow or other into the hands of devout persons. But there are other times when the children of believers fail to obtain such grace because there is some obstacle present which makes it impossible to come to their aid when they are in danger of death. Certainly, these things take place by the

hidden Providence of God "whose judgments are incomprehensible and whose ways are unsearchable."[1] Take a careful look at what the Apostle had said before which led him to say what he did. He was discussing the Jews and Gentiles when, writing to the Romans, to Gentiles, that is, he had said: "For as you at one time did not believe God, but now have obtained mercy by reason of their unbelief, so they too have not now believed by reason of the mercy shown you, that they too may obtain mercy. For God has shut up all in unbelief, that he may have mercy upon all."[2] And after he had reflected upon what he had said, filled, indeed, with wonderment over the real truth of his words, but astounded by their great depth, of how God had shut up all in unbelief to show them all mercy—as if doing evil that good might result—he exclaimed at once, saying: "O the depth of the riches of the wisdom and of the knowledge of God. How incomprehensible are his judgments and how unsearchable his ways."[3] But there are certain perverse men, thoughtless and censorious, who through their inability to understand what is meant by the incomprehensible judgments and unsearchable ways, have boastfully supposed that the Apostle was saying: "Let us do evil that good may come."[4] God forbid that the Apostle should ever say this! But this is what those who fail to understand the Apostle thought he meant when he said: "Now the Law intervened that the offense might abound. But where the offense has abounded, grace has abounded yet more."[5] Grace does of course result in this, that good works are now performed by those who before had done evil; it does not make them continue in doing evil in the belief that good will be given them in return. So they should not say: "Let us do evil that good may come," but rather: "We have done evil and good has come; let us now

---
1 Cf. Rom. 11.33.
2 Rom. 11.30-32.
3 Rom. 11.33.
4 Rom. 3.8.
5 Rom. 5.20.

do good so that we who have received good for evil in this world may receive good for good in the world to come." Thus is it written in the Psalm: "Mercy and judgment I will sing to thee."[6] Accordingly, the Son of Man did not first come into the world to judge the world, but came in order that the world might be saved through Him.[7] He first came out of mercy; He will come hereafter for judgment, to judge the living and the dead, though, even at the present time, there is no salvation without judgment, but it is a hidden judgment. This is why He says: "For judgment have I come into this world, that they who do not see may see, and they who see may become blind."[8]

Chapter 23

45. Accordingly, when you observe the case of infants who undoubtedly are all subject to the same condition of having contracted the hereditary sin from Adam, and you see that one is helped to receive baptism, but not another, so that he dies shackled in the very chains of this sin; or that one who was baptized and whose future wickedness was forseen by God, is abandoned in this life, while another is snatched from this life after baptism "lest wickedness should alter his understanding"[1]—you must refer these things to God's hidden judgments. You must not ascribe them to injustice or to a want of wisdom on the part of God in whom there is found the very source of justice and wisdom. Rather, as I exhorted you from the beginning of this treatise,[2] you are to walk according to the light already received. And God will disclose to you this mystery also, if not in this life, at least in the next, for "there is nothing concealed that will not

---

6 100.1.
7 Cf. John 3.17.
8 John 9.39.

1 Wisd. 4.11.
2 Cf. 1.1.

be disclosed."[3] Consequently, when you hear the Lord say: "I the Lord have deceived that prophet,"[4] or the words of the Apostle: "He has mercy on whom he will, and whom he wills he hardens,"[5] you must believe that there were evil merits in that man whom God permits to go astray and to become hardened, while, for the man upon whom He has mercy, you must acknowledge with an unswerving faith that this is a case of the grace of God who is not rendering evil for evil, but good for evil.[6] And you must not deny free will to Pharao just because God says in a number of places: "I have hardened Pharao," or, "I will harden the heart of Pharao,"[7] for it does not thereby follow that it was not Pharao himself who hardened his own heart. Furthermore, we read that this happened to Pharao after the plague of flies had been removed from the Egyptians, as the Scripture testifies: "And Pharao's heart was hardened so that neither this time would he let the people go."[8] Thus it was that both God and Pharao caused this hardening of the heart: God, by His just judgments, Pharao, by his free will.

You may be sure then that your efforts will not be in vain if only you persevere unto the end by going ahead with your good resolve. But God, who does not presently deal with those whom He sets free according to their works, will then render to each one according to his works. Being just, He will indeed render evil for evil; being good, He will render good for evil; being both good and just, He will render good for good. This only He will not do, namely, render evil for good, seeing that He is not unjust. He will, therefore, render evil for evil, and punishment for unrighteousness. He will also render good for evil, grace for unrighteousness, good for good, and grace for grace.

---

[3] Matt. 10.26.
[4] Ezech. 14.9.
[5] Rom. 9.18.
[6] Cf. 1 Peter 3.9.
[7] Exod. 4.21; 7.3; 9.12; 10.20, 27; 14.4.
[8] Cf. Matt. 16.27.

Chapter 24

46. Go over this treatise carefully in your mind. If you understand it, give thanks to God; where you fail to understand it, pray for understanding which God will give you. Recall the words of Scripture: "If anyone of us is wanting in wisdom, let him ask it of God, who gives abundantly to all men, and does not reproach; and it will be given to him."[1] As the Apostle himself expresses it, this is the wisdom "that descends from above."[2] But you must ward off from you, and pray that that kind of wisdom be not found in you which the Apostle abominated where he said: "But if you have bitter jealousy and contention in your hearts . . . this is not the wisdom that descends from above. It is earthly, sensuous, devilish. For where there is envy and contentiousness, there is instability and every wicked deed. But the wisdom that is from above is first of all chaste, then peaceable, moderate, docile . . . full of mercy and good fruits, without judging, without dissimulation."[3] What blessing, then, will that man not possess who has asked for and received this wisdom from the Lord? And this will give you an understanding of what grace is; for if this wisdom were from ourselves, it would not be from above and we would not have to ask for it from the same God who created us.

Pray for us also, brethren, that "we may live temperately and justly and piously in this world, looking for the blessed hope and manifestation of our Lord and Savior Jesus Christ,"[4] to whom belong honor and glory and kingdom, with the Father and the Holy Spirit, forever and ever. Amen.

---

1 James 1.5.
2 James 3.17.
3 James 3.14-17.
4 Titus 2.12-13.

INDICES

GENERAL INDEX

Abisai, 298.
Absalom, 300.
Achitophel, 300.
Adeodatus, 3, 65.
adultery, why evil, 76-78.
Aeneid 2.659, 10.
Ahias, 300.
Amasias, King, 301 f.
Ananias, 50.
Andria, of Terence, 18 n.
anima, animus, 88 n.
Assuerus, King, 302.
Augustine, St.:
 at Cassiciacum, 3; appreciation of son Adeodatus, 3 n.; Platonic reminiscence, 4 n., 5 n.; doctrine of "illumination," 5 n., 54 n., 73 n., 85, 110 n.; adherence to Academic doubt, 45 n.; on belief and understanding, 2, 50 f., 69; Platonic influence on, 51 n.; on sensation, 52 n.; on memory, 53 n.; knowledge of Punic language, 58 n.; program of liberal arts, 60 n.; coined term *soliloquia*, 65 n.; composition and scope of *The Free Choice of the Will*, 66, 70; on origin of Pelagianism, 67, 285 n.; ordained priest, 70; correspondence with Evodius, 70 n.; attracted by Manichaean dualism, 75 n.; on origin of the soul, 215-222; on existence of God, 113 ff.; refutation of skepticism, 114 n.; Pythagorean influence on, 140 n.; Christian humanism of, 147 n.; *De pulchro et apto*, lost work of, 151 n.; on God's foreknowledge and human freedom, 168 ff.; on the Divine Ideas, 177 n.; works on grace enumerated, 245 n.; and monks of Hadrumetum, 246 f.; correspondence

with Valentine of Hadrumetum, 246 n.; *Grace and Free Will*, purpose of, 247 f.; references to works not contained in this volume: *De beata vita*, 3 n., 33, 65, 114 n.; *De ordine*, 52 n., 65, 67, 140 n.; *Soliloquia*, 4, 51 n., 65, 73 n., 114 n.; *De quantitate animae*, 4, 65, 70; *De immortalitate animae*, 65; *De vera religione*, 52 n., 114 n.; *De utilitate credendi*, 51 n., 75 n.; *C. Secundinum*, 69, 147 n.; *De diversis quaestionibus 83*, 177 n.; *Confessiones*, 3, 53, 151 n., 285 n.; *De Trinitate*, 5, 50 n., 114 n., 146 n.; *Tractatus in evangelium Ioannis*, 51 n., 69 n.; *De Genesi ad litteram*, 146 n., 154 n.; *De sermone Domini in monte*, 9 n.; *De fide et operibus*, 269 n.; *De dono perseverantiae*, 67; *De correptione et gratia*, 289 n.; *De gestis Pelagii*, 266 n.; *Opus imperfectum contra Iulianum*, 218 n.; *Ep.* 120, 50 n.; *Ep.* 166, 69 n., 218 n.; *Ep.* 190, 245 n.; *Ep.* 194, 24 n.; *Ep.* 214, 246 n.; *Ep.* 215, 246, n.; *Sermo* 56, 9.

Augustinian School, on efficacious and ineffacacious grace, 289 n.

Azarias, 50.

Bañez, 173 n.

baptism, of children, 255 ff.

believing, and knowing, 50 f.; and understanding, 50 f., 112 f.

Bonner, G., 66 n., 78 n.

Boyer, C., 33 n., 69 n.

cardinal virtues, 97 f.

Cassiciacum, 3, 65.

Cassian, John, 248 n.

Celestius, Pelagian, 266 n.

certitude, implied in personal existence, 114.

Christ, the inner Teacher, 51; dwells in the inner man, 51; inner Oracle, 61.

Christian humanism, 147 n.

Cicero, *In Verrem*, 26; *Tusculanae disputationes*, 26 n.

Cilleruelo, L., 54 n.

cogito, Augustinian and Cartesian, 114 n.

concupiscentia and *libido*, 78 n.

Council of Carthage, 245.

Courcelle, P., 5 n.

creation, order in, 187 ff.; perfected by rational creatures, 205.

creationism, 218 n.

credere and *scire*, 50 n.

Cresconius, monk of Hadrumetum, 246.

Da quod jubes et jube quod vis, reaction of Pelagius to, 285 n.

David, King, 298 ff.
De auxiliis, 248 n.
de Plinval, 245 n.
Diospolis, Council of, 262 n., 266 n.
Divine Ideas, dependence of soul upon, 177; and Divine "illumination," 177 n.

Empedocles, 52 n.
Epistola tractoria, of Pope Zosimus, 245, 247.
eternal law, supreme wisdom, 85; definition of, 85; and happiness, 102 f.; and human laws, 85.
Eulogius, Primate of Palestine, 262 n.
evil, problem of, 72 ff.; Manichaean view of, 66 f.; cause of, 72 ff.; turning from changeless good, 162.
Evodius, 70 ff.; correspondence with Augustine, 70 n.; Bishop of Uzala, 246.
existence, always preferable to non-existence, 181 ff.; instinctive desire for, 185.

faith, primacy of, 75; and good works, 269 ff.; a gift, 269 f., 281 f.
Faustus of Riez, 248 n.
fear of the Lord, a grace, 295.
Felix, monk of Hadrumetum, 246.
Ferguson, J., 245 n.
form, and changeable reality, 154.

fortitude, 98.
four elements, theory of, 52 n.
free will, cause of evil, 106; why given to man, 107 ff.; taught by the Scriptures, 251 ff.

Gannon, M. A., 52 n.
Gellius, A., *Noctes Atticae*, 39 n.
Gilson, E., 88 n., 110 n., 113 n.
God, attributes of, 75 f.; existence of, demonstrated, 113 ff.; foreknowledge of, and human freedom, 168 ff.
good will, 95, 100.
good works, necessity of, 269 ff.
grace, Augustine's works on, 245 n.; taught by Scripture, 258 ff.; not result of merit, 265 ff.; not the Law, 275 ff.; not result of good will, 283 f.; *operans* and *cooperans*, 289 n.; efficacious and inefficacious, 289 n.; neither the Law nor knowledge of the Law nor mere remission of sins, 280; not destructive of freedom, 297; dispensation of, 306 f.
Grabowski, S., 173 n.
Green, W. M., 58 n., 70 n., 192 n.

Hadrumetum, monks of, 246.
Hagendahl, H., 26 n.
Hai, city of, 298.
Hamman, A., 246 n.

happy life, 100, 161; desired but not achieved by all, 100 f.; and eternal law, 102 f.
Heros, Bishop of Arles, 262 n.
Honoratus, friend of Augustine, 51 n.

"ignorance" and "difficulty," effects of original sin, 212 ff., 222 f.
"illumination," Divine, 4 f., 5 n., 51, 54 n., 73, 110 n.; and Divine Ideas, 177 n.
inner sense, existence and function of, 116 f.; superior to external senses, 121 f.
Inner Truth, 51, 54, 59.
Innocent, Pope, 247.
Institutio oratoria, of Quintilian, 39 n.
intellect, objects of, 53.
intellectus, 88 n.
intelligentia, 88 n.
intelligible realities, perceived in inner light, cannot be taught, 54 f.
"interior man," 8, 51, 54.

Jarom, 301.
Jeroboam, 300.
Jerome, St., 68, 218 n.
Joas, King of Israel, 301.
Josue, 298.
justice, 98.

knowledge, and belief, 50 f.; and understanding, 50 f.; sensual and intellectual, 52-54.

law, divine and human, 82 ff.; eternal and temporal, 84.
Lazarus, Bishop of Aix, 262 n.
Lecerf, J., 58 n.
Leckie, G., 5 n.
Lewis, G., 114 n.
love, perfect and imperfect, 288 f.; greater than knowledge, 297.
Lynch, L., 88 n.

man, defined, 37.
Manichaeism, embraced by Augustine, 66, 75 n.; dualism of, 66 f.; identifies sun with God, 180 n.
Marrou, H., 50 n.
Massilienses, 248 n.
memory, and sense impressions, 53.
Meno, of Plato, 5 n.
mens, 88 n.
Misael, 50.
Molina, 173 n.
Monica, St., mother of Augustine, 65, 70, 246 n.
Morán, J., 110 n.
Morin, Dom, 246 n.
Moses, 146 n.
Most, W., 140 n.

nature, every nature good, 199 f.; and substance, 200; how corrupted, 201 ff.; analogical term, 214.
Nebridius, 4 n.
Noctes Atticae, of Gellius, 39 n.
nomen, derivation of, 22.

nouns, and signs, 17, 22; definition of, 22; and other parts of speech, 23-25; and terms, 28; general and particular, 27-29.
number, perception of, 129 ff.; and wisdom, 133, 139 ff.; and beauty, 151 ff.
Nun, father of Josue, 298.

Ontologism, 146 n.
Optatus, Augustine's letter to, 245 n.
Oracle, Inner, 61.
original sin, cause of "ignorance" and "difficulty," 212 ff., 222 ff.; transmission of, 306.

passion *(libido)*, source of sin, 78; and desire, 78-80; evil effects of, 93 f.
Paul, St., 24 ff.; 251 *et passim*.
Pelagius, 67 ff.; at Council of Diospolis, 21 f., 266 n.; identified grace with the Law, 275 ff.; grace not needed to avoid sin, 279 ff.; reaction of, to Augustine's *Confessions,* 285 n.
Pelagianorum reliquiae, 248 n.
Persius 3.32, 41 f.
Phaedo, 45 n.
Pharao, 298.
philarguria, 209.
Plato, 5, 153 n.
Platonists, and Christian teaching, 52 n.

Plotinus, 51 n.; *Enneads* of, 151 n.; on evil, 165 n.
Porphyry, 51 n.
Possidius, Augustine's first biographer, 67 n.; *Indiculum* of, 72 n.
pronoun, defined, 22.
prudence, 97.
Puech, H. C., 66 n.
Punic language, 58.
Pythagoreanism, 140 n.

Quintilian, *Institutio oratoria,* 39 n.

ratio, 88 n.
rational creatures, apex of creation, 205.
reason, distinctive of man, 87, 123; and virtue, 89; knows itself and sense powers, 120.
Republic, of Plato, 153 n.
Retractations, Two Books of, Augustine's review of his works, 3, 52 n., 60 n., 65 n., 67 n., 68, 73; Book 1, Ch. 9, 235-241.
Ries, J., 66 n.
Roboam, 300.

Sage, A., 287 n.
sapientia, 50 n.
saraballae, 47 f.
scientia, 50 n.
Schützinger, C., 54 n., 110 n.
scire and *credere,* 50 n.
Secundinus, Manichaean, 69.
self-defense, morality of, 81 ff.
Semei, son of Gera, 298.

Semi-Pelagianism, 248.
seminal reasons, doctrine of, 52 n.
sensation, Augustine and Aquinas on, 52 n.
senses (external), messengers of mind, 52; objects of, 52; number and specific objects of, 115 ff.; known by reason, 116; *see also* inner sense.
Septuagint, 50 n., 75 n.
signs, and words, 10-12, 16; and gestures, 12-16; kinds of, 16, 29; and nouns, 17-22; indicated by other signs, 16; and "signifiables," 17; self-signifying, 20; reciprocal, 20-23; cannot alone engender knowledge, 46-49; compared with things and knowledge, 38-42; whether required to indicate actions, 42 ff.
sin, cause of, 72 ff.; turning from changeless good, 162 f.; an analogical term, 214.
Sixtus, Roman priest (later Sixtus III), 245.
Socrates, 39 n., 45 n.
soul, views on origin of, 215-222.
Sousse (Tunisia), identified with ancient Hadrumetum, 246 n.
spiritual generationism, 218 n.
suicide, 186 f.

Tagaste, birthplace of Augustine, 3, 65.

Teacher, the Inner, 51, 60, 61.
teaching, and recalling, 7-9.
temperance, 98.
temporal laws, jurisdiction of, 103 f.; and eternal law, 85.
Terence, *Andria,* 18 n.
Thomas Aquinas, St., 5 n.
truth, present in the mind, 51; and moral dispositions, 51; identified with Christ, 51; same for all, 137, 142 f.; superior to mind, 143 f.; and happiness, 144 ff.; Inner Teacher of, 148.

understanding, and belief, 50 f.
Uzala, 246.

Valentine, of Hadrumetum, 246.
verbum, derivation of, 22.
Vergil, *Aeneid,* 10 n.
Verrine Orations, of Cicero, 26.
vice, contrary to nature, 203.
videre and *credere,* 50 n.
vituperatio, derivation of, 203.

Weigel, G., 5.
will, self-determining, 96; root of happiness and unhappiness, 99 f., 106; an "intermediate" good, 160; necessary for moral life, 162; cause of sin, 209 ff.; subject to God, 303.
Wisdom, and highest good, 134 ff.; same for all, 139; and number, 139 ff.

words, defined, 18; and nouns, 18-20; naturally suggest realities, 37 f.; do not alone cause knowledge, 49 f., 55, 60.

Zosimus, Pope, *Epistola tractoria* of, 245, 247.

INDEX OF HOLY SCRIPTURE

(Books of the Old Testament)

Genesis
  2.5: 231.
Exodus
  4.21: 307.
  9.16: 298.
  20.17: 286.
Leviticus
  19.18: 292.
Deuteronomy
  6.4-5: 292.
  8.17-18: 268.
Josue
  7.12: 298.
  11.20: 298.
2 Kings
  15.31: 300.
  16.10: 298.
  16.11-12: 298.
  17.14: 300.
3 Kings
  12.15: 300.
4 Kings
  14.10: 302.

1 Paralipomenon
  28.9: 263.
2 Paralipomenon
  15.2: 262.
  21.16-17: 301.
  25.7-8: 301.
  25.20: 302.
Esther
  15.10-11: 302.
Psalms
  1.2: 253.
  4.5-6: 9.
  5.12: 272.
  13.1: 111, 157.
  18.13-14: 193.
  24.7: 211.
  26.9: 258, 265.
  26.33: 287.
  29.7: 265.
  29.8: 265.
  31.9: 253.
  31.9: 256.
  33.14: 286.

35.4: 256.
36.4: 144.
38.2: 287.
40.5: 169.
41.7: 231.
43.22: 268.
51.27: 154.
67.19: 261.
78.6: 256.
79.4: 284.
83.8: 293.
88.11: 234.
84.5-7: 284.
84.7.5: 262.
94.8: 282, 284.
100.1: 306.
102.4: 273.
104.25: 303.
140.3: 286, 287.
Proverbs
1.8: 253.
1.31: 253.
2.6: 297.
3.7: 253.
3.11: 253, 261.
3.16: 293.
3.27: 253.
3.29: 253.
5.2: 253.
8.35: 287.
9.14: 259.
19.3: 252, 303.
21.1: 302.
29.19: 257.

36.3: 253.
Canticle of Canticles
8.5: 265.
Wisdom
4.11: 306.
6.13: 156.
7.27: 155.
8.1: 140.
8.21: 260.
Ecclesiasticus [Sirach]
15.11-17: 253.
15.16: 285.
22.23: 286.
23.4-5: 286.
23.5: 286.
33.6: 286.
Isaia
1.18: 266.
7.9: 50, 75, 113.
11.2: 297.
11.23: 295.
Jeremia
17.5: 257.
Ezechiel
11.19: 282.
11.19-20: 282.
14.9: 302, 307.
18.31-32: 284.
36.22-27: 283.
36.26: 285.
36.27: 287.
Daniel
3.94: 47.

(BOOKS OF THE NEW TESTAMENT)

Matthew
5.17: 279.
6.6: 8.

6.12-13: 279.
6.19: 254.
7.7: 113.

10.26: 307.
10.28: 254.
11.30: 289.
16.24: 254.
16.27: 255, 272, 307.
18.11: 279.
19.10-11: 259.
22.40: 292.
26.41: 26.

Mark
12.28-31: 292.

Luke
2.14: 254.
12.4: 295.
12.5: 295.
12.48.47: 256.
19.10: 279.
20.36: 192.
22.32: 261.

John
1.16: 272.
3.27: 267.
6.66: 262.
8.31-32: 146.
9.39: 306.
13.34-35: 292.
14.37: 288.
15.5: 266, 271.
15.13: 288.
15.16: 294.
15.22: 251.
17.3: 113.

Romans
1.17: 269.
1.18-20: 252.
1.21: 231.
1.22: 231.
1.24: 26, 28, 303.
2.6: 270, 272.

2.12: 255.
3.8: 305.
3.20: 274.
3.28: 269.
4.4: 263, 270.
4.5: 284.
4.15: 274.
5.3-5: 295.
5.20: 305.
6.14: 278.
6.23: 271, 373.
7.6: 274.
7.7-13: 275.
7.19.18: 211.
8.12-13: 276.
8.14: 276.
8.28: 289.
8.35-39: 290.
8.36-37: 268.
9.16: 268.
9.18: 307.
9.22: 298.
10.3: 276.
10.14: 281.
11.5-6: 270.
11.30-32: 305.
11.33: 305.
11.36: 196.
12.1: 253.
12.3: 273, 281.
12.21: 257, 260.
13.8: 290.
13.8-10: 288.
16.18: 39.

1 Corinthians
1.19: 24.
1.23-24: 51.
2.12: 296.
3.2-3: 282.

3.5: 268.
3.6: 272.
3.16: 8.
3.17: 203.
4.7: 267.
4.15: 281.
5.17-18: 272.
6.1: 263.
6.3: 192.
7.7: 259, 273.
7.25: 269, 281.
7.32: 259.
7.36-37: 254.
7.37: 259.
8.1: 296.
8.11: 254.
9.17: 254.
11.16: 25.
12.31: 290.
13.1-8: 290.
13.4: 297.
13.13-14.1: 290.
15.9: 263.
15.10: 263, 264.
15.34: 254.
15.56: 260.
15.57: 260, 268.
16.14: 291.
2 Corinthians
1.19: 24.
3.2-3: 282.
3.5: 268.
3.6: 272.
4.15: 281.
5.17-18: 272.
6.1: 263.
11.16: 25.
Galatians
2.16: 275.

2.21: 279.
5.6: 270.
5.13-14: 290.
5.17: 211.
Ephesians
2.3: 214.
2.8: 269, 281.
2.9: 269.
3.14-17: 51.
3.16-17: 8.
3.19: 296.
4.8: 267, 271.
4.10: 271.
6.6-7: 254.
6.23: 281, 296.
Philippians
1.6: 289.
1.29: 281.
2.12: 273.
2.13: 273, 287, 289.
3.8-9: 277.
3.12: 251.
3.15: 251.
3.16: 25.
Colossians
3.14: 290.
1 Thessalonians
1.7-8: 256.
3.12: 294.
5.14-15: 291.
2 Thessalonians
1.3: 294.
2.10-11: 303.
3.2: 279.
1 Timothy
1.5: 291.
1.13: 211.
4.14: 254.
5.22: 259.

6.10: 209.
2 Timothy
  1.7: 295, 297.
  1.8-9: 264.
  3.12: 254.
  4.6-7: 266.
  4.7: 267.
  4.8: 266.
Titus
  2.2-13: 308.
  3.3: 264.
  3.4-7: 264.
James
  1.5: 308.
  1.7: 267.
  1.13-15: 252.
  1.14: 260.
  2.1: 254.
  2.8: 291.
  2.19: 270.
  3.14-17: 308.
  3.17: 308.
  4.11: 255.
  12.2: 260.
Philemon
  14: 254.
1 Peter
  3.9: 307.
  4.8: 291.
1 John
  1.5: 296.
  2.10: 291.
  2.15: 255.
  3.1: 296.
  3.10: 291.
  3.23: 291.
  4.7: 293, 297.
  4.16: 296.
  4.18: 288.
  4.19: 293.
  4.21: 291.
  5.2-3: 292.
2 John
  5: 292.

www.ingramcontent.com/pod-product-compliance
Lightning Source LLC
LaVergne TN
LVHW040613250326
834688LV00035B/529